POWER & RIGHTS IN US
CONSTITUTIONAL LAW

POWER & RIGHTS IN US CONSTITUTIONAL LAW

SECOND EDITION

THOMAS LUNDMARK

OXFORD
UNIVERSITY PRESS

OXFORD
UNIVERSITY PRESS

Oxford University Press, Inc., publishes works that further Oxford University's objective of excellence in research, scholarship, and education.

Oxford New York
Auckland Cape Town Dar es Salaam Hong Kong Karachi Kuala Lumpur Madrid Melbourne
Mexico City Nairobi New Delhi Shanghai Taipei Toronto

With offices in
Argentina Austria Brazil Chile Czech Republic France Greece Guatemala Hungary Italy
Japan Poland Portugal Singapore South Korea Switzerland Thailand Turkey Ukraine
Vietnam

Copyright © 2008 Oxford University Press

Published by Oxford University Press, Inc., 198 Madison Avenue, New York, New York 10016
www.oup.com

Oxford is a registered trademark of Oxford University Press

All rights reserved. No part of this publication may be reproduced, stored in a retrieval system, or transmitted, in any form or by any means, electronic, mechanical, photocopying, recording, or otherwise, without the prior permission of Oxford University Press.

Library of Congress Cataloging-in-Publication Data
Lundmark, Thomas.
  Power & rights in US constitutional law/by Thomas Lundmark—2nd ed.
     p. cm.
  Includes bibliographical references and index.
  ISBN-13: 978-0-19-536872-7 ((pbk.): alk. paper) 1. Constitutional law—United States. 2. Civil rights—United States. 3. United States—Politics and government. I. Title: Power and rights in United States constitutional law. II. Title.
  KF4550.Z9L86 2008
  342.73—dc22
                                                                                                2007052829

Printed in the United States of America on acid-free paper

Note to Readers
This publication is designed to provide accurate and authoritative information in regard to the subject matter covered. It is based upon sources believed to be accurate and reliable and is intended to be current as of the time it was written. It is sold with the understanding that the publisher is not engaged in rendering legal, accounting, or other professional services. If legal advice or other expert assistance is required, the services of a competent professional person should be sought. Also, to confirm that the information has not been affected or changed by recent developments, traditional legal research techniques should be used, including checking primary sources where appropriate.

(Based on the Declaration of Principles jointly adopted by a Committee of the American Bar Association and a Committee of Publishers and Associations.)

You may order this or any other Oxford University Press publication by visiting the Oxford University Press website at www.oup.com

Contents

Preface to the Second Edition. xi
About the Author. xiii
Introduction 1

PART ONE: GOVERNMENTAL POWER 3

Subpart A: The Federal Government 7
1. The Principle of Separation of Powers 8
   A. Checks and Balances 9
   B. On the Ambiguity of the Tri-Partite Demarcation 10
2. Legislative Powers 12
   A. On the Meaning of the Term "Legislative" 13
      I. The Text of the Constitution. 13
      II. Legislative Immunity 15
   B. Enumeration of Powers 16
      I. Taxing Power 16
      II. Spending Power 17
      III. Commerce Clause 19
         AA. Early Commerce Clause Jurisprudence 20
         BB. Recent Commerce Clause Jurisprudence. 21
      CASE: **Heart of Atlanta Motel v. United States**
      379 U.S. 241 (1964) 22
         CC. The *Lopez* Synthesis 25
      CASE: **United States v. Lopez**
      514 U.S. 549 (1995) 25
         DD. The Fallout from *Lopez*. 31
      CASE: **Gonzales v. Raich**
      545 U.S. 1 (2005) 32

EE. "Jurisdictional Elements" in Commerce
Clause Legislation............................ 35
IV. Necessary and Proper Clause 37
CASE: **McCulloch v. Maryland**
17 U.S. 316 (1819) 38
V. Section 5 of the Fourteenth Amendment........... 51
3. Executive Power...................................... 53
A. Foreign Affairs................................... 54
I. Treaties and Executive Agreements 55
II. Foreign Military Interventions 55
STATUTE: **The War Powers Resolution**
50 U.S.C. § 1541 (1973) 56
B. Domestic Affairs ("Emergency" Power) 58
CASE: **Youngstown Sheet & Tube Co. v.
Sawyer [Steel Seizure Case]**
343 U.S. 579 (1952) 58
C. Presidential Legislative Prerogatives 63
I. Presidential Veto 63
II. Delegation of Legislative Power 64
D. Election, Appointment, Removal, and Immunity....... 65
I. Election and Appointment 65
II. Removal (Impeachment) 66
CASE: **Morrison v. Olson**
487 U.S. 654 (1988) 69
III. Privilege and Immunity...........................70
CASE: **Clinton v. Jones**
520 U.S. 681 (1997) 70
4. Judicial Power 74
A. Express Grants of (and Limitations on) Judicial Power.. 76
I. Heads of Federal Judicial Power
(Subject Matter Jurisdiction)..................... 76
II. Limitation of Jurisdiction to "Cases or
Controversies" 77
B. Implied Grants of (and Limitations on) Judicial Power .. 79
I. Judicial Review of Constitutionality 79
CASE: **Marbury v. Madison**
5 U.S. 137 (1803) 81

CASE: **Martin v. Hunter's Lessee**
14 U.S. 304 (1816) 87
II. The "Political Question" Doctrine 90

Subpart B: The Governments of the States 93
1. The Supremacy Clause 94
   A. Concurrent Jurisdiction 94
   B. Preemption 97
2. The Tenth Amendment 99
   A. The Tenth Amendment in the Courts. 100
   CASE: **Printz v. United States**
   521 U.S. 98 (1997) 101
   B. A Principle of Localism or Subsidiarity? 105

PART TWO: CONSTITUTIONAL RIGHTS 107

1. "State Action". 112
2. Levels of Scrutiny. 115
   A. "Minimum Scrutiny" (Lawful or "Valid" Ends/Rational Means) 116
   B. "Strict Scrutiny" (Compelling Ends/Necessary Means) .. 118
   C. "Intermediate Scrutiny" (Important Ends/Substantially Related Means) 119
   CASE: **Plyler v. Doe**
   457 U.S. 202 (1982) 120
   CASE: **United States v. Virginia [Virginia Military Institute or "VMI" Case]**
   518 U.S. 515 (1996) 123

Subpart A: Liberty (Due Process) 125
1. Explicit Fundamental Rights 126
   A. Speech 128
      I. What is Speech for Constitutional Purposes? 129
      CASE: **United States v. Eichman**
      496 U.S. 310 (1990) 131
      II. What are the Categories of Unprotected Speech ("non-speech")? 132
         AA. Crimes Involving Speech 132

CASE: **Brandenburg v. Ohio**
395 U.S. 444 (1969) 133
    BB. Defamation and Other Torts 135
    CC. Fighting Words 136
    DD. Obscenity 138
CASE: **Jenkins v. Georgia**
418 U.S. 153 (1974) 139
  III. Is the Regulation Content-Based or
    Content-Neutral? 142
    AA. Content-Based Restrictions on Speech 142
CASE: **R.A.V. v. City of St. Paul**
505 U.S. 377 (1992) 143
    BB. Content-Neutral, Time, Place, and Manner
        Restrictions on Speech 146
  IV. Licensing and Other Traditionally Valid
    Restrictions on Speech 147
    AA. Licensing and Prior Restraints 147
    BB. Restricting "Symbolic Expression" 149
    CC. Restricting Commercial Speech 150
    DD. Free Speech Rights of Government Employees .. 151
  B. Religion 151
    I. Establishment of Religion 152
CASE: **Zelman v. Simmons-Harris**
536 U.S. 639 (2002) 153
    II. Free Exercise of Religion 156
CASE: **Wisconsin v. Yoder**
406 U.S. 205 (1972) 157
  2. Implicit Fundamental Rights 160
    A. The Judicial Recognition of Fundamental Rights 161
    B. Privacy and Other Implicit Rights 162
CASE: **Roe v. Wade**
410 U.S. 113 (1973) 164

Subpart B: Equality (Equal Protection) 169
  1. Discrimination 172
    A. *De jure* Discrimination 175
      I. Explicit Discriminations 175

CASE: **Korematsu v. United States**
323 U.S. 214 (1944) 175
CASE: **City of Richmond v. J.A. Croson Co.**
488 U.S. 469 (1989) 179
    ii. Implicit Discriminations 184
        B. *De facto* Discrimination 185
CASE: **Washington v. Davis**
426 U.S. 229 (1976) 185
  2. Protected Groups 187
      A. Suspect Classifications 188
CASE: **Brown v. Board of Education [Brown I]**
347 U.S. 483 (1954) 188
CASE: **Brown v. Board of Education [Brown II]**
349 U.S. 294 (1955) 191
      B. Quasi-Suspect Classifications 193
CASE: **Saenz v. Roe**
526 U.S. 489 (1999) 197

Attachments 201

  Attachment A: The Declaration of Independence 201

  Attachment B: The Articles of Confederation
              (ratified 1781) 205

  Attachment C: The Constitution of the United States of
              America (ratified 1788) 212

  Attachment C-1: The Bill of Rights (ratified 1791) 222

  Attachment C-2: Constitutional Amendments 11–27 224

  Attachment D: Individual Rights Found in the Text of the
              Constitution Excluding the Amendments .. 231

  Attachment E: The Emancipation Proclamation (1863) ... 232

Bibliography 235

Table of Cases 239

Preface to the Second Edition

Experience over the past ten years has shown that the organization, coverage, and method of the first edition are well-adapted to conveying the basic principles of American constitutional law, particularly to foreign lawyers. On the other hand, the first edition did have various shortcomings, as was pointed out to me in thoughtful comments and suggestions by, among others, Professor Brandon L. Garrett, University of Virginia School of Law, and Matthew LeMieux, Lecturer in Law at the University of Münster. At Brandon and Matt's urging, I revamped the coverage of the Commerce Clause and the First Amendment, and restructured the discussion of levels of scrutiny. I would like to thank both Brandon and Matt for their thoughtful suggestions. Also, thanks to my secretary, Christine Pilz, for formatting the manuscript.

Everything has been brought up to date for the second edition. Cases and materials that are no longer current, or were rarely discussed in class, have been replaced or omitted.

A book that relies on U.S. Supreme Court decisions can never be current, for new decisions are constantly being handed down. To get around this problem, I have presented the materials in the context of the interests and policies that inspire constitutional law in general, and the decisions of the courts in particular. I try not to place too much emphasis on "blackletter" case-law. By employing this method, I hope to convey that court decisions, like congressional statutes and presidential pronouncements, are voices in an ongoing democratic conversation.

Thomas Lundmark
Münster, November 2007

About the Author

Thomas Lundmark studied literature at San Diego State University and the University of Uppsala and holds a Bachelor of Arts degree in comparative literature, awarded in 1972. Mr. Lundmark studied law at the University of California, Berkeley, where he earned the juris doctor degree in 1976, and at the Albert-Ludwigs-Universität Freiburg as a Fulbright Scholar in 1976–77. Years later, in 1995, he was granted the degree Doktor der Rechte (Dr. jur.) by the Rheinische Friedrich-Wilhelms-Universität Bonn.

Returning to San Diego in 1977, Mr. Lundmark worked as a litigation and trial lawyer, first in private, then in public, practice. Coincidentally with a change in the focus of his law practice, Mr. Lundmark was appointed in 1986 an adjunct professor of law at the University of San Diego, teaching part-time until 1991, when he was appointed to a Fulbright professorship at the Rheinische Friedrich-Wilhelms-Universität Bonn. In Bonn, he lectured and wrote primarily on American constitutional law. Mr. Lundmark's Fulbright status was extended for two years to enable him to teach and write on constitutional and other topics at the Universität Rostock and the Ernst Moritz Arndt Universität Greifswald. In the spring of 1995 he taught British and American constitutional law as a guest professor at the Friedrich-Schiller-Universität Jena. At the end of 1995, Mr. Lundmark returned to San Diego to practice law, teach, and write.

Mr. Lundmark was appointed a professor of law at the Westfälische Wilhelms-Universität Münster in early 1997. There he holds the chair in Common Law and Comparative Legal Theory and serves on the editorial board of the periodical *Rechtstheorie* ("Legal Theory"). He is the faculty advisor to the Foreign Law Program and regularly teaches U.S. constitutional law. He has published widely in English and German in the areas of constitutional and environmental law, comparative law, and jurisprudence. He is also the author of the *Talking Law Dictionary*, a German-English law dictionary in which the terms are pronounced by leading judges from Germany and the common law world, including United States Supreme Court Associate Justice Stephen Breyer.

Introduction

THIS BOOK IS ABOUT DEMOCRATIC GOVERNMENT AND ITS CITIZENS. GOVERNMENT possesses power. Citizens enjoy rights that protect them against untoward exercises of this power. All exercises of governmental power are traceable to, and legitimated by, the people, making them democratic.

To be meaningful and effective, democracy demands accountability. In American government, accountability is realized most immediately in the direct election of legislators. Accountability, and thereby democracy, is also fostered by the assignment of distinct governmental functions to discrete branches of government in accordance with the principle of separation of powers. Similar democratic considerations help account for the vertical division of governmental power in accordance with the principle of federalism.

But the principles of separation of powers and federalism also operate to split the monopoly of sovereign power. This splitting is believed to create a climate more hospitable to the promotion and conservation of liberty. When this device fails, judicial intervention becomes necessary to protect human rights from majoritarian zeal.

The materials covered in this book could be presented in any number of ways. A political scientist might stress political aspects, and focus on democracy. A historian might trace economic, political, and cultural developments. Jurists, on the other hand, tend to emphasize ultimate questions of governmental power and constitutional rights, and to center on the role of the courts. They attempt to fashion concepts and institutions into rigid frameworks. All of these approaches have their strengths and weaknesses. The lawyer's approach of plotting outer boundaries is valid and necessary because ultimate questions must often be confronted and decided in legislating, enforcing, and in interpreting law and constitutional rights. However, this approach has the unavoidable side effect of suggesting that government in fact exercises all of its power to the maximum allowable limit, and that liberty ceases at the constitutional frontier. Neither is, of course, true. In particular, by focusing on constitutional rights, this approach disregards the multiplicity of far-reaching rights created by statute.

One half of this book is devoted each to governmental power and constitutional rights. The first half (Part One) sketches the structure of the federal government of the United States, focusing on the core principle of separation of powers (Subpart A). Part One also discusses so-called "checks and balances," which are deliberate departures from the principle of strict separation of powers. Federalism (Subpart B) refers to the interplay between the federal and state governments of the United States. The materials on federalism end by suggesting that democratic "localism," known in Europe as the principle of subsidiarity, be recognized as a justiciable principle of American constitutional law.

Part One features a number of fundamental decisions of the United States Supreme Court, such as *Heart of Atlanta Motel* v. *United States, United States* v. *Lopez, Gonzales* v. *Raich, McCulloch* v. *Maryland, Youngstown Sheet & Tube Co.* v. *Sawyer [Steel Seizure Case], Morrison* v. *Olson, Clinton* v. *Jones, Marbury* v. *Madison, Martin* v. *Hunter's Lessee,* and *Printz* v. *United States.* Part Two includes *Plyler* v. *Doe, United States* v. *Virginia [Virginia Military Institute Case], United States* v. *Eichman, Brandenburg* v. *Ohio, Jenkins* v. *Georgia, R. A. V.* v. *City of St. Paul, Zelman* v. *Simmons-Harris, Wisconsin* v. *Yoder, Roe* v. *Wade, Korematsu* v. *United States, City of Richmond* v. *J. A. Croson Co., Washington* v. *Davis, Brown* v. *Board of Education [Brown I and II],* and *Saenz* v. *Roe.*

Part Two appraises the panoply of explicit and implicit constitutional rights protected by the Constitution. In the past half century, the Supreme Court has been much more active in the subject matter of this part of the book than in that of the first. For ease of understanding and study, constitutional rights are subsumed under the concepts of liberty and equality. Liberty rights can usefully be thought of as individual rights. They include the "fundamental rights" recognized by the Constitution and by the Supreme Court, such as freedom of speech and the right of privacy. Equality rights are those enjoyed as a member of a protected group. According to reigning doctrine, the protected groups are known as "suspect" and "quasi-suspect classes." Racial classifications, for example, belong to the former group; gender classifications, to the latter.

PART ONE

GOVERNMENTAL POWER

Part One of this book addresses sovereign power and the structure of the government of the United States of America. The first of the two subparts (Subpart A) primarily treats the horizontal distribution of authority among the three limbs of the federal government. This distribution is known as separation of powers. The tactic of separating powers assigns responsibility for legislative, executive, and judicial functions to more or less independent branches, regardless of the subject matter or purpose of the governmental action. This tactic is tempered by theoretical limitations and by deliberate use of "checks and balances."

Subpart A introduces and expounds upon the theme that the federal government is one of limited, enumerated powers. This theme is taken up in Subpart B, which faces the topic of federalism, that is, the constitutional and prudential roles of the state and local governments vis-à-vis the federal government. The stratagem of American federalism is to cleave federal matters from non-federal matters, to allocate the former more or less exclusively to the federal government, and to reserve the latter for more or less independent resolution by the states. Subpart B concludes by asking whether the value of democratic "localism," known in Europe as the principle of subsidiarity, ought not be recognized as a justiciable constitutional principle in the United States.

By splitting governmental authority, federalism is thought, among other things, to promote democratic accountability and to lessen the risk and gravity of undivided, extensive attacks on civil liberties. Coincidentally, these same purposes—pursuit of freedom and democracy—underpin the principle of separation of powers that is the principal focus of Subpart A.

SUBPART A

The Federal Government

THIS BOOK IS ABOUT CORE PRINCIPLES. ONE SUCH CORE PRINCIPLE IS DEMOCRACY. The U.S. Constitution begins with the emphatic words "We the People." Public officials are routinely criticized for being out of touch with the will of the people, and public debate often centers on conflicting interpretations of that will. However, the U.S. Constitution does not create a direct democracy. There is no provision for direct law-making, for example, by initiative. While federal legislators are elected, there is no provision for their recall. There is no provision for recall of the president or even for a parliamentary vote of "no confidence." Only two executive officials, the president and vice president, and none of the judges, are elected. Private individuals cannot demand enforcement of federal laws unless they have a personal stake ("standing"). While members of the public who serve as jurors hear many federal cases, they are acting in an official, representative capacity. Even then their verdict is ineffective unless reduced to judgment by a judge. All federal governmental action, whether legislative, executive, or judicial, is therefore democratically indirect.

Many fascinating questions regarding democracy, such as, Why is democracy good?, are not addressed in this book.[1] But democratic ideals are fundamental to the U.S. Constitution and to the United States, and should not be ignored in considering the materials here presented. In particular when exploring the boundaries of constitutional rights one must ask whether the judicial safeguarding of those rights does not imply a failure of democratic institutions.

The Constitution took effect upon ratification by the ninth state on June 21, 1788, but the important states of Virginia and New York did not ratify until June 25, 1788 and July 26, 1789 respectively. The Founding Fathers of the American Constitution did not abide by the procedure called for in Article XIII of the Articles of Confederation (Attach. B). Does this mean that the Constitution is illegitimate, and that the Articles are still in effect?

The structure of the federal government of the United States is characterized by perhaps the most pronounced application of the principle of separation of powers in any country. A discussion of that principle provides

---

[1] See Dahl. For further thoughts see Lundmark, *Forms* and Lundmark, *East Germany*.

a background against which the three branches of the federal government are presented. These are introduced in the order that they were created by the Constitution: the legislative, the executive, and the judiciary.

1. THE PRINCIPLE OF SEPARATION OF POWERS

The government of a state is thought to consist of three categories of powers: legislative, executive, and judicial, respectively making, enforcing, and interpreting law. Political theorist John Locke (1632–1704) favored a government of limited powers, one that was consequently less likely to violate the individual's life, health, liberty, and possessions. For the same reason, that is, the avoidance of despotic rule, Locke, in *Of Civil Government*, advocated entrusting the legislative and executive functions to distinct branches of government. The Lockean tradition of separation of powers is echoed in Justice Brandeis's dissenting opinion in *Myers v. United States*:

> The doctrine of the separation of powers was adopted by the convention of 1787 not to promote efficiency but to preclude the exercise of arbitrary power. The purpose was not to avoid friction, but, by means of the inevitable friction incident to the distribution of the governmental powers among three departments, to save the people from autocracy. In America, as in England, the conviction prevailed then that the people must look to representative assemblies for the protection of their liberties. And protection of the individual … from the arbitrary or capricious exercise of power was then believed to be an essential of free government.[2]
>
> The divorcing of the judiciary from the legislature was championed most famously by Charles de Montesquieu (1689–1755) in *De l'esprit des loix*, published in 1748. When it came to the principle of separation of powers, Montesquieu's sympathies were more democratic than Locke's. According to Montesquieu, the arbitrary judicial *parlements* must be stripped of all law-making power. In turn, this power must be vested in a democratically elected and accountable legislature.[3] The theories of these two men, Locke and Montesquieu, formed the philosophical basis for the division of the federal government in the United States into three more or less distinct branches. While not treated here, there is a pronounced doctrinal similarity between the federal and the state constitutional conceptions of separation of powers.[4]

---

[2] 272 U.S. 52 (1926).
[3] See Merryman.
[4] Gardner at p. 111.

In the American conception of separation of powers, almost all governmental actions require the agreement of two branches; and any governmental action that limits an individual's constitutional rights must ordinarily navigate its way through all three organs of government, each of which must weigh the action's constitutionality.

The partition of powers into branches of government is not complete in the United States. This lack of complete separation is due to at least two reasons, one deliberate, and one inescapable, discussed here under the headings checks and balances and the ambiguity of the tri-partite demarcation.

a.   Checks and Balances

One reason why the partition of governmental powers in the federal government is incomplete is that the U.S. Constitution contains various "checks and balances," that is, procedures for one branch to superintend the other. While these devices may violate the letter of the principle of separation of powers, they do not violate its spirit, which is the avoidance of capricious or "despotic" rule. Indeed, the Framers of the American Constitution deliberately followed Montesquieu's exhortation when they granted the president the power to veto a bill before it becomes law,[5] an action more akin to law-making than law enforcement. Again *à la* Montesquieu the Framers bestowed upon the parliament (the Congress) the power to remove the president from office, although they limited the grounds for removal to conviction of "Treason, Bribery, or other high Crimes and Misdemeanors."[6] The impeachment process is hardly legislative, being a procedure more akin to criminal indictment (executive) and conviction (judicial).

Other examples of deliberate checks and balances include the requirement that the president secure the approval of two-thirds of the senators to conclude a treaty[7] and the condition that a majority of the Senate shall confirm the presidential appointment of ambassadors, federal judges, and other federal officers.[8] The popular election of the president,[9] rather than appointment by the parliament, might also be understood in this vein. So too can the institution of judicial review of legislative enactments, and of executive decisions, for conformity with the Constitution.

---

[5] Art. I, § 7.
[6] Art. II, § 4.
[7] Art. II, § 2, cl. 2.
[8] Art. II, § 2, cl. 2.
[9] Art. II, § 1.

b. On the Ambiguity of the Tri-Partite Demarcation

The second reason why the separation of powers in the U.S. is not complete is that the various powers do not lend themselves to clear theoretical and practical demarcation. In part this is true because they overlap to an uncertain, but, nevertheless, considerable, degree.

The theoretical division of the tripartite powers of government according to the principle of separation of powers is shaped by the proposition that the legislature, as the law giver, is the only branch that should be making law. But an internally consistent demarcation among the several powers with respect to law-making is impossible to construct. Legislation ordinarily refers to formal norms deliberately created by the legislature, which is the organ of government assembled for this purpose. The definition thus excludes custom. It also excludes the pronouncements of judicial tribunals. What then of the major areas of law that can only be found in judicial opinions? To take the crassest example: What of the many constitutional rights—privacy, for example—that are only vaguely subsumable, if at all, under textual provisions of the Constitution? Are these rights not law? Or what of "interstitial" law-making by the courts, which fills gaps sometimes left deliberately in legislation? Has the legislature somehow delegated law-making authority to the courts? And, most importantly for the United States, what of the common law, which regulated most all aspects of private law before the ascendancy of statutory law in this century? Does anyone contend that the Framers of the American Constitution meant to demote the stature of common law to delegated law-making or sub-law?

Legislation also differs from judicial pronouncements in that legislation looks to the future. It alters existing conditions by making a new rule for prospective application. Legislation is said to take effect *ex nunc*. *Ex post facto* laws are even specifically prohibited by the U.S. Constitution.[10] Judicial judgments are pronounced *post factum*. One might think that the Anglo-American doctrine of *stare decisis*, which makes previous judicial decisions binding on future decisions, offends this distinction and, thus, transgresses against the separation of powers principle. Actually, the opposite is true. By adhering to legal rules announced in previous decisions, judges are actually reducing the opportunity for judicial law-making and thus are promoting separation of powers. Of course judges may return to the rule and change it if it has proved to be wrong (corrective overruling). Further, they may determine that society has changed, perhaps through the passage of legislation, making a change in the rule necessary (renovative overruling). Merely changing a rule because the members of the court no longer agree with it (legislative overruling) should generally be condemned

---

[10] Art. I, §§ 9 and 10.

because, among other reasons, it violates notions of separation of powers.[11]

Execution of the laws means, most fundamentally, that every action of the executive must be based on law. "Law" for purposes of this truism must be read to include the Constitution, since the executive may have occasion to enforce the Constitution directly. In cases of perceived conflict between legislative and constitutional law, the executive would be required to comply with one or the other (depending upon one's conception of the state). But in making this determination, isn't the executive acting judicially? And what of instances of great public importance where the legislature has not acted? Locke would recognize executive prerogative in such cases, an innate privilege that might even supersede legislation. Here the executive would be acting legislatively. To stay with the executive for sake of example, can the executive be authorized to "legislate" interstitially, at least if based on specifically drafted authorizing legislation? Or what about informal, consistent practice of the executive in carrying out the law? Does this practice ever ripen into "law" and bind the executive? If so, can it not be said that the executive is "making law" by custom and practice? (These are issues dealt with below under the rubrics "executive privilege" and "delegation.")

Returning to the legislature, legislation ordinarily possesses general normative character. But this is not always the case. The Constitution has been interpreted to allow Congress to enact special "private" bills that benefit particular individuals, for example, by conferring the Congressional Medal of Honor, or by chartering a bank. These and other activities, though undertaken by the Congress by legislative enactment, have more of an administrative than legislative character.

Finally, the tremendous growth in the importance of administrative agencies and of federal departments in the past decades has prompted a reexamination of the accuracy of the tri-partite conception of the state, and of the efficacy of the principle of separation of powers in meeting its traditional objectives. Administrative agencies routinely exercise all three traditional governmental functions. They promulgate (legislate) regulations, they enforce (execute) these regulations and the laws on which they are based, and they adjudicate (judge) claims arising out of the application of the laws and regulations. Perhaps administrative agencies can best be understood as subordinate governmental subject-matter bodies, subordinate in the sense that municipalities are subordinate to the states. But if one thinks of them in this way, what has happened to democratic rule and to the constitutional guarantee of a republican form of government?[12]

---

[11] Lundmark, Juristische Technik at pp.162, 178–180.
[12] See Art. IV, § 4.

2. Legislative Powers

The Congress created by the Articles of Confederation (Attach. B) was unicameral. But the present Congress has two houses, the House of Representatives and the Senate. The bifurcation, which was suggested by the bifurcation in the British Parliament, resulted when the colonies with smaller populations refused to join a strengthened union in which their representation would be determined solely by their population. The smaller states preferred the New Jersey Plan, whereby each state would have an equal number of representatives. The New Jersey Plan was in turn rejected by the states with larger populations, like Virginia and New York. What resulted was the Great Compromise, which provided for equal representation by two representatives each in the upper house (Senate), and representation in proportion to population in the lower house (House of Representatives). In addition, the small states were guaranteed at three votes for president and vice president in the electoral college.[13] Each state, regardless of population, is also entitled to at least one member in the House.[14]

Another (in)famous compromise concerned slavery. At the constitutional convention, the delegates from the northern states wanted the Congress to have the power to forbid trade in slaves. Most southern states opposed this. However, for purposes of representation in the House, the southern states wanted to count slaves even though slaves enjoyed neither citizenship nor the franchise. According to the compromise, Congress was not able to forbid the foreign slave trade until 1808,[15] which it promptly did. In return, the southern states were allowed to count each slave as three-fifths of a person for purposes of representation in the House of Representatives.[16]

The Senate is composed of two senators from each state, elected for staggered, six-year terms.[17] Originally chosen by the state legislatures, senators have been popularly elected since 1913.[18] Members of the House of Representatives are elected to two-year terms,[19] the shortest of any legislative body. In 1911, Congress fixed the total number of representatives at 435, elected in first-past-the-post elections in each of as many districts. The population of all districts is approximately the same. Presently, the average population of each congressional district is 690,000. California, with the largest population, has 53 representatives. The seven smallest states in

---

[13] See Art. I, § 1, cl. 2.
[14] Art. I, § 2, cl. 3.
[15] Art. I, § 9, cl. 1.
[16] Art. I, § 2, cl. 3.
[17] Art. I, § 3, cl. 1.
[18] Amend. 17.
[19] Art. I, § 2, cl. 1. Art. I, § 2, cl. 1

population have only one representative each. The District of Columbia, Guam, U.S. Virgin Islands, Northern Mariana Islands, and American Samoa are each represented by one non-voting delegate, and Puerto Rico elects a non-voting resident commissioner to the House.

Each house of Congress is the judge of the qualifications of its members.[20] Each house has the power to punish its members for disorderly behavior by majority vote, and to expel a member by two-thirds' vote.[21] Both the House and the Senate have adopted procedural rules, as specifically provided in the Constitution.[22] Whereas the House rules strictly limit debate, senators, by contrast, are allowed to speak as long as they want unless 60 senators vote for closure. Abuse of this privilege to block a vote is referred to as a "filibuster."

With one exception—tax bills — a bill may originate in either house.[23] A bill becomes law only if it is passed by majority vote in both houses and is either signed by the president or, if the bill is vetoed by the president, if the veto is overridden by a two-thirds' vote in each house of Congress.[24]

a. On the Meaning of the Term "Legislative"

In order to apply the principle of separation of powers, one must have some conception of what is meant by "legislative." One approach, employed above, is to attempt general, abstract definitions. Another, discussed in a later section, is to ask which actions of the Congress are subject to presidential veto.

The following discussion approaches the question in two additional ways. First, it explores the text of the Constitution. Second, it examines the question of what actions are so inherently legislative that legislators enjoy absolute immunity when engaged in them.

i. *The Text of the Constitution*

According to the first sentence of the first article of the U.S. Constitution, all legislative powers granted by the Constitution are vested in the Congress. The term "legislative powers" is not defined in the Constitution. Obviously, the term was meant by the Framers of the Constitution to differentiate the legislative powers of Congress from the executive powers of the President and from the judicial powers of the Supreme Court.

Some inkling of what the Framers meant by "legislative powers" can be deduced from the text of the first article, which in part enumerates

---

[20] Art. I, § 5, cl. 1.
[21] Art. I, § 5, cl. 2.
[22] Art. I, § 5, cl. 2.
[23] Art. I, § 7, cl. 1.
[24] Art. I, § 7, cl. 2.

congressional powers. The powers there enumerated can roughly be classified as follows (with examples in parentheses):

- Administrative powers: The power of Congress to organize its affairs (Art. I, § 2, cl. 5; Art. I, § 3, cl. 5; Art. I, § 4; Art. I, § 5; Art. I, 7, 3).
- Taxing and spending powers: The powers to raise money by imposing taxes, to borrow money, and to spend for the general welfare of the United States (Art. I, § 8, cls. 1, 2, and 6). The spending power is discussed below.
- Supervisory powers: The power to impeach, and try those officials charged with impeachable offenses (Art. I, § 2, cl. 5; Art. I, § 3, cl. 6).[25]
- Establishment powers: The powers to establish post offices, to coin money, to establish federal courts, to grant patents and copyrights (cls. 5, 7, 8, and 9), and to acquire property (Art. 4, § 3). The power to coin money includes the power to print paper money.[26]
- War power, and powers over external affairs, including the treaty power shared with the president (Art. II, § 2, cl. 2): The powers to provide for defense, to declare war, and to punish violations of international law (Art. I, § 2, cls. 10–16). This congressional authority continues after cessation of hostilities to remedy evils, such as housing shortages, attributable to the war.[27]
- Regulatory powers, including the power to investigate matters of legislative concern: The powers to regulate naturalization and bankruptcies, "To regulate Commerce with foreign Nations and among the several States, and with the Indian Tribes," to govern the District of Columbia (Art. I, § 8, cls. 3, 4, and 17), and to consent to compacts between states or between a state and a foreign power (Art. I, § 10, cl. 3). The authority of Congress over the admission of non-citizens aliens is plenary.[28]

Of these classifications, only the last fits squarely within the definition of legislation proposed in the preceding section, that is, formal norms deliberately created by the legislature. Nevertheless, all of the specified powers, whether legislative in character or not, may, without question, constitutionally be exercised by the Congress.

---

[25] The determination of the procedures for trying an impeached official is constitutionally entrusted to the Senate and is consequently not reviewable by the courts (Nixon v. United States, 506 U.S. 224 (1993)).
[26] Legal Tender Cases (Knox v. Lee), 79 U.S. 457 (1871).
[27] Woods v. Cloyd W. Miller Co., 333 U.S. 138 (1948).
[28] Kleindienst v. Mandel, 408 U.S. 753 (1972). The commerce clause is discussed in some detail below.

Before moving on, consider the classification of the following powers that are specifically enumerated in various amendments:

- To enforce the amendment banning slavery (Amend. 13, § 2)
- To enforce the provisions of the Fourteenth Amendment, which, among other things, guarantee due process and equal protection (Amend. 14, § 5)
- To enforce voting rights (Amends. 15, § 2; 19, § 2; 23, § 2; 24, § 2; 26, § 2)

ii. Legislative Immunity

The distinction between legislative and non-legislative congressional activities is important for more than reasons of separation of powers. It is important in deciding what actions of the Congress are subject to presidential veto. It is also crucial to the existence and scope of congressional immunity.

The Constitution provides that, "for any Speech or Debate in either House," senators and representatives "shall not be questioned in any other Place."[29] This so-called "speech and debate clause" has been construed to forbid criminal or civil proceedings against members of Congress for "legislative acts."[30] The clause has also been extended to protect congressional aides who engage in acts that would be immune if performed by the legislator.[31]

To enjoy the protection of congressional immunity under the speech and debate clause, the conduct must be "legislative." Legislative conduct includes, in addition to statements on the floor of the Congress, matters such as conducting committee hearings, introducing material into the record at such hearings, and preparing committee reports; but it does not extend to the public distribution of committee reports, even when authorized by statute.[32] Nor does it extend to republication of defamatory statements originally made on the floor of the Congress.[33] And, while the speech and debate clause ordinarily protects a legislator's motivation for her legislative acts from judicial sanction, the clause does not prevent prosecution for bribery to influence legislation.[34]

---

[29] Art. I, § 6, cl. 1.
[30] United States v. Johnson, 383 U.S. 169 (1966).
[31] Gravel v. United States, 408 U.S. 606 (1972).
[32] Doe v. McMillan, 412 U.S. 306 (1973).
[33] Hutchinson v. Proxmire, 443 U.S. 111 (1979).
[34] United States v. Brewster, 408 U.S. 501 (1972).

b. Enumeration of Powers

The federal government is one of limited jurisdiction (power). This characteristic is felt most keenly in Article I, section 8, in which specified ("enumerated") powers are delegated by the individual states or directly by the people to the newly formed federal state. Copyrights, patents, bankruptcies, national defense, and "piracies and felonies committed on the high seas" possessed sufficient national import to merit inclusion among the enumerated powers. Criminal law and private law, which fell under the jurisdiction of the common law (state) courts, did not.

There is one broad exception to the doctrine that the federal government's powers are limited to those specifically enumerated in the Constitution. This exception encompasses external and foreign affairs, where the federal government's powers are considered inherent and plenary despite not being expressly recited in the Constitution.[35] This exception is discussed below.

As mentioned above, the Constitution was drafted against the backdrop of the Articles of Confederation (Attach. B). The federal government formed by the Articles was seen as too weak because, among other things, it lacked the powers to tax and to regulate interstate commerce. As a result, that first federal government was dependent on voluntary contributions of money from the states. These in turn had taken to imposing import taxes on goods from other states, in effect competing against each other. As shown in the following subsections, both of these shortcomings were addressed in the new constitution in, respectively, the taxing and spending clauses and the commerce clause. The discussion also addresses the necessary and proper clause of Article I, section 8, clause 18.

i. *Taxing Power*

In the words of the Constitution, "The Congress shall have Power To lay and collect Taxes, Duties, Imposts and Excises, to pay the Debts and provide for the common Defence and general Welfare of the United States."[36] "Duties" are import taxes. "Excises" or "excise taxes" are taxes on the sale, use, and production of goods, and sometimes on the privilege of doing business. "Imposts" is a term that generally includes both duties and excise taxes.

The Supreme Court was confronted for the first time in 1869 with the question whether the taxing power could be used to regulate. At issue was a federal law that imposed a tax on banknotes issued by state banks. The tax had the effect, and most certainly the intent, of taxing state-issued banknotes out of existence. The Court upheld the tax under Congress's

---

[35] United States v. Curtiss-Wright Export Corp., 299 U.S. 304 (1936).
[36] Art. I, § 8, cl. 1.

power to "regulate the Value" of money.[37] The Congress may do indirectly by taxation that which it might have done directly by regulation.[38]

What then of a tax that cannot be justified by resort to an enumerated power? Here one must look to the dominant intent of the tax to determine whether its objective is to raise revenue or to regulate or prohibit specific activities. However, the Supreme Court has not been consistent in applying this test. For example, it upheld a tax on yellow margarine that was 40 times higher than the tax on white margarine despite the obvious purpose of supporting the dairy industry.[39]

In 1894, Congress enacted the federal government's first income tax law, one which taxed income derived from property. The Supreme Court ruled the tax unconstitutional because, as a "direct tax," it must be apportioned according to population as provided in Article II.[40] In response, Congress proposed the following amendment, which was ratified to become the Sixteenth Amendment in 1913:

> The Congress shall have power to lay and collect taxes on incomes, from whatever source derived, without apportionment among the several States, and without regard to any census or enumeration.[41]

The revenues generated under the power to collect income taxes have dramatically changed the complexion of the federal government, and have multiplied the importance of the spending power, discussed in the following subsection.

ii. Spending Power

The spending clause empowers Congress "to pay the Debts and provide for the common Defence and general Welfare of the United States." By limiting expenditures to those that serve the general welfare, the Constitution requires that expenditures must be for the "common benefit as distinguished from some mere local purpose."[42] But does this mean that, supposing the requirement of "common benefit" is met, Congress may regulate indirectly by spending that which it could not constitutionally have regulated directly? Theoretically, the answer must be No, for otherwise the federal government would lose its fundamental character as a

---

[37] Art. I, § 5.
[38] Veazie Bank v. Fenno, 75 U.S. 533 (1869).
[39] McCray v. United States, 195 U.S. 27 (1904).
[40] Art. II, § 2, cl. 3 and § 9, cl. 4; Pollock v. Farmers' Loan & Trust Co., 157 U.S. 429 (1895).
[41] Compare the last clause of the 16th Amendment with the last clause of Article I, section 8, clause 1.
[42] United States v. Gerlach Live Stock Co., 339 U.S. 725 (1950).

government of limited, enumerated powers. But making the distinction in theory and in practice are two different things, as illustrated by the decision of the United States Supreme Court in *Helvering* v. *Davis*, discussed in the following paragraph. (The extent to which state autonomy may limit federal conditional spending programs is discussed in a later section.)

In 1935, Congress enacted the Social Security Act. Titles II and VIII of that Act impose a tax on employers and employees, and provide for the payment of old-age benefits. Traditionally, social programs had been the province of state and local governments, and there was no specific grant of power upon which Congress could rely. Nevertheless, the United States Supreme Court upheld the constitutionality of the legislation in *Helvering* v. *Davis*.[43] In doing so, the Supreme Court seemed to suggest that there is an implied federal legislative power to aid and cooperate with the states. Justice Cardozo wrote for the majority:

> The line must still be drawn between one welfare and another, between particular and general. Where this shall be placed cannot be known through a formula in advance of the event. The discretion, however, is not confided to the courts. The discretion belongs to Congress, unless the choice is clearly wrong, a display of arbitrary power, not an exercise of judgment. This is now familiar law .... Nor is the concept of the general welfare static. Needs that were narrow or parochial a century ago may be interwoven in our day with the well-being of the nation. What is critical or urgent changes with the times.
>
> ...
>
> Congress did not improvise a judgment when it was found that the award of old age benefits would be conducive to the general welfare .... The problem is plainly national in area and dimensions. Moreover, laws of the separate states cannot deal with it effectively. Congress, at least, had a basis for that belief. States and local governments are often lacking in the resources that are necessary to finance an adequate program of security for the aged .... Apart from the failure of resources, states and local governments are at times reluctant to increase so heavily the burden of taxation to be borne by their residents for fear of placing themselves in a position of economic disadvantage. We have seen this in our study of the problem of unemployment compensation. [*Steward Machine Co.* v. *Davis*, 301 U.S. 548 (1937), upheld Title IX of the same Act, which imposes a payroll tax on employers and provides for unemployment insurance.] A system of old age pensions has

---

[43] 301 U.S. 619 (1937).

special dangers of its own, if put in force in one state and rejected in another. The existence of such a system is a bait to the needy and dependent elsewhere, encouraging them to migrate and seek a haven of repose. Only a power that is national can serve the interests of all.

...

When money is spent to promote the general welfare, the concept of welfare or the opposite is shaped by Congress, not the states. So the concept be not arbitrary, the locality must yield. Constitution, art. 6, par. 2.

The spending power is probably the most important federal power in terms of its impact on the daily lives of Americans. Federal funding of social programs, especially in cooperation with the states (called "cooperative federalism"), has grown astronomically since the 1930s. Just three federal social programs—Social Security (retirement), Medicare (medical care for the aged and handicapped), and Medicaid (medical care for the poor)—are now responsible for almost forty percent (40%) of the federal budget.[44] (Defense spending accounts for one-fifth.) Other social programs which are based on the federal spending power include Temporary Assistance for Needy Families (TANF) and Food Stamps (coupons with which to buy foodstuffs). Four million families with a total of five million children receive TANF.[45] The federal Food Stamp Program provides benefits to 26 million people every month.[46]

Can public funding of presidential election campaigns be justified under the spending clause as promoting the general welfare?[47]

iii. Commerce Clause

According to the text of the commerce clause, the federal power over commerce extends to international commerce, to interstate commerce, and to commerce with the Indian tribes. Power to regulate intrastate commerce therefore rests textually with the states.

Because of the importance of the commerce clause as a basis for federal legislation, and the vague contours of its authority, the following discussion will trace the congressional employment of the clause and the judicial response, which will include an abstract from the 1964 decision in *Heart of Atlanta Motel*. The discussion culminates with the Supreme Court

---

[44] Congressional Budget Office, January 2007.
[45] TANF Seventh Annual Report to Congress, December 2006.
[46] United States Department of Agriculture, Food and Nutrition Services, Food Stamps - Persons Participating Report, September 2007.
[47] See *Buckley* v. *Valeo*, 424 U.S. 1 (1976).

decisions in *United States* v. *Lopez*[48] and *Gonzales* v. *Raich*,[49] treated at length below.

aa. Early Commerce Clause Jurisprudence

The interstate commerce clause was originally intended to prevent Balkanization and to encourage creation of a national market.[50] During the nineteenth century the federal courts employed the commerce clause, if at all, when the law of a single state was claimed to interfere with the interstate transportation and commerce in goods, for, stated generally, the commerce clause prohibits states from imposing unreasonable burdens upon interstate commerce.

In order to decide these cases, federal judges had to define what was meant by "commerce" and by "interstate." According to the Supreme Court in 1824, commerce that was "interstate" was commerce which concerned more states than one.[51] In other words, interstate commerce presupposed a geographical transborder element. The judges of the federal courts employed a mercantile definition of commerce, holding that commerce consisted of buying and selling. Thus, in *United States* v. *E.C. Knight Co.*,[52] the Supreme Court held: "Contracts to buy, sell, or exchange goods to be transported among the several States, the transportation and its instrumentalities ... may be regulated, but this is because they form part of interstate trade or commerce." According to this definition, production, manufacturing, and mining were merely precursors of commerce, but not commerce themselves. Therefore, they could not be regulated by Congress under the commerce clause.[53]

By construing the commerce clause so narrowly, the federal judges avoided having to declare protectionist policies of the state governments unconstitutional even though they had or could have had a detrimental effect on interstate commerce. For example, in one case the federal judges held that a ferry monopoly was intrastate because the ferry never crossed a border, even though passengers and freight moved across state lines.[54] In another case, the Supreme Court ruled that brewing and packaging of intoxicating beverages did not constitute buying and selling ("commerce"), but rather merely "production." Thus, the states could forbid the production of alcoholic beverages without doing violence to the commerce clause.[55]

---

[48] 514 U.S. 549 (1995).
[49] 545 U.S. 1 (2005).
[50] See Hughes v. Oklahoma, 441 U.S. 322, 325 (1979).
[51] Gibbons v. Ogden, 22 U.S. 1 (1824).
[52] 156 U.S. 1 (1895).
[53] Wickard v. Filburn, 317 U.S. 111 (1942).
[54] Veazie v. Moor, 55 U.S. 568 (1853).
[55] Kidd v. Pearson, 128 U.S. 1 (1888).

The mercantile test for commerce survived into the late 19th century, which was a time of expanding federal preoccupation with commerce. Examples of federal legislation stemming from this time period include the Interstate Commerce Act of 1887 and the Sherman Antitrust Act of 1890. As a result of this new federal legislative interest in commerce, the commerce clause became a handy weapon for attacks upon federal legislation. New federal regulations of production, manufacturing, and mining were held to be unconstitutional because, not being commerce, Congress had no power to regulate them.

In *E.C. Knight*, cited above, a federal agency sought to block the acquisition of a sugar refinery on the ground that its acquisition would give rise to a monopoly unlawful under the Sherman Antitrust Act. The federal judges theorized that the manufacture of sugar was a precondition of commerce, but not exactly commerce itself; as such, it could not be part of interstate commerce over which the federal government had jurisdiction.[56] The same reasoning was applied to the federal Child Labor Act, which forbade the transportation of goods manufactured with the help of child labor. According to the Supreme Court at the time, manufacture was not commerce, at least not interstate commerce.[57] The same reasoning was followed for mining. "Mining," according to the Court, "brings the subject matter of commerce into existence. Commerce disposes of it"; and thus Congress could not legislate a nationwide minimum wage for miners, because mining was not commerce.[58] Even if mercantile commerce as then defined was involved, the federal judges would differentiate between measures that directly (constitutionally) and indirectly (unconstitutionally) regulated commerce. Applying this ancillary test, the federal judges held a federal law setting maximum working hours and minimum wages for the poultry industry to be unconstitutional because the effects of the law on commerce were indirect, not direct.[59]

bb. Recent Commerce Clause Jurisprudence

The great shift in the opinion of the Supreme Court came in 1937 shortly after President Roosevelt announced his "Court Packing Plan." According to Roosevelt's legislative plan, the number of judges on the Supreme Court was to be increased in order to ensure that younger judges—those sympathetic to Roosevelt's legislation—had a majority on the Court. Even though Roosevelt's plan met with opposition in Congress, the Court

---

[56] United States v. E.C. Knight Co., 156 U.S. 1 (1895).
[57] Hammer v. Dagenhart, 247 U.S. 251 (1918).
[58] Carter v. Carter Coal Co., 298 U.S. 238, 304 (1936).
[59] Schechter Poultry Corp. v. United States, 295 U.S. 495 (1935), in which the Supreme Court declared the National Industrial Recovery Act of 1933 unconstitutional, in part as an unlawful delegation of legislative power to the executive without sufficient standards.

began backing down from its protection of the supremacy of the states in economic matters.

In the seminal opinion, *National Labor Relations Board* v. *Jones & Laughlin Steel Corporation*,[60] the Supreme Court not only abandoned the direct-indirect test, it went further: Even intrastate activities were reachable by Congress under the commerce clause if they had such a close and substantial relation to interstate commerce that their control was essential or appropriate to protect that commerce from burdens and obstructions. Using this new standard, the Supreme Court upheld the National Labor Relations Act of 1935 which, among other things, outlawed unfair employment practices such as firing employees for union activity. There followed decisions which emphasized the cumulative effect of the regulated activity on commerce and interstate commerce. Following the lead of Congress, the Supreme Court so expanded the reach of the commerce clause that all activity could be regulated if it had some conceivable, if only cumulative, effect on an interstate transaction. Thus the Supreme Court upheld laws which forbade local, usurious credit transactions[61]; which prohibited discrimination in privately owned restaurants[62]; which regulated the harvest and consumption of small quantities of wheat[63]; and which punished arson attacks on apartment buildings.[64] The Court even stopped calling production, manufacture, and mining a precursor to commerce. Indeed, one case exclusively concerned the regulation of intrastate mining, yet the federal regulation was upheld on the strength of the commerce clause.[65]

CASE: Heart of Atlanta Motel v. United States
379 U.S. 241 (1964)

MR. JUSTICE CLARK delivered the opinion of the Court.

...

The case comes here on admissions and stipulated facts. Appellant owns and operates the Heart of Atlanta Motel which has 216 rooms available to transient guests. The motel is located on Courtland Street, two blocks from downtown Peachtree Street. It is readily accessible to interstate highways 75 and 85 and state highways 23 and 41. Appellant solicits patronage from outside the State

---

[60] 301 U.S. 1 (1937).
[61] Perez v. United States, 402 U.S. 146, 155–156 (1971).
[62] Katzenbach v. McClung, 379 U.S. 294 (1964).
[63] Wickard v. Filburn, 317 U.S. 111 (1942).
[64] Russell v. United States, 471 U.S. 858 (1985).
[65] Hodel v. Virginia Surface Mining & Reclamation Assn., Inc., 452 U.S. 264 (1981).

of Georgia through various national advertising media, including magazines of national circulation; it maintains over 50 billboards and highway signs within the State, soliciting patronage for the motel; it accepts convention trade from outside Georgia and approximately 75% of its registered guests are from out of State. Prior to passage of the Act the motel had followed a practice of refusing to rent rooms to Negroes, and it alleged that it intended to continue to do so. In an effort to perpetuate that policy this suit was filed.

The appellant contends that Congress in passing this Act exceeded its power to regulate commerce under Art. I, 8, cl. 3, of the Constitution of the United States; that the Act violates the Fifth Amendment because appellant is deprived of the right to choose its customers and operate its business as it wishes, resulting in a taking of its liberty and property without due process of law and a taking of its property without just compensation; and, finally, that by requiring appellant to rent available rooms to Negroes against its will, Congress is subjecting it to involuntary servitude in contravention of the Thirteenth Amendment.

Congress first evidenced its interest in civil rights legislation in the Civil Rights or Enforcement Act of April 9, 1866. There followed four Acts, with a fifth, the Civil Rights Act of March 1, 1875, culminating the series. In 1883 this Court struck down the public accommodations sections of the 1875 Act in the *Civil Rights Cases*, 109 U.S. 3. No major legislation in this field had been enacted by Congress for 82 years when the Civil Rights Act of 1957 became law. It was followed by the Civil Rights Act of 1960. Three years later, on June 19, 1963, the late President Kennedy called for civil rights legislation in a message to Congress to which he attached a proposed bill. Its stated purpose was

> to promote the general welfare by eliminating discrimination based on race, color, religion, or national origin in ... public accommodations through the exercise by Congress of the powers conferred upon it ... to enforce the provisions of the fourteenth and fifteenth amendments, to regulate commerce among the several States, and to make laws necessary and proper to execute the powers conferred upon it by the Constitution.

...

In light of our ground for decision, it might be well at the outset to discuss the *Civil Rights Cases*, supra, which declared provisions of the Civil Rights Act of 1875 unconstitutional. We think that decision inapposite, and without precedential value in determining the constitutionality of the present Act. Unlike Title II of the present legislation, the 1875 Act broadly proscribed discrimination in "inns, public conveyances on land or water, theaters, and other places of public amusement," without limiting the categories of affected businesses to those impinging upon interstate commerce. In contrast, the applicability of Title II is carefully limited to enterprises having a direct and substantial relation to the interstate flow of goods and people, except where state action is involved. Further, the fact that certain kinds of businesses may not in 1875 have been sufficiently involved in interstate commerce to warrant bringing them within the ambit of the commerce power is not necessarily dispositive of the same question today. Our populace had not reached its present mobility, nor were facilities, goods and services circulating as readily in interstate commerce as they are today ...

...

The same interest in protecting interstate commerce which led Congress to deal with segregation in interstate carriers and the white-slave traffic has prompted it to extend the exercise of its power to gambling ...; to criminal enterprises ...; to deceptive practices in the sale of products ...; to fraudulent security transactions ...; to misbranding of drugs ...; to wages and hours ...; to members of labor unions ...; to crop control ...; to discrimination against shippers ...; to the protection of small business from injurious price cutting ...; to resale price maintenance ...; to professional football ...; and to racial discrimination by owners and managers of terminal restaurants ....

That Congress was legislating against moral wrongs in many of these areas rendered its enactments no less valid. In framing Title II of this Act Congress was also dealing with what it considered a moral problem. But that fact does not detract from the overwhelming evidence of the disruptive effect that racial discrimination has had on commercial intercourse. It was this burden which empowered Congress to enact appropriate legislation, and, given this basis for the exercise of its power, Congress was not restricted by the fact that the particular obstruction to interstate commerce with which it was dealing was also deemed a moral and social wrong.

It is said that the operation of the motel here is of a purely local character. But, assuming this to be true, "[i]f it is interstate commerce that feels the pinch, it does not matter how local the operation which applies the squeeze." ...

...

We find no merit in the remainder of appellant's contentions, including that of "involuntary servitude." As we have seen, 32 States prohibit racial discrimination in public accommodations. These laws but codify the common-law innkeeper rule which long predated the Thirteenth Amendment. It is difficult to believe that the Amendment was intended to abrogate this principle .... We could not say that the requirements of the Act in this regard are in any way "akin to African slavery."...

We, therefore, conclude that the action of the Congress in the adoption of the Act as applied here to a motel which concededly serves interstate travelers is within the power granted it by the Commerce Clause of the Constitution, as interpreted by this Court for 140 years. It may be argued that Congress could have pursued other methods to eliminate the obstructions it found in interstate commerce caused by racial discrimination. But this is a matter of policy that rests entirely with the Congress not with the courts. How obstructions in commerce may be removed—what means are to be employed—is within the sound and exclusive discretion of the Congress. It is subject only to one caveat—that the means chosen by it must be reasonably adapted to the end permitted by the Constitution. We cannot say that its choice here was not so adapted. The Constitution requires no more.
Affirmed.
[Concurring opinions omitted.]

cc. The Lopez Synthesis

Until the decision by the Supreme Court in *United States* v. *Lopez*, abstracted below, the commerce clause seemed not to limit Congress's legislative prerogative in any way. Indeed, since the New Deal of the 1930s, not a single piece of commerce clause legislation had been held unconstitutional for lack of jurisdiction. The last case declaring a commerce clause regulation unconstitutional for want of federal legislative jurisdiction was *Railroad Retirement Board* v. *Alton Railway Co.*[66] Professors Nowak and Rotunda wrote in their textbook *Constitutional Law* in 1991: "The Supreme Court today interprets the commerce clause as a complete grant of power."[67]

CASE: **United States v. Lopez**
514 U.S. 549 (1995)

CHIEF JUSTICE REHNQUIST delivered the opinion of the Court [in which O'Connor, Scalia, Kennedy, and Thomas joined].

---

[66] 295 U.S. 330 (1935).
[67] Nowark & Rotunda at p. 154.

In the Gun-Free School Zones Act of 1990, Congress made it a federal offense "for any individual knowingly to possess a firearm at a place that the individual knows, or has reasonable cause to believe, is a school zone." The Act neither regulates a commercial activity nor contains a requirement that the possession be connected in any way to interstate commerce. We hold that the Act exceeds the authority of Congress "to regulate Commerce ... among the several States ...."

We start with first principles. The Constitution creates a Federal Government of enumerated powers. See U.S. Const., Art. I, 8. As James Madison wrote, "[t]he powers delegated by the proposed Constitution to the federal government are few and defined. Those which are to remain in the State governments are numerous and indefinite." The Federalist No. 45, pp. 292–293 (C. Rossiter ed. 1961). This constitutionally mandated division of authority "was adopted by the Framers to ensure protection of our fundamental liberties." *Gregory* v. *Ashcroft* .... "Just as the separation and independence of the coordinate branches of the Federal Government serves to prevent the accumulation of excessive power in any one branch, a healthy balance of power between the States and the Federal Government will reduce the risk of tyranny and abuse from either front." Ibid.

...

Jones & Laughlin Steel, *Darby*, and *Wickard* ushered in an era of Commerce Clause jurisprudence that greatly expanded the previously defined authority of Congress under that Clause. In part, this was a recognition of the great changes that had occurred in the way business was carried on in this country. Enterprises that had once been local or at most regional in nature had become national in scope. But the doctrinal change also reflected a view that earlier Commerce Clause cases artificially had constrained the authority of Congress to regulate interstate commerce.

But even these modern-era precedents which have expanded congressional power under the Commerce Clause confirm that this power is subject to outer limits. In *Jones & Laughlin Steel*, the Court warned that the scope of the interstate commerce power "must be considered in the light of our dual system of government and may not be extended so as to embrace effects upon interstate commerce so indirect and remote that to embrace them, in view of our complex society, would effectually obliterate the distinction between what is national and what is local and create a completely centralized government."...

Consistent with this structure, we have identified three broad categories of activity that Congress may regulate under its commerce power. First, Congress may regulate the use of the channels of interstate commerce .... Second, Congress is empowered to regulate and protect the instrumentalities of interstate commerce, or persons or things in interstate commerce, even though the threat may come only from intrastate activities .... Finally, Congress' commerce authority includes the power to regulate those activities having a substantial relation to interstate commerce, *Jones & Laughlin Steel*, i.e., those activities that substantially affect interstate commerce. [*Wirtz*]

Within this final category, admittedly, our case law has not been clear whether an activity must "affect" or "substantially affect" interstate commerce in order to be within Congress' power to regulate it under the Commerce Clause .... We conclude, consistent with the great weight of our case law, that the proper test requires an analysis of whether the regulated activity "substantially affects" interstate commerce.

We now turn to consider the power of Congress, in the light of this framework, to enact § 922(q). The first two categories of authority may be quickly disposed of: § 922(q) is not a regulation of the use of the channels of interstate commerce, nor is it an attempt to prohibit the interstate transportation of a commodity through the channels of commerce; nor can § 922(q) be justified as a regulation by which Congress has sought to protect an instrumentality of interstate commerce or a thing in interstate commerce. Thus, if § 922(q) is to be sustained, it must be under the third category as a regulation of an activity that substantially affects interstate commerce.

First, we have upheld a wide variety of congressional Acts regulating intrastate economic activity where we have concluded that the activity substantially affected interstate commerce. Examples include the regulation of intrastate coal mining; [*Hodel*], intrastate extortionate credit transactions, [*Perez*], restaurants utilizing substantial interstate supplies, [*McClung*], inns and hotels catering to interstate guests, [*Heart of Atlanta Motel*], and production and consumption of home-grown wheat, [*Wickard*]. These examples are by no means exhaustive, but the pattern is clear. Where economic activity substantially affects interstate commerce, legislation regulating that activity will be sustained.

Even *Wickard*, which is perhaps the most far reaching example of Commerce Clause authority over intrastate activity, involved economic activity in a way that the possession of a gun in a school zone does not. Roscoe Filburn operated a small farm in Ohio, on which, in the year involved, he raised 23 acres of wheat. It was his practice to sow winter wheat in the fall, and after harvesting it in July to sell a portion of the crop, to feed part of it to poultry and livestock on the farm, to use some in making flour for home consumption, and to keep the remainder for seeding future crops. The Secretary of Agriculture assessed a penalty against him under the Agricultural Adjustment Act of 1938 because he harvested about 12 acres more wheat than his allotment under the Act permitted. The Act was designed to regulate the volume of wheat moving in interstate and foreign commerce in order to avoid surpluses and shortages, and concomitant fluctuation in wheat prices, which had previously obtained. The Court said, in an opinion sustaining the application of the Act to Filburn's activity:

> One of the primary purposes of the Act in question was to increase the market price of wheat and to that end to limit the volume thereof that could affect the market. It can hardly be denied that a factor of such volume and variability as home-consumed wheat would have a substantial influence on price and market conditions. This may arise because being in marketable condition such wheat overhangs the market and, if induced by rising prices, tends to flow into the market and check price increases. But if we assume that it is never marketed, it supplies a need of the man who grew it which would otherwise be reflected by purchases in the open market. Home-grown wheat in this sense competes with wheat in commerce.

Section 922(q) is ... not an essential part of a larger regulation of economic activity in which the regulatory scheme could be undercut unless the intrastate activity were regulated ....

Second, § 922(q) contains no jurisdictional element which would ensure, through case-by-case inquiry, that the firearm possession in question affects interstate commerce ....

The Government's essential contention, *in fine*, is that we may determine here that § 922(q) is valid because possession of a firearm in a local school zone does indeed substantially affect interstate commerce. The Government argues that possession of a firearm in a school zone may result in violent crime and that violent crime can be expected to affect the functioning of the national economy in two ways. First, the costs of violent crime are substantial, and, through the mechanism of insurance, those costs are spread throughout the population. Second, violent crime reduces the willingness of individuals to travel to areas within the country that are perceived to be unsafe. Cf. *Heart of Atlanta Motel* .... The Government also argues that the presence of guns in schools poses a substantial threat to the educational process by threatening the learning environment. A handicapped educational process, in turn, will result in a less productive citizenry. That, in turn, would have an adverse effect on the Nation's economic well-being. As a result, the Government argues that Congress could rationally have concluded that § 922(q) substantially affects interstate commerce.

We pause to consider the implications of the Government's arguments. The Government admits, under its "costs of crime" reasoning, that Congress could regulate not only all violent crime, but all activities that might lead to violent crime, regardless of how tenuously they relate to interstate commerce. Similarly, under the Government's "national productivity" reasoning, Congress could regulate any activity that it found was related to the economic productivity of individual citizens: family law (including marriage, divorce, and child custody), for example. Under the theories that the Government presents in support of § 922(q), it is difficult to perceive any limitation on federal power, even in areas such as criminal law enforcement or education where States historically have been sovereign. Thus, if we were to accept the Government's arguments, we are hard-pressed to posit any activity by an individual that Congress is without power to regulate.

...

... The possession of a gun in a local school zone is in no sense an economic activity that might, through repetition elsewhere, substantially affect any sort of interstate commerce. Respondent was a local student at a local school; there is no indication that he had recently moved in interstate commerce, and there is no requirement that his possession of the firearm have any concrete tie to interstate commerce.

To uphold the Government's contentions here, we would have to pile inference upon inference in a manner that would bid fair to convert congressional authority under the Commerce Clause to a general police power of the sort retained by the States .... The broad language in these [prior] opinions has suggested the possibility of additional expansion, but we decline here to proceed any further. To do so would require us to conclude ... that there never will be a distinction between what is truly national and what is truly local .... This we are unwilling to do.

For the foregoing reasons the judgment of the Court of Appeals is affirmed.

JUSTICE KENNEDY, with whom JUSTICE O'CONNOR joins, concurring.

...

The theory that two governments accord more liberty than one requires for its realization two distinct and discernable lines of political accountability: one between the citizens and the Federal

Government; the second between the citizens and the States. If, as Madison expected, the federal and state governments are to control each other, see The Federalist No. 51, and hold each other in check by competing for the affections of the people, see The Federalist No. 46, those citizens must have some means of knowing which of the two governments to hold accountable for the failure to perform a given function. [Were] the Federal Government to take over the regulation of entire areas of traditional state concern, areas having nothing to do with the regulation of commercial activities, the boundaries between the spheres of federal and state authority would blur and political responsibility would become illusory. The resultant inability to hold either branch of the government answerable to the citizens is more dangerous even than devolving too much authority to the remote central power.

...

An interference of these dimensions occurs here, for it is well established that education is a traditional concern of the States. The proximity to schools, including of course schools owned and operated by the States or their subdivisions, is the very premise for making the conduct criminal. In these circumstances, we have a particular duty to insure that the federal-state balance is not destroyed.

...

If a State or municipality determines that harsh criminal sanctions are necessary and wise to deter students from carrying guns on school premises, the reserved powers of the States are sufficient to enact those measures. Indeed, over 40 States already have criminal laws outlawing the possession of firearms on or near school grounds.

...

JUSTICE BREYER, with whom JUSTICE STEVENS, JUSTICE SOUTER, and JUSTICE GINSBURG join, dissenting.

...

I recognize that we must judge this matter independently. "[S]imply because Congress may conclude that a particular activity substantially affects interstate commerce does not necessarily make it so." *Hodel* ...

Applying these principles to the case at hand, we must ask whether Congress could have had a rational basis for finding a significant (or substantial) connection between gun related school violence and interstate commerce..... As long as one views the commerce connection, not as a "technical legal conception," but as "a practical one," *Swift & Co.* v. *United States* ..., the answer to this question must be yes.

... For one thing, reports, hearings, and other readily available literature make clear that the problem of guns in and around schools is widespread and extremely serious.... And, they report that this widespread violence in schools throughout the Nation significantly interferes with the quality of education in those schools.... Based on reports such as these, Congress obviously could have thought that guns and learning are mutually exclusive .... And, Congress could therefore have found a substantial educational problem—teachers unable to teach, students unable to learn—and concluded that guns near schools contribute substantially to the size and scope of that problem.

Having found that guns in schools significantly undermine the quality of education in our Nation's classrooms, Congress could also have found, given the effect of education upon interstate and foreign commerce, that gun related violence in and around schools is a commercial, as well as a human, problem. Education, although far more than a matter of economics, has long been inextricably intertwined with the Nation's economy.... In recent years the link between secondary education and business has strengthened.... Increasing global competition also has made primary and secondary education economically more important....

The economic links I have just sketched seem fairly obvious. Why then is it not equally obvious, in light of those links, that a widespread, serious, and substantial physical threat to teaching and learning also substantially threatens the commerce to which that teaching and learning is inextricably tied? That is to say, guns in the hands of six percent of inner city high school students and gun related violence throughout a city's schools must threaten the trade and commerce that those schools support. The only question, then, is whether the latter threat is (to use the majority's terminology) "substantial." And, the evidence of (1) the extent of the gun related violence problem, (2) the extent of the resulting negative effect on classroom learning, and (3) the extent of the consequent negative commercial effects, when taken together, indicate a threat to trade and commerce that is "substantial." At the very least, Congress could rationally have concluded that the links are "substantial."

[Other concurring and dissenting opinions omitted.]

---

dd. The Fallout from Lopez

Faced with statistical evidence that states were not prosecuting crimes against women as vigorously as crimes against men, Congress, in 1994, passed the Violence Against Women Act which granted victims of gender-based violence, regardless of sex, the right to sue their assailants in federal court for compensatory and punitive damages. (Congress cited section 5 of the Fourteenth Amendment, discussed in the next section, as well as the commerce clause as its legislative authority). In a 5–4 decision, the Supreme Court in *United States* v. *Morrison*,[68] relying on its reasoning in *Lopez*, ruled the creation of the civil action unconstitutional.

In the case that follows, residents of California and of other states where medical use of marijuana is legal challenged the constitutionality of the federal Controlled Substances Act to the extent it prevented them from using cannabis for their personal medical use. This time the Court upheld the federal enactment in a 6–3 decision. Justice Scalia, who voted with the majority in *Lopez* and *United States* v. *Morrison*, attempts to reconcile these decisions in the following excerpt from his concurring opinion.

CASE: **Gonzales v. Raich**
545 U.S. 1 (2005)

JUSTICE SCALIA, concurring in the judgment.

...

[O]ur cases have mechanically recited that the Commerce Clause permits congressional regulation of three categories: (1) the channels of interstate commerce; (2) the instrumentalities of interstate commerce, and persons or things in interstate commerce; and (3) activities that "substantially affect" interstate commerce .... The first two categories are self-evident, since they are the ingredients of interstate commerce itself .... The third category, however, is different in kind, and its recitation without explanation is misleading and incomplete.

It is misleading because ... activities that substantially affect interstate commerce are not themselves part of interstate commerce, and thus the power to regulate them cannot come from the Commerce Clause alone. Rather, as this Court has acknowledged ..., Congress's regulatory authority over intrastate activities that are not themselves part of interstate commerce (including activities that have a substantial effect on interstate commerce) derives from the Necessary and Proper Clause .... And the category of "activities that substantially affect interstate commerce" ... is incomplete because the authority to enact laws necessary and

---

[68] 529 U.S. 598 (2000).

proper for the regulation of interstate commerce is not limited to laws governing intrastate activities that substantially affect interstate commerce. Where necessary to make a regulation of interstate commerce effective, Congress may regulate even those intrastate activities that do not themselves substantially affect interstate commerce.

...

... Congress's authority to enact laws necessary and proper for the regulation of interstate commerce is not limited to laws directed against economic activities that have a substantial effect on interstate commerce .... As the Court put it in *Wrightwood Dairy*, where Congress has the authority to enact a regulation of interstate commerce, "it possesses every power needed to make that regulation effective."...

Although this power "to make ... regulation effective" commonly overlaps with the authority to regulate economic activities that substantially affect interstate commerce, and may in some cases have been confused with that authority, the two are distinct. The regulation of an intrastate activity may be essential to a comprehensive regulation of interstate commerce even though the intrastate activity does not itself "substantially affect" interstate commerce. Moreover, as the passage from *Lopez* quoted above suggests, Congress may regulate even noneconomic local activity if that regulation is a necessary part of a more general regulation of interstate commerce .... The relevant question is simply whether the means chosen are "reasonably adapted" to the attainment of a legitimate end under the commerce power ....

...

The application of these principles to the case before us is straightforward. In the CSA, Congress has undertaken to extinguish the interstate market in Schedule I controlled substances, including marijuana .... To effectuate its objective, Congress has prohibited almost all intrastate activities related to Schedule I substances—both economic activities (manufacture, distribution, possession with the intent to distribute) and noneconomic activities (simple possession) .... That simple possession is a noneconomic activity is immaterial to whether it can be prohibited as a necessary part of a larger regulation. Rather, Congress's authority to enact all of these prohibitions of intrastate controlled-substance activities depends only upon whether they are appropriate means of achieving the legitimate end of eradicating Schedule I substances from interstate commerce.

By this measure, I think the regulation must be sustained. Not only is it impossible to distinguish "controlled substances manufactured and distributed intrastate" from "controlled substances manufactured and distributed interstate," but it hardly makes sense to speak in such terms. Drugs like marijuana are fungible commodities. As the Court explains, marijuana that is grown at home and possessed for personal use is never more than an instant from the interstate market—and this is so whether or not the possession is for medicinal use or lawful use under the laws of a particular State .... Congress need not accept on faith that state law will be effective in maintaining a strict division between a lawful market for "medical" marijuana and the more general marijuana market ....

Many congressional statutes, including a large number of the criminal provisions, have, using the terminology of *Lopez*, "jurisdictional elements" which limit their application to transborder affairs. These are discussed below in the section entitled "Jurisdictional Elements" in Commerce Clause Legislation. This discussion addresses federal statutes, like the Gun-Free School Zone Act, that do not mention commerce or interstate commerce at all. Because of the breadth of the topic, the discussion can make only observations of a general nature.

Federal social programs—such as old-age benefits (Social Security), medical care for the poor (Medicaid), and medical care for the aged and handicapped (Medicare)—are based on the federal spending power and, as such, are not directly affected by the *Lopez* decision. Tax laws enjoy their own base of federal legislative jurisdiction, even when employed as instruments of indirect regulation.[69]

The *Lopez* case will have little effect on the constitutionality of federal environmental legislation because most of the laws are not based exclusively on the "affecting commerce" aspect of the commerce clause. If they are, then jurisdictional problems may arise in the application of an otherwise constitutional statute. The Clean Water Act seeks to control the discharge of pollutants into the "waters of the United States." Overzealous administrative extension of this territorial jurisdiction can bring invalidity of an action.[70] Another very important piece of environmental legislation, the Clean Air Act, is not affected by the reasoning of the *Lopez* decision because it employs a system of incentives to the states to entice them to prepare and enforce State Implementation Plans. The Endangered Species Act[71] can in part be considered an exercise of the power of the

---

[69] Sonzinsky v. United States, 300 U.S. 506 (1937), rev'd on other grounds.
[70] E.g., Hoffman Homes, Inc. v. EPA, 999 F.2d 256, 261 (7th Cir. 1993).
[71] See Gibbs v. Babbitt, 214 F.3d 483 (4th Cir. 2000), upholding protection of red wolves under the ESA.

federal government to enter into treaties with foreign countries.[72] Federal laws implementing treaties are binding on the states without a separate ground of federal legislative jurisdiction.[73] The National Environmental Policy Act, like many federal environmental laws, affects federal agencies and projects that are supported by federal funds, in other words, projects which would fall under Congress's spending power. As such they are not affected by the Lopez decision.

Other federal environmental laws, on the other hand, are exclusively based on the interstate commerce clause. Exemplary is the Surface Mining Control and Reclamation Act of 1977, which dictates mining practices for open-space mining and requires restoration after mining. In 1981, the Supreme Court upheld the constitutionality of the law despite the fact that it only indirectly (if at all) regulated interstate commerce.[74] The Supreme Court would likely reach the same result today, because mining is a commercial activity with a substantial impact on interstate and foreign commerce.

ee. "Jurisdictional Elements" in Commerce Clause Legislation

In *Lopez*, the Court criticized the Gun-Free School Zones Act for not having a "jurisdictional element which wo uld ensure, through case-by-case inquiry, that the firearm possession in question affects interstate commerce." More than 100 federal laws in the United States Code, including more than 25 criminal provisions, employ the words "affecting commerce." Others, like the Safe Homes for Women Act,[75] refine their reach with words like "interstate" or "crossing states lines."

Can *Lopez* and *Morrison* be circumvented simply by inserting a "jurisdictional element" into a statutory scheme?[76] Should the courts save Congress the trouble of amending its legislation by simply construing federal statutes under the commerce clause to possess this element?

Doctrinally, the presence of a jurisdictional element removes the statute from the "affecting commerce" prong of the Supreme Court's commerce clause test, allowing it to be judged under the "instrumentalities" or "channels" prong. Thus, for example, the Civil Rights Act of 1964 at issue in *Heart of Atlanta Motel*[77] and similarly legislation do not have to satisfy *Lopez* and *Morrison* because they regulate hotels, restaurants, and the workplace, which are "instrumentalities." An example of a

---

[72] Missouri v. Holland, 252 U.S. 416 (1920).
[73] Ware v. Hylton, 3 U.S. 199 (1796).
[74] Hodel v. Virginia Surface Mining & Reclamation Assn., Inc., 452 U.S. 264 (1981).
[75] 42 U.S.C. §§ 40201-40295.
[76] See generally Stuckey.
[77] 379 U.S. 241 (1964).

constitutional[78] "channels" regulation is the 1968 Gun Control Act,[79] which makes it a crime for anyone convicted of domestic violence to "possess in or affecting commerce, any firearm or ammunition which has been shipped or transported in interstate or foreign commerce." Further, it is unlawful "for any [licensed] importer, manufacturer, dealer, or collector ... to ship or transport in interstate or foreign commerce any firearm to any person other than a licensed importer, licensed manufacturer, licensed dealer, or licensed collector ...."[80] Post-*Lopez*, courts have upheld federal convictions for carjacking,[81] possession of a machine gun,[82] and blocking access to an abortion clinic[83] using this reasoning. The same would hold true for drug smuggling, kidnapping,[84] and for crimes which employ the channels of commerce, including telephones and the post office. And, of course, federal criminal law protecting federal persons or property can be sustained on other jurisdictional grounds.

Not every invocation of a "jurisdictional element" has been successful in saving federal legislation. To cite one example, a number of federal appellate courts have held that Congress exceeded its regulatory powers under the commerce clause in enacting the Child Support Recovery Act of 1992, which establishes a national program to aid states in enforcing child support across state lines.[85] Others have upheld the act.[86]

To this point we have only discussed challenges to statutes on their face. In judging the constitutionality of a statute as applied, the court may, of course, conclude in any given case that the jurisdictional element has not been met. In *United States v. Denalli*,[87] for example, the Eleventh Circuit refused to allow federal prosecution for arson on a private residence, and in *United States v. Pappadopoulos*,[88] the Ninth Circuit ruled that the burning

---

[78] E.g., United States v. Gallimore, 247 F.3d 134, 138 (4th Cir. 2001), United States v. Napier, 233 F.3d 394, 400 (6th Cir. 2000), and United States v. Dorris, 236 F.3d 582 (10th Cir. 2000), cert. denied, 532 U.S. 586 (2001). See also United States v. Johnson, 22 F.3d 106, 108–09 (6th Cir. 1994), construing a statute, 18 U.S.C. § 2119, that criminalizes carjacking a motor vehicle "that has been transported, shipped, or received in interstate or foreign commerce."
[79] 18 U.S.C. § 922(g)(9).
[80] 18 U.S.C. § 922(a)(2).
[81] United States v. Bishop, 66 F.3d 569 (3d Cir. 1995).
[82] United States v. Wilks, 58 F.3d 1518 (10th Cir. 1995).
[83] Cheffer v. Reno, 55 F.3d 1517 (11th Cir. 1995).
[84] United States v. Cummings, 281 F.3d 1046 (9th Cir. 2002), rejecting a constitutional challenge to the International Parental Kidnapping Crime Act.
[85] United States v. Mussari, 95 F.3d 787 (9th Cir. 1996) and United States v. Faasse, 265 F.3d 475 (6th Cir. 2001).
[86] United States v. Bongiorno, 106 F.3d 1027 (1st Cir. 1997), United States v. Lewko, 269 F.3d 64 (1st Cir. 2001), and United States v. Monts, 311 F.3d 993 (10th Cir. 2002). See also Kilroy v. Winter, 54 Cal. App. 4th 793 (1997).
[87] 73 F.3d 328 (11th Cir. 1996).
[88] 64 F.3d 522 (9th Cir. 1995).

of a private home is not within Congress's power to punish if the only link to commerce is that the home receives its fuel supply from another state.

iv. Necessary and Proper Clause

The final power enumerated in Article I, section 8, is clause 18:

> [The Congress shall have Power] To make all Laws which shall be necessary and proper for carrying into Execution the foregoing Powers, and all other Powers vested by this Constitution in the Government of the United States, or in any Department thereof.

This clause was construed by the United States Supreme Court in the famous and historically fascinating case of *McCulloch* v. *Maryland*,[89] which has been consistently followed ever since. Briefly, Congress chartered (created) a bank called the Bank of the United States in 1790, but that bank's charter expired in 1811. The bank was rechartered in 1816, with the federal government owning 20 percent. The bank was unpopular with the states and with state-chartered banks. Some states enacted laws prohibiting the Bank of the United States from transacting business on state soil. Other states, such as Maryland, taxed it. When the Bank of the United States refused to pay the tax, Maryland sued McCulloch, who was the bank's head cashier in Baltimore, Maryland. McCulloch and his federal employer, who lost in the Maryland courts, appealed to the United States Supreme Court.

Before ruling that the state could not constitutionally tax a federal facility, the Supreme Court had to rule on the constitutionality of the bank's creation. The Supreme Court marshaled three arguments to sustain the creation of the bank. First, the Supreme Court indicated that the unchallenged existence of the bank had in effect conferred a presumption of constitutionality upon it. Second, the Court broadly construed the powers of Congress under Article I. Even though the Constitution does not enumerate a power to create a bank, Chief Justice Marshall wrote:

> A constitution, to contain an accurate detail of all the subdivisions of which its great powers will admit, and of all the means by which they may be carried into execution, would partake of the prolixity of a legal code, and could scarcely be embraced by the human mind .... In considering this question, then, we must never forget that this is a constitution we are expounding.

---

[89] 17 U.S. 316 (1819).

In short, Marshall was pleading for a liberal interpretation of the Constitution in favor of grants of power to the federal government.

The third argument, and the one that concerns us here, is that Congress may incorporate a national bank as a "necessary and proper" means of carrying out its delegated powers to coin money (Art. I, §8, cl. 5), lay and collect taxes (cl. 1), borrow money (cl. 2), regulate commerce among the several states (cl. 3), declare and conduct war (cl. 11), and raise and support armies and a navy (cls. 12 and 13). On this point, the Court, in *McCulloch* v. *Maryland*, held that "necessary and proper" means "any appropriate or proper means" to achieve the ends specified in an enumerated power. Restated somewhat differently: Resort to the necessary and proper clause does not obviate the need for a constitutionally enumerated ends; but the "necessity" of the means in this context is for Congress to judge, not the Court.

When we get to constitutional rights we will see that, when a law infringes a constitutionally protected right, the necessity of the means does become subject to judicial review.

CASE: **McCulloch v. Maryland**
17 U.S. 316 (1819)

MARSHALL, Ch. J., delivered the opinion of the court.

In the case now to be determined, the defendant, a sovereign state, denies the obligation of a law enacted by the legislature of the Union, and the plaintiff, on his part, contests the validity of an act which has been passed by the legislature of that state. The constitution of our country, in its most interesting and vital parts, is to be considered; the conflicting powers of the government of the Union and of its members, as marked in that constitution, are to be discussed; and an opinion given, which may essentially influence the great operations of the government. No tribunal can approach such a question without a deep sense of its importance, and of the awful responsibility involved in its decision. But it must be decided peacefully, or remain a source of hostile legislation, perhaps, of hostility of a still more serious nature; and if it is to be so decided, by this tribunal alone can the decision be made. On the supreme court of the United States has the constitution of our country devolved this important duty.

The first question made in the cause is, has congress power to incorporate a bank?

It has been truly said, that this can scarcely be considered as an open question, entirely unprejudiced by the former proceedings of the nation respecting it. The principle now contested was introduced at a very early period of our history, has been recognized by many successive legislatures, and has been acted upon by the judicial department, in cases of peculiar delicacy, as a law of undoubted obligation.

It will not be denied, that a bold and daring usurpation might be resisted, after an acquiescence still longer and more complete than this. But it is conceived, that a doubtful question, one on which human reason may pause, and the human judgment be suspended, in the decision of which the great principles of liberty are not concerned, but the respective powers of those who are equally the representatives of the people, are to be adjusted; if not put at rest by the practice of the government, ought to receive a considerable impression from that practice. An exposition of the constitution, deliberately established by legislative acts, on the faith of which an immense property has been advanced, ought not to be lightly disregarded.

The power now contested was exercised by the first congress elected under the present constitution. The bill for incorporating the Bank of the United States did not steal upon an unsuspecting legislature, and pass unobserved. Its principle was completely understood, and was opposed with equal zeal and ability. After being resisted, first, in the fair and open field of debate, and afterwards, in the executive cabinet, with as much persevering talent as any measure has ever experienced, and being supported by arguments which convinced minds as pure and as intelligent as this country can boast, it became a law. The original act was permitted to expire; but a short experience of the embarrassments to which the refusal to revive it exposed the government, convinced those who were most prejudiced against the measure of its necessity, and induced the passage of the present law. It would require no ordinary share of intrepidity, to assert that a measure adopted under these circumstances, was a bold and plain usurpation, to which the constitution gave no countenance.

These observations belong to the cause; but they are not made under the impression, that, were the question entirely new, the law would be found irreconcilable with the constitution.

In discussing this question, the counsel for the state of Maryland have deemed it of some importance, in the construction of the constitution, to consider that instrument, not as emanating from the people, but as the act of sovereign and independent states. The powers of the general government, it has been said, are delegated by the states, who alone are truly sovereign; and must be exercised in subordination to the states, who alone possess supreme dominion.

It would be difficult to sustain this proposition. The convention which framed the constitution was indeed elected by the state legislatures. But the instrument, when it came from their hands, was a mere proposal, without obligation, or pretensions to it. It was reported to the then existing congress of the United States, with a request that it might 'be submitted to a convention of delegates, chosen in each state by the people thereof, under the recommendation of its legislature, for their assent and ratification.' This mode of proceeding was adopted; and by the convention, by congress, and by the state legislatures, the instrument was submitted to the people. They acted upon it in the only manner in which they can act safely, effectively and wisely, on such a subject, by assembling in convention. It is true, they assembled in their several states—and where else should they have assembled? No political dreamer was ever wild enough to think of breaking down the lines which separate the states, and of compounding the American people into one common mass. Of consequence, when they act, they act in their states. But the measures they adopt do not, on that account, cease to be the measures of the people themselves, or become the measures of the state governments.

From these conventions, the constitution derives its whole authority. The government proceeds directly from the people; is 'ordained and established,' in the name of the people; and is declared to be ordained, 'in order to form a more perfect union, establish justice, insure domestic tranquillity, and secure the blessings of liberty to themselves and to their posterity.' The assent of the states, in their sovereign capacity, is implied, in calling a convention, and thus submitting that instrument to the people. But the people were at perfect liberty to accept or reject it; and their act was final. It required not the affirmance, and could not be negatived, by the state governments. The constitution, when thus adopted, was of complete obligation, and bound the state sovereignties ....

The government of the Union, then (whatever may be the influence of this fact on the case), is, emphatically and truly, a government of the people. In form, and in substance, it emanates from them. Its powers are granted by them, and are to be exercised directly on them, and for their benefit.

This government is acknowledged by all, to be one of enumerated powers. The principle, that it can exercise only the powers granted to it, [is] now universally admitted. But the question respecting the extent of the powers actually granted, is perpetually arising, and will probably continue to arise, so long as our system shall exist.

In discussing these questions, the conflicting powers of the general and state governments must be brought into view, and the supremacy of their respective laws, when they are in opposition, must be settled.

If any one proposition could command the universal assent of mankind, we might expect it would be this-that the government of the Union, though limited in its powers, is supreme within its sphere of action. This would seem to result, necessarily, from its nature. It is the government of all; its powers are delegated by all; it represents all, and acts for all. Though any one state may be willing to control its operations, no state is willing to allow others to control them. The nation, on those subjects on which it can act, must necessarily bind its component parts. But this question is not left to mere reason: the people have, in express terms, decided it, by saying, 'this constitution, and the laws of the United States, which shall be made in pursuance thereof,' 'shall be the supreme law of the land,' and by requiring that the members of the state legislatures, and the officers of the executive and judicial departments of the states, shall take the oath of fidelity to it ....

Among the enumerated powers, we do not find that of establishing a bank or creating a corporation. But there is no phrase in the instrument which, like the articles of confederation, excludes incidental or implied powers; and which requires that everything granted shall be expressly and minutely described. Even the 10th amendment, which was framed for the purpose of quieting the excessive jealousies which had been excited, omits the word 'expressly,' and declares only, that the powers 'not delegated to the United States, nor prohibited to the states, are reserved to the states or to the people;' thus leaving the question, whether the particular power which may become the subject of contest, has been delegated to the one government, or prohibited to the other, to depend on a fair construction of the whole instrument. The men who drew and adopted this amendment had experienced the embarrassments resulting from the insertion of this word in the articles of confederation, and probably omitted it, to avoid those embarrassments. A constitution, to contain an accurate detail of all the subdivisions of which its great powers will admit, and of all the means by which they may be carried into execution, would partake of the prolixity of a legal code, and could scarcely be embraced by the human mind. It would, probably, never be understood by the public. Its nature, therefore, requires, that only its great outlines should be marked, its important objects designated, and the minor ingredients which compose those objects, be deduced from the nature of the objects themselves.

That this idea was entertained by the framers of the American constitution, is not only to be inferred from the nature of the instrument, but from the language. Why else were some of the limitations, found in the 9th section of the 1st article, introduced? It is also, in some degree, warranted, by their having omitted to use any restrictive term which might prevent its receiving a fair and just interpretation. In considering this question, then, we must never forget that it is a constitution we are expounding.

Although, among the enumerated powers of government, we do not find the word 'bank' or 'incorporation,' we find the great powers, to lay and collect taxes; to borrow money; to regulate commerce; to declare and conduct a war; and to raise and support armies and navies. The sword and the purse, all the external relations, and no inconsiderable portion of the industry of the nation, are intrusted to its government. It can never be pretended, that these vast powers draw after them others of inferior importance, merely because they are inferior. Such an idea can never be advanced. But it may with great reason be contended, that a government, intrusted with such ample powers, on the due execution of which the happiness and prosperity of the nation so vitally depends, must also be intrusted with ample means for their execution. The power being given, it is the interest of the nation to facilitate its execution. It can never be their interest, and cannot be presumed to have been their intention, to clog and embarrass its execution, by withholding the most appropriate means. Throughout this vast republic, from the St. Croix to the Gulf of Mexico, from the Atlantic to the Pacific, revenue is to be collected and expended, armies are to be marched and supported. The exigencies of the nation may require, that the treasure raised in the north should be transported to the south, that raised in the east, conveyed to the west, or that this order should be reversed. Is that construction of the constitution to be preferred, which would render these operations difficult, hazardous and expensive? Can we adopt that construction (unless the words imperiously require it), which would impute to the framers of that instrument, when granting these powers for the public good, the intention of impeding their exercise, by withholding a choice of means?...

It is not denied, that the powers given to the government imply the ordinary means of execution. That, for example, of raising revenue, and applying it to national purposes, is admitted to imply the power of conveying money from place to place, as the exigencies of the nation may require, and of employing the usual means of conveyance ....

But the constitution of the United States has not left the right of congress to employ the necessary means, for the execution of the powers conferred on the government, to general reasoning. To its enumeration of powers is added, that of making 'all laws which shall be necessary and proper, for carrying into execution the foregoing powers, and all other powers vested by this constitution, in the government of the United States, or in any department thereof.'

The counsel for the state of Maryland have urged various arguments, to prove that this clause, though, in terms, a grant of power, is not so, in effect; but is really restrictive of the general right, which might otherwise be implied, of selecting means for executing the enumerated powers ....

[The] argument on which most reliance is placed, is drawn from that peculiar language of this clause. Congress is not empowered by it to make all laws, which may have relation to the powers conferred on the government, but such only as may be 'necessary and proper' for carrying them into execution. The word 'necessary' is considered as controlling the whole sentence, and as limiting the right to pass laws for the execution of the granted powers, to such as are indispensable, and without which the power would be nugatory. That it excludes the choice of means, and leaves to congress, in each case, that only which is most direct and simple.

Is it true, that this is the sense in which the word 'necessary' is always used? Does it always import an absolute physical necessity, so strong, that one thing to which another may be termed necessary, cannot exist without that other? We think it does not. If reference be had to its use, in the common affairs of the world, or in approved authors, we find that it frequently imports no more than that one thing is convenient, or useful, or essential to another. To employ the means necessary to an end, is generally understood as employing any means calculated to produce the end, and not as being confined to those single means, without which the end would be entirely unattainable. Such is the character of human language, that no word conveys to the mind, in all situations, one single definite idea; and nothing is more common than to use words in a figurative sense. Almost all compositions contain words, which, taken in their rigorous sense, would convey a meaning different from that which is obviously intended. It is essential to just construction, that many words which import something excessive, should be understood in a more mitigated sense—in that sense which common usage justifies. The word 'necessary' is of this description. It has not a fixed character, peculiar to itself. It admits of all degrees of comparison; and is often connected with other words, which increase or diminish the impression the mind receives of the urgency it imports. A thing may be necessary, very necessary, absolutely or indispensably necessary. To no mind would the same idea be conveyed by these several phrases. The comment on the word is well illustrated by the passage cited at the bar, from the 10th section of the 1st article of the constitution. It is, we think, impossible to compare the sentence which prohibits a state from laying 'imposts, or duties on imports or exports, except what may be *absolutely* necessary for executing its inspection laws,' with that which authorizes congress 'to make all laws which shall be necessary and proper for carrying into execution' the powers of the general government, without feeling a conviction, that the convention understood itself to change materially the meaning of the word 'necessary,' by prefixing the word 'absolutely.' This word, then, like others, is used in various senses; and, in its construction, the subject, the context, the intention of the person using them, are all to be taken into view.

Let this be done in the case under consideration. The subject is the execution of those great powers on which the welfare of a nation essentially depends. It must have been the intention of those who gave these powers, to insure, so far as human prudence could insure, their beneficial execution. This could not be done, by confiding the choice of means to such narrow limits as not to leave it in the power of congress to adopt any which might be appropriate, and which were conducive to the end. This provision is made in a constitution, intended to endure for ages to come, and consequently, to be adapted to the various crises of human affairs. To have prescribed the means by which government should, in all future time, execute its powers, would have been to change, entirely, the character of the instrument, and give it the properties of a legal code. It would have been an unwise attempt to provide, by immutable rules, for exigencies which, if foreseen at all, must have been seen dimly, and which can be best provided for as they occur. To have declared, that the best means shall not be used, but those alone, without which the power given would be nugatory, would have been to deprive the legislature of the capacity to avail itself of experience, to exercise its reason, and to accommodate its legislation to circumstances. If we apply this principle of construction to any of the powers of the government, we shall find it so pernicious in its operation that we shall be compelled to discard it ....

So, with respect to the whole penal code of the United States: whence arises the power to punish, in cases not prescribed by the constitution? All admit, that the government may, legitimately, punish any violation of its laws; and yet, this is not among the enumerated powers of Congress. The right to enforce the observance of law, by punishing its infraction, might be denied, with the more plausibility, because it is expressly given in some cases. Congress is empowered 'to provide for the punishment of counterfeiting the securities and current coin of the United States,' and 'to define and punish piracies and felonies committed on the high seas, and offences against the law of nations.' The several powers of congress may exist, in a very imperfect state, to be sure, but they may exist and be carried into execution, although no punishment should be inflicted, in cases where the right to punish is not expressly given.

Take, for example, the power 'to establish post-offices and post-roads.' This power is executed, by the single act of making the establishment. But, from this has been inferred the power and duty of carrying the mail along the post-road, from one post-office to another. And from this implied power, has again been inferred the right to punish those who steal letters from the post-office, or rob the mail. It may be said, with some plausibility, that the right to carry the mail, and to punish those who rob it, is not indispensably necessary to the establishment of a post-office and post-road. This right is indeed essential to the beneficial exercise of the power, but not indispensably necessary to its existence. So, of the punishment of the crimes of stealing or falsifying a record or process of a court of the United States, or of perjury in such court. To punish these offences, is certainly conducive to the due administration of justice. But courts may exist, and may decide the causes brought before them, though such crimes escape punishment.

The baneful influence of this narrow construction on all the operations of the government, and the absolute impracticability of maintaining it, without rendering the government incompetent to its great objects, might be illustrated by numerous examples drawn from the constitution, and from our laws ....

In ascertaining the sense in which the word 'necessary' is used in this clause of the constitution, we may derive some aid from that with which it is associated. Congress shall have power 'to make all laws which shall be necessary and proper to carry into execution' the powers of the government. If the word 'necessary' was used in that strict and rigorous sense for which the counsel for the state of Maryland contend, it would be an extraordinary departure from the usual course of the human mind, as exhibited in composition, to add a word, the only possible effect of which is, to qualify that strict and rigorous meaning; to present to the mind the idea of some choice of means of legislation, not strained and compressed within the narrow limits for which gentlemen contend.

But the argument which most conclusively demonstrates the error of the construction contended for by the counsel for the state of Maryland, is founded on the intention of the convention, as manifested in the whole clause. To waste time and argument in proving that, without it, congress might carry its powers into execution, would be not much less idle, than to hold a lighted taper to the sun. As little can it be required to prove, that in the absence of this clause, congress would have some choice of means. That it might employ those which, in its judgment, would most advantageously effect the object to be accomplished. That any means adapted to the end, any means which tended directly to the execution of the constitutional powers of the government, were in themselves constitutional. This clause, as construed by the state of Maryland, would abridge, and almost annihilate, this useful and necessary right of the legislature to select its means. That this could not be intended, is, we should think, had it not been already controverted, too apparent for controversy.

We think so for the following reasons:

1st. The clause is placed among the powers of Congress, not among the limitations on those powers.

2d. Its terms purport to enlarge, not to diminish the powers vested in the government. It purports to be an additional power, not a restriction on those already granted. No reason has been, or can be assigned, for thus concealing an intention to narrow the discretion of the national legislature, under words which purport to enlarge it ....

The result of the most careful and attentive consideration bestowed upon this clause is, that if it does not enlarge, it cannot be construed to restrain the powers of Congress, or to impair the right of the legislature to exercise its best judgment in the selection of measures to carry into execution the constitutional powers of the government. If no other motive for its insertion can be suggested, a sufficient one is found in the desire to remove all doubts respecting the right to legislate on that vast mass of incidental powers which must be involved in the constitution, if that instrument be not a splendid bauble.

We admit, as all must admit, that the powers of the government are limited, and that its limits are not to be transcended. But we think the sound construction of the constitution must allow to the national legislature that discretion, with respect to the means by which the powers it confers are to be carried into execution, which will enable that body to perform the high duties assigned to it, in the manner most beneficial to the people. Let the end be legitimate, let it be within the scope of the constitution, and all means which are appropriate, which are plainly adapted to that end, which are not prohibited, but consist with the letter and spirit of the constitution, are constitutional ....

...

... Should congress, in the execution of its powers, adopt measures which are prohibited by the constitution; or should congress, under the pretext of executing its powers, pass laws for the accomplishment of objects not intrusted to the government; it would become the painful duty of this tribunal, should a case requiring such a decision come before it, to say, that such an act was not the law of the land. But where the law is not prohibited, and is really calculated to effect any of the objects intrusted to the government, to undertake here to inquire into the decree of its necessity, would be to pass the line which circumscribes the judicial department, and to tread on legislative ground. This court disclaims all pretensions to such a power ....

It being the opinion of the court, that the act incorporating the bank is constitutional; and that the power of establishing a branch in the state of Maryland might be properly exercised by the bank itself, we proceed to inquire—

2. Whether the State of Maryland may, without violating the constitution, tax that branch?

That the power of taxation is one of vital importance; that it is retained by the States; that it is not abridged by the grant of a similar power to the government of the Union; that it is to be concurrently exercised by the two governments: are truths which have never been denied. But such is the paramount character of the constitution, that its capacity to withdraw any subject from the action of even this power, is admitted. The States are expressly forbidden to lay any duties on imports or exports, except what may be absolutely necessary for executing their inspection laws. If the obligation of this prohibition must be conceded—if it may restrain a State from the exercise of its taxing power on imports and exports—the same paramount character would seem to restrain, as it certainly may restrain, a State from such other exercise of this power, as is in its nature incompatible with, and repugnant to, the constitutional laws of the Union. A law, absolutely repugnant to another, as entirely repeals that other as if express terms of repeal were used.

On this ground, the counsel for the bank place its claim to be exempted from the power of a State to tax its operations. There is no express provision for the case, but the claim has been sustained on a principle which so entirely pervades the constitution, is so intermixed with the materials which compose it, so interwoven with its web, so blended with its texture, as to be incapable of being separated from it, without rending it into shreds.

This great principle is, that the constitution and the laws made in pursuance thereof are supreme; that they control the constitution and laws of the respective States, and cannot be controlled by them. From this, which may be almost termed an axiom, other propositions are deduced as corollaries, on the truth or error of which, and on their application to this case, the cause has been supposed to depend. These are, 1st. That a power to create implies a power to preserve. 2d. That a power to destroy, if wielded by a different hand, is hostile to, and incompatible with these powers to create and to preserve. 3d. That where this repugnancy exists, that authority which is supreme must control, not yield to that over which it is supreme ....

That the power of taxing it by the States may be exercised so as to destroy it, is too obvious to be denied. But taxation is said to be an absolute power, which acknowledges no other limits than those expressly prescribed in the constitution, and like sovereign power of every other description, is intrusted to the discretion of those who use it. But the very terms of this argument admit, that the sovereignty of the State, in the article of taxation itself, is subordinate to, and may be controlled by the constitution of the United States. How far it has been controlled by that instrument, must be a question of construction. In making this construction, no principle, not declared, can be admissible, which would defeat the legitimate operations of a supreme government. It is of the very essence of supremacy, to remove all obstacles to its action within its own sphere, and so to modify every power vested in subordinate governments, as to exempt its own operations from their own influence. This effect need not be stated in terms. It is so involved in the declaration of supremacy, so necessarily implied in it, that the expression of it could not make it more certain. We must, therefore, keep it in view, while construing the constitution.

The argument on the part of the State of Maryland, is, not that the states may directly resist a law of congress, but that they may exercise their acknowledged powers upon it, and that the constitution leaves them this right, in the confidence that they will not abuse it.

Before we proceed to examine this argument, and to subject it to test of the constitution, we must be permitted to bestow a few considerations on the nature and extent of this original right of taxation, which is acknowledged to remain with the States. It is admitted, that the power of taxing the people and their property, is essential to the very existence of government, and may be legitimately exercised on the objects to which it is applicable, to the utmost extent to which the government may choose to carry it. The only security against the abuse of this power, is found in the structure of the government itself. In imposing a tax, the legislature acts upon its constituents. This is, in general, a sufficient security against erroneous and oppressive taxation.

The people of a State, therefore, give to their government a right of taxing themselves and their property, and as the exigencies of government cannot be limited, they prescribe no limits to the exercise of this right, resting confidently on the interest of the legislator, and on the influence of the constituent over their representative, to guard them against its abuse. But the means employed by the government of the Union have no such security, nor is the right of a State to tax them sustained by the same theory. Those means are not given by the people of a particular State, not given by the constituents of the legislature, which claim the right to tax them, but by the people of all the States. They are given by all, for the benefit of all—and upon theory, should be subjected to that government only which belongs to all ....

We find, then, on just theory, a total failure of this original right to tax the means employed by the government of the Union, for the execution of its powers. The right never existed, and the question whether it has been surrendered, cannot arise.

But, waiving this theory for the present, let us resume the inquiry, whether this power can be exercised by the respective States, consistently with a fair construction of the constitution?

That the power to tax involves the power to destroy; that the power to destroy may defeat and render useless the power to create; that there is a plain repugnance in conferring on one government a power to control the constitutional measures of another, which other, with respect to those very measures, is declared to be supreme over that which exerts the control, are propositions not to be denied. But all inconsistencies are to be reconciled by the magic of the word CONFIDENCE. Taxation, it is said, does not necessarily and unavoidably destroy. To carry it to the excess of destruction, would be an abuse, to presume which, would banish that confidence which is essential to all government.

But is this a case of confidence? Would the people of any one State trust those of another with a power to control the most insignificant operations of their State government? We know they would not. Why, then, should we suppose, that the people of any one State should be willing to trust those of another with a power to control the operations of a government to which they have confided their most important and most valuable interests? In the legislature of the Union alone, are all represented. The legislature of the Union alone, therefore, can be trusted by the people with the power of controlling measures which concern all, in the confidence that it will not be abused. This, then, is not a case of confidence, and we must consider it is as it really is ....

If we apply the principle for which the State of Maryland contends, to the constitution, generally, we shall find it capable of changing totally the character of that instrument. We shall find it capable of arresting all the measures of the government, and of prostrating it at the foot of the States .... If the states may tax one instrument, ... they may tax any and every other instrument. [The] American people [did] not design to make their government dependent on the states ....

It has also been insisted, that, as the power of taxation in the general and State governments is acknowledged to be concurrent, every argument which would sustain the right of the general government to tax banks chartered by the States, will equally sustain the right of the States to tax banks chartered by the general government.

But the two cases are not on the same reason. The people of all the States have created the general government, and have conferred upon it the general power of taxation. The people of all the States, and the States themselves, are represented in Congress, and, by their representatives, exercise this power. When they tax the chartered institutions of the States, they tax their constituents; and these taxes must be uniform. But when a State taxes the operations of the government of the United States, it acts upon institutions created, not by their own constituents, but by people over whom they claim no control. It acts upon the measures of a government created by others as well as themselves, for the benefit of others in common with themselves. The difference is that which always exists, and always must exist, between the action of the whole on a part, and the action of a part on the whole—between the laws of a government declared to be supreme, and those of a government which, when in opposition to those laws, is not supreme.

But if the full application of this argument could be admitted, it might bring into question the right of Congress to tax the State banks, and could not prove the rights of the States to tax the Bank of the United States ....

[We] conclude that the states have no power, by taxation or otherwise, to retard, impede, burden, or in any manner control, the operations of the constitutional laws enacted by Congress ....

This opinion does not deprive the States of any resources which they originally possessed. It does not extend to a tax paid by the real property of the bank, in common with the other real property within the State, nor to a tax imposed on the interest which the citizens of Maryland may hold in this institution, in common with other property of the same description throughout the State. But this is a tax on the operations of the bank, and is, consequently, a tax on the operation of an instrument employed by the government of the Union to carry its powers into execution. Such a tax must be unconstitutional.

[Reversed.]

In 2001, a real estate developer named Basim Omar Sabri offered bribes to a city councilman in Minneapolis, Minnesota. Sabri was charged under a federal statute making it a crime to give or offer to give anything of value to an agent of a local government to influence a decision, provided the local government had received federal funds. Sabri filed a motion to dismiss the indictment on the ground that the statute was unconstitutional because it does not require that the bribery involve a program funded by federal funds. In a 9–0 ruling, the Supreme Court rejected the challenge.[90] Congress, according to the Court, was within its prerogative to ensure that local administrators on the take do not menace expenditures under the spending clause, particularly because federal funds are often mixed with other funds, and it would be difficult for prosecutors to prove that the funds affected by an attempted bribe were federal funds.

Is this holding compatible with *Lopez* and *United States* v. *Morrison*? Is the standard of "necessary and proper" less demanding for expenditures under the spending clause, such as under the Child Abuse Prevention and Treatment Act[91] or the Howard M. Metzenbaum Multi-Ethnic Placement Act of 1994,[92] than it is for regulations under the commerce clause?

v. Section 5 of the Fourteenth Amendment

The Fourteenth Amendment, like the Thirteenth, and Fifteenth, Nineteenth, Twenty-third, Twenty-fourth, Twenty-sixth, and repealed Eighteenth

---

[90] Sabri v. United States, 541 U.S. 600 (2004).
[91] 42 U.S.C. § 5101 *et seq.* and § 5116 *et seq.*
[92] 42 U.S.C. §§622, 671, and 1996a.

Amendments, has an enforcement clause. The enforcement clause of the Fourteenth Amendment reads as follows:

Section 5. The Congress shall have power to enforce, by appropriate legislation, the provisions of this article.

The most important "provisions of this article" are the due process and equal protection clauses that are the subject of Part Two of this book

In its decision in *United States* v. *Morrison*,[93] the Supreme Court rejected the argument that the federal cause of action created by the Violence Against Women Act could be sustained under section 5 of the Fourteenth Amendment:

[T]he language and purpose of the Fourteenth Amendment place certain limitations on the manner in which Congress may attack discriminatory conduct. These limitations are necessary to prevent the Fourteenth Amendment from obliterating the Framers' carefully crafted balance of power between the States and the National Government .... Foremost among these limitations is the time-honored principle that the Fourteenth Amendment, by its very terms, prohibits only state action.[94]

In *Gonzales* v. *Carhart*,[95] the recent case upholding Partial-Birth Abortion Ban Act of 2003, there is no discussion of state action. However, this act, in contrast to the Violence Against Women Act, contains a jurisdictional element under the commerce clause: "Any physician who, in or affecting interstate or foreign commerce, knowingly performs a partial-birth abortion and thereby kills a human fetus shall be fined under this title or imprisoned not more than 2 years, or both."[96]

The Religious Freedom Restoration Act of 1933, in contrast to the Violence Against Women Act, was aimed specifically at the states and their political subdivisions: "Government [including a branch, department, agency, instrumentality, and official (or other person acting under color of law) of the United States, a State, or a subdivision of a State] shall not substantially burden a person's exercise of religion even if the burden results from a rule of general applicability ..."[97] Despite the requirement of state action, the Religious Freedom Restoration Act was

---

[93] 529 U.S. 598 (2000).
[94] 529 U.S. 598, 620–621 (2000).
[95] 127 S. Ct. 1610 (2007).
[96] §1531(a).
[97] § 3(a).

held unconstitutional in *City of Boerne* v. *Flores*[98] because it "contradict[ed] vital principles necessary to maintain separation of powers and the federal balance."

> [Under section 5, Congress] has been given the power to "enforce," not the power to determine what constitutes a constitutional violation. Were it not so, what Congress would be enforcing would no longer be, in any meaningful sense, the "provisions of [the Fourteenth Amendment]." While the line between measures that remedy or prevent unconstitutional actions and measures that make a substantive change in the governing law is not easy to discern, and Congress must have wide latitude in determining where it lies, the distinction exists and must be observed. There must be a congruence and proportionality between the injury to be prevented or remedied and the means adopted to that end. Lacking such a connection, legislation may become substantive in operation and effect. History and our case law support drawing the distinction, one apparent from the text of the Amendment.[99]

In other words, the Supreme Court, and not Congress, is the sole interpreter of the Constitution.

In addition to the *Morrison* case above, the Supreme Court since *Boerne* has struck down the damages remedy for state employees under two other civil rights statutes, the Age Discrimination in Employment Act[100] and Americans with Disabilities Act.[101]

Can this line of cases be circumvented by enacting legislation employing the treaty power?[102]

3. EXECUTIVE POWER

The second article of the Constitution provides for and governs the executive power of the United States government. Clause 1 reads:

> The executive Power shall be vested in a President of the United States of America.

---

[98] 521 U.S. 507 (1997).
[99] 521 U.S. 507, 519–520 (1997).
[100] 29 U.S.C. §§ 621–634, ruled unconstitutional to the extent it allows state employees to sue for damages in Kimel v. Florida Board of Regents, 528 U.S. 62 (2000).
[101] 42 U.S.C. § 12101 *et seq.*, ruled unconstitutional to the extent it allows state employees to sue for damages in Board of Trustees of the University of Alabama v. Garrett, 531 U.S. 356 (2001).
[102] See Missouri v. Holland, 252 U.S. 416 (1920), see generally Fischer.

There is a textual discrepancy between the constitutional creation of the presidency, on the one hand, and the Congress and the Supreme Court on the other. In creating the Congress, the Constitution reads "All legislative Powers herein granted," and for the Supreme Court, "The judicial Power of the United States." Does this subtle difference in wording betray an intent on behalf of the Framers to create, or at least to recognize the existence of, inherent presidential powers? This position was taken by no less a constitutional expert than Alexander Hamilton, chief author of the essays *The Federalist*. The contrary, and historically more likely, view was espoused by James Madison, who has been dubbed the "Father of the Constitution" for his pivotal role at the Constitutional Convention. According to Madison, the addition of the words "of the United States" in the first clause of the second article would have been superfluous, since it is obvious that the federal government is one of limited powers.[103] Further, the president is specifically commanded to "take Care that the Laws be faithfully executed."[104]

The debate between Hamilton and Madison concerned the power of President George Washington, the first president elected under the Constitution, to issue a Neutrality Proclamation declaring that the United States would remain neutral in a European war. In the centuries since that debate, commentators and courts have come to accept that the federal government—and not just the president alone—enjoys inherent power over foreign affairs. The Constitution grants Congress the power to regulate foreign commerce, to punish offenses against international law, to raise and support military forces, and to declare war; and the Constitution names the president commander in chief of the army and navy,[105] grants him (with the advice and consent of the Senate) certain treaty-making powers (with two-third's vote of the Senate),[106] and provides that he appoint (with advice and consent of the Senate) ambassadors and receive foreign ambassadors.[107] Conceptually, these and other powers over foreign affairs were never possessed by the colonies turned states; rather, they passed directly to the federal government as a sovereign nation from the sovereign nation of Great Britain.

a. Foreign Affairs

Having determined that the federal power over foreign affairs is plenary and exclusive, it is another matter to demarcate the scope of the respective

---

[103] Chemerinksy, Constitutional Law, at pp. 337–338.
[104] Art. II, § 3.
[105] Art. II, § 2, cl. 1.
[106] Art. II, § 2, cl. 2.
[107] Art. II, § 2, cl. 2.

powers of the Congress and the president over foreign affairs. The following discussion confines itself to the making of treaties and to military interventions.

i. Treaties and Executive Agreements

The Constitution empowers the president, "by and with the Advice and Consent of the Senate, to make Treaties, provided two thirds of the Senators present concur."[108] Treaties that do not expressly or impliedly require Congress to enact effectuating legislation are self-executing, that is, they create judicially enforceable rights and liabilities without the necessity of further action by Congress. Where there is a conflict between a treaty and an act of Congress, they are of equal weight. Thus, the last expression will control.[109] The United States might, however, remain accountable of the basis of the treaty under international law; but the dispute is not justiciable in American courts.[110]

Formal treaties are much less common than so-called "executive agreements" that the president enters into with foreign countries. Because these agreements are not considered to be treaties, they do not require the consent of the Senate. In *United States v. Belmont*[111] and *United States v. Pink*,[112] the Supreme Court upheld the Litvinov Agreement, by which the United States recognized the Soviet Union as a nation in exchange for the Soviet Union's assignment of its interests in the assents of a nationalized Russian insurance company in New York, whose assets were used to pay claims of the U.S. and others against the Soviet Union. A more recent example is the agreement that President Carter negotiated with Iran by which Iran would release American hostages in return for the lifting of a (presidentially ordered) freeze on Iranian assets in the United States.[113]

Executive agreements have a dignity "similar" to that of treaties in that they can be self-executing, and they prevail over inconsistent state law.[114] However, unlike treaties, an executive agreement will not prevail over an inconsistent federal law.[115]

ii. Foreign Military Interventions

As detailed above, the Constitution splits power to commit foreign troops abroad between the Congress and the president. By committing the powers

---

[108] Art. II, § 2, cl. 2. The Senate has approved over 1,500 treaties and rejected only 21. Crandall § 25.
[109] Head Money Cases, 112 U.S. 580 (1884).
[110] Clark v. Allen, 331 U.S. 503 (1947).
[111] 301 U.S. 324 (1937).
[112] 315 U.S. 203 (1942).
[113] Dames & Moore v. Regan, 453 U.S. 654 (1981).
[114] United States v. Pink, 315 U.S. 203 (1942).
[115] United States v. Guy W. Capps, Inc., 204 F.2d 655 (4th Cir. 1953), aff'd on other grounds, 438 U.S. 296 (1955); see Lundmark & McNeece.

to appropriate money, to raise armies, and to declare war (Is this power legislative or executive?) to the Congress, the Constitution is giving the Congress the upper hand. But what of insurrection or invasion? May the president deploy military forces without waiting for a congressional declaration of war? This question was answered in the affirmative in the *Prize Cases*,[116] which upheld the presidential blockade of southern ports during the Civil War in the absence of a congressional declaration of war. The court wrote:

If a war be made by invasion of a foreign nation, the president is not only authorized but bound to resist force by force. He does not initiate the war, but is bound to accept the challenge without waiting for any special legislative authority. And whether the hostile party be a foreign invader, or States organized in rebellion, it is nonetheless a war, although the declaration of it be unilateral.[117]

In 1973, Congress enacted a statute entitled "The War Powers Resolution," abstracted below, over President Nixon's veto. Critics claim that this law unconstitutionally limits the president's prerogatives as commander in chief, and enacts an impermissible legislative veto. Since its passage it has often been ignored.[118] All presidents since its passage have asserted that the War Powers Resolution is unconstitutional.[119]

STATUTE: **The War Powers Resolution** 50 U.S.C. § 1541 (1973)

SECTION 2. PURPOSE AND POLICY

(a) It is the purpose of this joint resolution to fulfill the intent of the framers of the Constitution of the United States and insure that the collective judgment of both the Congress and the President will apply to the introduction of United States Armed Forces into hostilities, or into situations where imminent involvement in hostilities is clearly indicated by the circumstances, and to the continued use of such forces in hostilities or in such situations.

(b) Under article I, section 8, of the Constitution, it is specifically provided that the Congress shall have the power to make all laws necessary and proper for carrying into execution, not only its own powers but also all other powers vested by the Constitution

---

[116] 67 U.S. 635 (1863).
[117] At p. 668.
[118] Koh at pp. 39–40.
[119] Treanor at p. 704.

in the Government of the United States, or in any department or officer thereof.

(c) The constitutional powers of the President as Commander-in-Chief to introduce United States Armed Forces into hostilities, or into situations where imminent involvement in hostilities is clearly indicated by the circumstances, are exercised only pursuant to (1) a declaration of war, (2) specific statutory authorization, or (3) a national emergency created by attack upon the United States, its territories or possessions, or its armed forces.

SECTION 3. CONSULTATION

The President in every possible instance shall consult with Congress before introducing United States Armed Forces into hostilities or into situation where imminent involvement in hostilities is clearly indicated by the circumstances, and after every such introduction shall consult regularly with the Congress ....

SECTION 4. REPORTING

(a) In the absence of a declaration of war, in any case in which United States Armed Forces are introduced—

(1) into hostilities or into situations where imminent involvement in hostilities is clearly indicated by the circumstances;

(2) into the territory, airspace or waters of a foreign nation, while equipped for combat ...; or

(3) in numbers which substantially enlarge United States Armed Forces equipped for combat already located in a foreign nation;

the president shall submit within 48 hours to the Speaker of the House of Representatives and to the President pro tempore of the Senate a report, in writing, setting forth [the circumstances necessitating the introduction of armed forces other information requested by the Congress].

...

SECTION 5. CONGRESSIONAL ACTION

...

(b) Within sixty calendar days after a report is submitted or is required to be submitted ..., the President shall terminate any use of United States Armed Forces with respect to which such report was submitted (or required to be submitted), unless the Congress (1) has declared war or has enacted a specific authorization for such use of United States Armed Forces, (2) has extended by law such sixty-day period, or (3) is physically unable to meet as a result of an armed attack upon the United States ....

(c) Notwithstanding subsection (b), at any time that United States Armed Forces are engaged in hostilities outside the territory of the United States, [without] a declaration of war or specific statutory authorization, such forces shall be removed by the President if the Congress so directs by concurrent [resolution].

...

---

b. Domestic Affairs ("Emergency") Power)

At this juncture we consider whether the president might not enjoy some inherent power to act domestically even in the absence of express constitutional or statutory authority. The leading case addressing the existence and scope of any such power is *Youngstown Sheet & Tube Co. v. Sawyer*.[120] That case arose in 1952 when the United Steelworkers Union announced a nationwide strike during the hostilities in Korea. Congress took no action. Fearing that the strike would endanger national defense and jeopardize the war effort, President Truman ordered his Secretary of Commerce to take possession of the steel mills and to keep them running. The Supreme Court, by a 6–3 vote, in seven different opinions, declared the seizure unconstitutional.

In the majority opinion, authored by Justice Black, the Court denies the existence of any inherent presidential power: "The President's power, if any, to issue the order must stem either from an act of Congress or from the Constitution itself."[121] Considering the case before him, Justice Black found neither, and therefore declared the action unconstitutional. Justice Jackson filed a concurring opinion, which is also abstracted below. Jackson's practical approach, which is considered by most to be authoritative, delineates three categories of presidential power.

CASE: **Youngstown Sheet & Tube Co. v. Sawyer [Steel Seizure Case]** 343 U.S. 579 (1952)

MR. JUSTICE BLACK delivered the opinion of the Court.

[We] are asked to decide whether [President Truman] was acting within his constitutional power when he issued an order directing the Secretary of Commerce [Sawyer] to take possession of and operate most of the Nation's steel mills. The mill owners argue that the President's order amounts to lawmaking, a legislative

---

[120] 343 U.S. 579 (1952).
[121] At p. 585.

function which the Constitution has expressly confided to the Congress and not to the President. The Government's position is that the order was made on findings of the President that his action was necessary to avert a national catastrophe which would inevitably result from a stoppage of steel production, and that in meeting this grave emergency the President was acting within the aggregate of his constitutional powers as the Nation's Chief Executive and the Commander in Chief of the [Armed Forces]. The issue emerges here from the following series of events:

In the latter part of 1951 [during the Korean War], a dispute arose between the steel companies and their employees [for] new collective bargaining agreements. [Efforts to settle the dispute—including reference to the Federal Wage Stabilization Board—failed.] On April 4, 1952, the [Steelworkers'] Union gave notice of a nation-wide strike called to begin [on] April 9. The indispensability of steel as a component of substantially all weapons and other war materials led the President to believe that the proposed work stoppage would immediately jeopardize our national defense and that governmental seizure of the steel mills was necessary in order to assure the continued availability of steel. [Accordingly,] the President, a few hours before the strike was to begin, issued Executive Order 10340, [directing] the Secretary of Commerce to take possession of most of the steel mills and keep them running. The Secretary immediately issued his own possessory orders, calling upon the presidents of the various seized companies to serve as operating managers for the United States. [The] next morning the President sent a message to Congress reporting his [action]. Congress has taken no action. Obeying the Secretary's orders under protest, the companies brought proceedings against him in the District Court, [which] on April 30 issued a preliminary injunction restraining the Secretary from "continuing the seizure and possession of the plants [and] from acting under the purported authority of Executive Order No. 10340." On the same day the Court of Appeals stayed the District Court's injunction. Deeming it best that the issues raised be promptly decided by this Court, we granted certiorari on May 3 and set the cause for argument on May 12. [This decision was announced soon after, on June 2, 1952.]

The President's power, if any, to issue the order must stem either from an act of Congress or from the Constitution itself. There is no statute that expressly authorizes the President to take possession of property as he did here. Nor is there any act of Congress to which our attention has been directed from which such a power can fairly be implied ....

It is clear that if the President had authority to issue the order he did, it must be found in some provision of the Constitution. And it is not claimed that express constitutional language grants this power to the President. The contention is that presidential power should be implied from the aggregate of his powers under the Constitution. Particular reliance is placed on provisions in Article II which say that "The executive Power shall be vested in a President ..."; that "he shall take Care that the Laws be faithfully executed"; and that he "shall be Commander in Chief of the [Army and Navy]." The order cannot properly be sustained as an exercise of the President's military power as Commander in Chief of the Armed Forces .... Even though "theater of war" be an expanding concept, we cannot with faithfulness to our constitutional system hold that the Commander in Chief of the Armed Forces has the ultimate power as such to take possession of private property in order to keep labor disputes from stopping production. This is a job for the Nation's lawmakers, not for its military authorities .... In the framework of our Constitution, the President's power to see that the laws are faithfully executed refutes the idea that he is to be a lawmaker. The Constitution limits his functions in the lawmaking process to the recommending of laws he thinks wise and the vetoing of laws he thinks bad. And the Constitution is neither silent nor equivocal about who shall make laws which the President is to execute ....

...

[Affirmed.]

MR. JUSTICE JACKSON, concurring in the judgment and opinion of the Court.

... We may well begin by a somewhat over-simplified grouping of practical situations in which a President may doubt, or others may challenge, his powers, and by distinguishing roughly the legal consequences of this factor of relativity.

1. When the President acts pursuant to an express or implied authorization of Congress, his authority is at its maximum, for it includes all that he possesses in his own right plus all that Congress can delegate ....

2. When the President acts in absence of either a congressional grant or denial of authority, he can only rely upon his own independent powers, but there is a zone of twilight in which he and Congress may have concurrent authority, or in which its distribution is uncertain. Therefore, congressional inertia, indifference or quiescence may sometimes, at least as a practical matter, enable, if not invite, measures on independent presidential responsibility. In this area, any actual test of power is likely to depend on the

imperatives of events and contemporary imponderables rather than on abstract theories of law.

3. When the President takes measures incompatible with the expressed or implied will of Congress, his power is at its lowest ebb, for then he can rely only upon his own constitutional powers minus any constitutional powers of Congress over the matter. Courts can sustain exclusive presidential control in such a case only by disabling the Congress from acting upon the subject. Presidential claim to a power at once so conclusive and preclusive must be scrutinized with caution, for what is at stake is the equilibrium established by our constitutional system.

Into which of these classifications does this executive seizure of the steel industry fit? It is eliminated from the first by admission, for it is conceded that no congressional authorization exists for this seizure. [Can] it then be defended under flexible tests available to the second category? It seems clearly eliminated from that class because Congress has not left seizure of private property an open field but has covered it by three statutory policies inconsistent with this seizure. [This] leaves the current seizure to be justified only by the severe tests under the third grouping, where it can be supported only by any remainder of executive power after subtraction of such powers as Congress may have over the subject. In short, we can sustain the President only by holding that seizure of such strike-bound industries is within his domain and beyond control by Congress.

...

In view of the ease, expedition and safety with which Congress can grant and has granted large emergency powers, certainly ample to embrace this crisis, I am quite unimpressed with the argument that we should affirm possession of them without statute. Such power either has no beginning or it has no end. If it exists, it need submit to no legal restraint. I am not alarmed that it would plunge us straightway into dictatorship, but it is at least a step in that wrong direction. As to whether there is imperative necessity for such powers, it is relevant to note the gap that exists between the President's paper powers and his real powers. The Constitution does not disclose the measure of the actual controls wielded by the modern presidential [office]. Vast accretions of federal power, eroded from that reserved by the States, have magnified the scope of presidential [activity].

Executive power has the advantage of concentration in a single head in whose choice the whole Nation has a part, making him the focus of public hopes and expectations. In drama, magnitude and finality his decisions so far overshadow any others that almost alone he fills the public eye and ear. No other personality in public life can begin to compete with him in access to the public mind through modern methods of communications. By his prestige as head of state and his influence upon public opinion he exerts a leverage upon those who are supposed to check and balance his power which often cancels their effectiveness. Moreover, rise of the party system has made a significant extra constitutional supplement to real executive power. [I] have no illusion that any decision by this Court can keep power in the hands of Congress if it is not wise and timely in meeting its problems. A crisis that challenges the President equally, or perhaps primarily, challenges Congress. If not good law, there was worldly wisdom in the maxim attributed to Napoleon that "The tools belong to the man who can use them." We may say that power to legislate for emergencies belongs in the hands of Congress, but only Congress itself can prevent power from slipping through its [fingers]. With all its defects, delays and inconveniences, men have discovered no technique for long preserving free government except that the Executive be under the law, and that the law be made by parliamentary deliberations. Such institutions may be destined to pass away. But it is the duty of the Court to be last, not first, to give them up.

[Other concurring and dissenting opinions omitted.]

The Supreme Court revisited Justice Jackson's framework for judging claims of inherent presidential power in 2004, in the case *Hamdi* v. *Rumsfeld*,[122] involving Yaser Hamdi, an American citizen, who was captured in Afghanistan and classified as an "enemy combatant" for allegedly taking up arms with the Taliban. In response to a petition for a writ of habeas corpus filed by Yaser's father on his behalf, the government argued that the detention was legal pursuant to the president's inherent executive powers, and also that it was authorized by Congress's Authorization for Use of Military Force (AUMF) resolution, enacted shortly after the September 11, 2001 attacks, empowering the president to "use all necessary and appropriate force" against "nations, organizations, or persons" that he determines "planned, authorized, committed, or aided" in the attacks. Four members of the Supreme Court found that Congress did indeed authorize the president to act as he did, but that, despite the authorization, constitutional due process demands that a citizen held in the United States as an enemy combatant be given a meaningful opportunity

---

[122] 542 U.S. 507 (2004).

to contest the factual basis for that detention before a neutral decision maker. Two members of the Court considered Hamdi's detention to be unlawful, but they joined with the plurality to hold that Hamdi be accorded a meaningful opportunity to offer evidence that he is not an enemy combatant.

On another issue, can the president impound (i.e., refuse to spend) money that Congress has mandated be spent? Would doing so violate the principle of separation of powers? The Impoundment Control Act of 1974[123] effectively forbids the practice.[124]

c.   Presidential Legislative Prerogatives

This section addresses two abashedly legislative functions discharged by the executive branch of the federal government. One, the veto power, is expressly provided for in the Constitution. The other, the delegation of legislative power to the executive, finds no textual support in the Constitution.

i. Presidential Veto

The presidential veto power is expressly provided for in Article I, section 7, clause 2:

> Every Bill which shall have passed the House of Representatives and the Senate, shall, before it becomes a Law, be presented to the President of the United States; If he approve he shall sign it, but if not he shall return it, with his Objections to that House in which it shall have originated .... If any Bill shall not be returned by the President within ten Days (Sundays excepted) after it shall have been presented to him, the Same shall be a Law, in like Manner as if he had signed it, unless the Congress by their Adjournment prevent its Return, in which Case it shall not be a Law.

The veto power extends to legislative measures ("bills") that are presented to the president before they become law. The veto power also extends to "Every Order, Resolution, or Vote to which the Concurrence of the Senate and House of Representatives may be necessary (except on a question of Adjournment)."[125] The veto power therefore does not extend to actions by the Congress that are not legislative, at least if they are not in the form of a bill. Exceptions from the president's veto power therefore include (non-binding) resolutions, adoption of procedures to organize

---

[123] 31 U.S.C. § 1301.
[124] See Train v. New York, 420 U.S. 35 (1975).
[125] Art. I, § 7, cl. 3.

Congress's affairs, and acts that are committed to the discretion of the Congress. This last group (comprising congressional acts excluded from the reach of the president's veto power) includes declarations of war, consent to treaties and appointments, and impeachment proceedings.

Governmental officials are subject to official and unofficial oversight by Congress. This oversight ranges from informal telephonic inquiries to the submission of reports and testimony before congressional committees. One provision of the Immigration and Nationality Act allowed either house of Congress to overturn a decision of the Immigration and Naturalization Service to suspend deportation. The provision was declared unconstitutional on separation of powers grounds.[126]

ii. Delegation of Legislative Power

While extremely difficult to justify on separation of powers grounds, and while arguably unconstitutional for violation of the opening sentence of the Constitution, delegations of regulatory power to administrative agencies is a twentieth- and twenty-first-century necessity. In light of the complexity of the law and the need for specialized knowledge, the only alternative would be to increase the staff of the Congress manyfold and to force members of Congress to vote on volumes of measures that they could never hope to comprehend.

During the 1930s, Congress would sometimes, at the president's request, make wholesale delegations to the executive. The National Industrial Recovery Act, for example, authorized the president to adopt "codes of fair competition" for various industries. When these delegations reached the courts, they were condemned as unconstitutional abdications of legislative authority.[127] For an example of the use by a state court of the non-delegation doctrine, see *Bayside Timber Co. v. Board of Supervisors*.[128]

It is popular among constitutional scholars to say that the delegation doctrine is dead. While it is true that no decision since 1935 has invalidated a congressional delegation of power, and that the Supreme Court has been liberal with what it considers "intelligible standards," a resurrection of the doctrine cannot be ruled out. Should it be ruled out? Is there no chance that even broad-based agencies might act capriciously or despotically? Are the courts a sufficient final refuge if they do?

---

[126] Immigration and Naturalization Service v. Chadha, 462 U.S. 919 (1983).
[127] E.g., Panama Refining Co. v. Ryan, 293 U.S. 388 (1935) and Schechter Poultry Corp. v. United States, 295 U.S. 495 (1935). To survive judicial review, the legislative delegation must contain "intelligible standards" that confine the discretion of the agency. Yankus v. United States, 321 U.S. 414 (1944).
[128] 20 Cal. App. 3d 1 (1971), discussed in Lundmark, *Regulation*.

d. Election, Appointment, Removal, and Immunity

The qualifications of the president are prescribed in Article II, section 1, clause 5:

> No Person except a natural born Citizen, or a Citizen of the United States, at the time of the Adoption of this Constitution, shall be eligible to the Office of President; neither shall any person be eligible to that Office who shall not have attained to the Age of thirty five Years, and been fourteen Years a Resident within the United States

The youngest person to become president was forty-year-old Theodore Roosevelt.

i. Election and Appointment

The president is not appointed by the Congress. Rather, he is popularly, but indirectly, elected. At the time the Constitution was written, representatives chosen by the states would have to travel great distances to the electoral college to cast their votes. The voters of the states voted by proxy via the electoral college. As part of a political compromise to gain the consent of the small states, representation in the electoral college for each state is equivalent to the sum of its senators and representatives,[129] which totals 535. The electoral college operates on a "winner takes all" rule. This is an extra-constitutional practice, codified in the laws of all the states but two, by which the candidate who receives the largest number of votes in a state receives all of that state's electoral votes.[130] It has come to pass that candidates with more popular votes have lost to candidates with more electoral college votes, but all three instances were in the nineteenth century.[131] The most recent occurrence was in November 2000, when George W. Bush defeated Albert Gore, Jr.

The procedure for the election of the president has been changed once by amendment to the Constitution. Since the ratification of the Twelfth Amendment in 1804, electors must vote for one person as president and for another as vice president. The amendment resulted from the presidential election of 1800, which saw two men, Aaron Burr and Thomas Jefferson, tie. Previously, the candidate with the most votes became president; the runner-up became vice president. Incidentally, the tie vote between Burr and Jefferson was broken by a vote in the House of Representatives.

---

[129] U.S. Const., Art. II, §1, cl. 2; Williams v. Rhodes, 393 U.S. 23 (1968) at p. 43, n. 2.
[130] Mikva at p. 800.
[131] Farber & Sherry at pp. 94–99.

Elections and voting rights have been the chief topic addressed in the seventeen amendments ratified since the Bill of Rights (the first ten amendments). In addition to the amendments granting the suffrage to former slaves,[132] to women,[133] to citizens of the District of Columbia to vote for president and vice president, but not for members of Congress,[134] and to eighteen-year-olds,[135] other amendments have been ratified to abolish poll (head) taxes as a qualification for voting[136] and to govern the election of senators[137] and of the president.

The date on which the newly elected president and vice president would begin serving was moved up to the twentieth day of January by the Twentieth Amendment, ratified in 1933. Until Franklin D. Roosevelt, no other president had run for election to more than two consecutive terms. The Twenty-second Amendment wrote this custom into the Constitution. The Twenty-fifth Amendment, ratified in 1967, provides a procedure for presidential appointment, and congressional confirmation, of a replacement vice president. (Previously vacancies had remained unfilled until the next election.) In 1973, Gerald Ford became the first person chosen to be vice president under the Twenty-fifth Amendment. The following year, Ford became president upon President Nixon's resignation. Nelson Rockefeller was chosen vice president under the same procedure.

ii. Removal (Impeachment)

The government of the United States is not parliamentary. There is no procedure for a vote of no confidence. There is no procedure for popular referendum to remove a wayward president. The exclusive means of removal is set forth in Article II, section 4, of the Constitution:

> The President, Vice President and all civil Officers of the United States, shall be removed from Office on Impeachment for, and Conviction of, Treason, Bribery, or other high Crimes and Misdemeanors.

Impeachment consists of an act of the House of Representatives charging the official with "Treason, Bribery, or other high Crimes and Misdemeanors." History is vague on what this originally meant, and commentators have varied widely in their interpretations. Many people

---

[132] Amend. 15.
[133] Amend. 19.
[134] Amend. 23.
[135] Amend. 26.
[136] Amend. 24.
[137] Amend. 17.

share the conviction of (then Congressman) Gerald Ford when he said, "An impeachable offense is whatever a majority of the House of Representatives considers it to be."

The Senate must try the president on the charges in the impeachment resolution. The original proposal was to have the Supreme Court try the president, but this was changed to make the impeachment procedure more democratic. A two-thirds' vote of the members present is required to convict and remove the president from office.[138] Conviction does not bring a prison term or monetary fine:

> Judgment in Cases of Impeachment shall not extend further than to removal from Office, and disqualification to hold and enjoy any Office of honor, Trust or Profit under the United States: but the Party convicted shall nevertheless be liable and subject to Indictment, Trial, Judgment and Punishment, according to Law.[139]

Five federal judges have been removed by impeachment and conviction. The last was district court judge Walter Nixon, who was convicted of making false statements to a grand jury, and was sentenced to prison. The House impeached Nixon. Rather than hold a trial with all of its members present, the Senate created a committee which held hearings and made recommendations to the full Senate. By two-thirds' vote of the members present,[140] the Senate removed Judge Nixon from office. The Supreme Court refused to set aside the conviction, ruling the procedure valid, or at least nonjusticiable.[141]

President Andrew Johnson, who became president on the death of Abraham Lincoln, was impeached in 1867 for firing Secretary of War Edwin Stanton who had openly challenged the president's authority. The House charged that, in doing so, Johnson had violated the Tenure in Office Act, which specifically provided that the firing of a department head would be deemed a "high misdemeanor."[142] The Senate failed by one vote to convict Johnson on the charge. President Nixon resigned after the House Judiciary Committee voted three articles of impeachment against him, but before he was impeached by the House. (The articles charged the president with obstruction of justice in connection with the Watergate cover-up, using government agencies, such as the FBI and the IRS, for

---

[138] Art. I, § 3, cl. 6.
[139] Art. I, § 3, cl. 7.
[140] Art. I, § 3.
[141] Nixon v. United States, 506 U.S. 224 (1993).
[142] Years later the Supreme Court invalidated the Tenure in Office Act on separation of powers grounds. Myers v. United States, 272 U.S. 52 (1926).

political purposes, and failing to comply with subpoenas.) The only elected president ever to have been impeached was President Clinton, who was charged in 1998 by the House of Representatives with committing perjury and obstruction of justice. The Senate failed to convict him on the charges.

In the wake of the Watergate Scandal under President Nixon, Congress enacted the Ethics in Government Act of 1978,[143] which allows for the appointment of an "independent counsel" to investigate and prosecute wrongdoing by high executive officials on the assumption that the executive itself could not be counted on to do so. Nevertheless, the first step in the process must be taken by the Attorney General, a presidential appointee. If, following a preliminary investigation, she determines, as Attorney General Janet Reno did in the case of President Clinton, that there are "reasonable grounds to believe that further investigation is warranted," she refers the matter to a panel of federal judges, chosen from different courts, one of which must be the Court of Appeals for the District of Columbia Circuit. These three judges in turn appoint the independent counsel and define her prosecutorial jurisdiction. In Clinton's case they appointed Kenneth Starr.

The constitutionality of the appointment procedure of the Ethics in Government Act was attacked on the grounds that they (1) violated the appointments clause,[144] (2) breached the limitations placed on federal judges by Article III, and (3) unconstitutionally interfered with executive functions and therefore contravened the principle of separation of powers. In the case that follows, the Supreme Court upheld the law. On the first point, it held that the independent counsel, Alexia Morrison in this case, was an "inferior" officer and as such need not be named by the president. On the second point, the Court held that the judges' power to define the jurisdiction of the independent counsel did not conflict with Article III because the appointing judges had no power whatsoever to supervise the independent counsel in the exercise of her investigative and prosecutorial authority. And, as to the third point, Justice Rehnquist wrote: "Most importantly, the Attorney General retains the power to remove the counsel for 'good cause.' [In short, the] Act gives the Executive Branch sufficient control over the independent counsel to ensure that the President is able to perform his constitutionally assigned [duties]." Justice Kennedy did not participate in the case. There was only one dissenter. His main argument on the separation-of-powers point follows.

---

[143] 28 U.S.C. §§ 591–599.
[144] Art. II, § 2, cl. 2.

CASE: **Morrison v. Olson**
487 U.S. 654 (1988)

JUSTICE SCALIA, dissenting.

...

The purpose of the separation and equilibration of powers in general, and of the unitary Executive in particular, was not merely to assure effective government but to preserve individual freedom. Those who hold or have held offices covered by the Ethics in Government Act are entitled to that protection as much as the rest of us, and I conclude my discussion by considering the effect of the Act upon the fairness of the process they receive. [Under] our system of government, the primary check against prosecutorial abuse is a political one. The prosecutors who exercise this awesome discretion are selected and can be removed by a President, whom the people have trusted enough to elect. Moreover, when crimes are not investigated and prosecuted fairly, nonselectively, with a reasonable sense of proportion, the President pays the cost in political damage to his administration. [That] is the system of justice the rest of us are entitled to, but what of that select class consisting of present or former high-level Executive Branch officials? If an allegation is made against them of any violation of any federal criminal law [the] Attorney General must give it his attention. That in itself is not objectionable. But if, after a 90-day investigation without the benefit of normal investigatory tools, the Attorney General is unable to say that there are "no reasonable grounds to believe" that further investigation is warranted, a process is set in motion that is *not* in the full control of persons "dependent on the people," and whose flaws cannot be blamed on the President. An independent counsel is selected, and the scope of his or her authority prescribed, by a panel of judges. What if they are politically partisan, as judges have been known to be, and select a prosecutor antagonistic to the [administration]? There is no remedy for that, not even a political one.

[The] ad hoc approach to constitutional adjudication has real attraction, even apart from its work-saving potential. It is guaranteed to produce a result, in every case, that will make a majority of the Court happy with the law. The law is, by definition, precisely what the majority thinks, taking all things into account, it *ought* to be. I prefer to rely upon the judgment of the wise men who constructed our system, and of the people who approved it, and of two centuries of history that have shown it to be sound. Like it or not, that judgment says, quite plainly, that "[t]he executive Power shall be vested in a President of the United States."

---

iii. Privilege and Immunity

Although not expressly mentioned in the Constitution, the Supreme Court has recognized a privilege to prevent disclosure of confidential communications made between the president and his advisors. The claim of executive privilege is given utmost deference by the courts when the communications relate to military, diplomatic, or sensitive national security secrets.[145] Executive privilege does not extend to evidence of meetings, or to conversations overheard by third persons, such as bodyguards.[146]

In the civil context, the president, whether sitting or former, enjoys absolute immunity from claims predicated on his official acts.[147] Can a sitting president be prosecuted criminally? Does a sitting president enjoy immunity from civil law suits arising before taking office, or based on unofficial acts? Consider the following case.

CASE: Clinton v. Jones
520 U.S. 681 (1997)

Justice Stevens delivered the opinion of the Court.

This case raises a constitutional and a prudential question concerning the Office of the President of the United States. Respondent, a private citizen, seeks to recover damages from the current occupant of that office based on actions allegedly taken before his term began. The President submits that in all but the most exceptional cases the Constitution requires federal courts to defer such litigation until his term ends and that, in any event, respect for the office warrants such a stay. Despite the force of the arguments supporting the President's submissions, we conclude that they must be rejected.

Petitioner, William Jefferson Clinton, was elected to the Presidency in 1992, and re elected in 1996. His term of office expires on January 20, 2001. In 1991 he was the Governor of the State

---

[145] United States v. Nixon, 418 U.S. 683 (1974).
[146] In re Sealed Case, 148 F.3d 1073 (D.C. Cir. 1998), cert. denied in Rubin v. United States, 525 U.S 990 (1998).
[147] Nixon v. Fitzgerald, 457 U.S. 731 (1982).

of Arkansas. Respondent, Paula Corbin Jones, is a resident of California. In 1991 she lived in Arkansas, and was an employee of the Arkansas Industrial Development Commission. On May 6, 1994, she commenced this action in the United States District Court for the Eastern District of Arkansas by filing a complaint naming petitioner and Danny Ferguson, a former Arkansas State Police officer, as defendants. The complaint alleges two federal claims, and two state law claims over which the federal court has jurisdiction because of the diverse citizenship of the parties. As the case comes to us, we are required to assume the truth of the detailed—but as yet untested—factual allegations in the complaint.

Those allegations principally describe events that are said to have occurred on the afternoon of May 8, 1991, during an official conference held at the Excelsior Hotel in Little Rock, Arkansas. The Governor delivered a speech at the conference; respondent—working as a state employee—staffed the registration desk. She alleges that Ferguson persuaded her to leave her desk and to visit the Governor in a business suite at the hotel, where he made "abhorrent" sexual advances that she vehemently rejected. She further claims that her superiors at work subsequently dealt with her in a hostile and rude manner, and changed her duties to punish her for rejecting those advances. Finally, she alleges that after petitioner was elected President, Ferguson defamed her by making a statement to a reporter that implied she had accepted petitioner's alleged overtures, and that various persons authorized to speak for the President publicly branded her a liar by denying that the incident had occurred.

...

Petitioner's principal submission—that "in all but the most exceptional cases" ..., the Constitution affords the President temporary immunity from civil damages litigation arising out of events that occurred before he took office—cannot be sustained on the basis of precedent.

Only three sitting Presidents have been defendants in civil litigation involving their actions prior to taking office. Complaints against Theodore Roosevelt and Harry Truman had been dismissed before they took office; the dismissals were affirmed after their respective inaugurations. Two companion cases arising out of an automobile accident were filed against John F. Kennedy in 1960 during the Presidential campaign. After taking office, he unsuccessfully argued that his status as Commander in Chief gave him a right to a stay under the Soldiers' and Sailors' Civil Relief Act of 1940 .... The motion for a stay was denied by the District

Court, and the matter was settled out of court. Thus, none of those cases sheds any light on the constitutional issue before us.

...

It does not follow, however, that separation of powers principles would be violated by allowing this action to proceed. The doctrine of separation of powers is concerned with the allocation of official power among the three co-equal branches of our Government. The Framers "built into the tripartite Federal Government ... a self executing safeguard against the encroachment or aggrandizement of one branch at the expense of the other .... Thus, for example, the Congress may not exercise the judicial power to revise final judgments ..., or the executive power to manage an airport .... Similarly, the President may not exercise the legislative power to authorize the seizure of private property for public use. *Youngstown* .... And, the judicial power to decide cases and controversies does not include the provision of purely advisory opinions to the Executive, or permit the federal courts to resolve nonjusticiable questions.

Of course the lines between the powers of the three branches are not always neatly defined .... But in this case there is no suggestion that the Federal Judiciary is being asked to perform any function that might in some way be described as "executive." Respondent is merely asking the courts to exercise their core Article III jurisdiction to decide cases and controversies. Whatever the outcome of this case, there is no possibility that the decision will curtail the scope of the official powers of the Executive Branch. The litigation of questions that relate entirely to the unofficial conduct of the individual who happens to be the President poses no perceptible risk of misallocation of either judicial power or executive power.

...

First, we have long held that when the President takes official action, the Court has the authority to determine whether he has acted within the law. Perhaps the most dramatic example of such a case is our holding [in *Youngstown*] that President Truman exceeded his constitutional authority when he issued an order directing the Secretary of Commerce to take possession of and operate most of the Nation's steel mills in order to avert a national catastrophe .... Our holding was an application of the principle established in *Marbury* v. *Madison*, 1 Cranch 137 (1803), that "[i]t is emphatically the province and duty of the judicial department to say what the law is."

Second, it is also settled that the President is subject to judicial process in appropriate circumstances. Although Thomas Jefferson apparently thought otherwise, Chief Justice Marshall, when presiding in the treason trial of Aaron Burr, ruled that a subpoena duces tecum could be directed to the President .... We unequivocally and emphatically endorsed Marshall's position when we held that President Nixon was obligated to comply with a subpoena commanding him to produce certain tape recordings of his conversations with his aides .... As we explained, "neither the doctrine of separation of powers, nor the need for confidentiality of high level communications, without more, can sustain an absolute, unqualified Presidential privilege of immunity from judicial process under all circumstances."

Sitting Presidents have responded to court orders to provide testimony and other information with sufficient frequency that such interactions between the Judicial and Executive Branches can scarcely be thought a novelty. President Monroe responded to written interrogatories ..., President Nixon—as noted above—produced tapes in response to a subpoena duces tecum ..., President Ford complied with an order to give a deposition in a criminal trial ..., and President Clinton has twice given videotaped testimony in criminal proceedings .... Moreover, sitting Presidents have also voluntarily complied with judicial requests for testimony. President Grant gave a lengthy deposition in a criminal case under such circumstances ... and President Carter similarly gave videotaped testimony for use at a criminal trial ....

...

The decision to postpone the trial was, furthermore, premature. The proponent of a stay bears the burden of establishing its need .... In this case, at the stage at which the District Court made its ruling, there was no way to assess whether a stay of trial after the completion of discovery would be warranted. Other than the fact that a trial may consume some of the President's time and attention, there is nothing in the record to enable a judge to assess the potential harm that may ensue from scheduling the trial promptly after discovery is concluded. We think the District Court may have given undue weight to the concern that a trial might generate unrelated civil actions that could conceivably hamper the President in conducting the duties of his office. If and when that should occur, the court's discretion would permit it to manage those actions in such fashion (including deferral of trial) that interference with the President's duties would not occur. But no such impingement upon the President's conduct of his office was shown here.

...

The Federal District Court has jurisdiction to decide this case. Like every other citizen who properly invokes that jurisdiction, respondent has a right to an orderly disposition of her claims. Accordingly, the judgment of the Court of Appeals is affirmed.

It is so ordered.

[Concurring opinion omitted.]

In accordance with the Supreme Court's decision, Paula Jones was allowed to prosecute her civil action against the president. At a deposition, the president was asked under oath about an alleged affair with Monica Lewinsky. The federal judge presiding over the deposition, Susan Webber Wright, a Clinton appointee, ruled the question relevant. Rather than refusing to answer and seeking review in the appellate court, the president denied under oath having "sexual relations" with her. DNA analysis of semen stains on Monica Lewinsky's dress proved that the president had been telling less than the whole truth at his deposition. His involvement of governmental officials, including the Secretary of State, in covering up the affair formed the basis of the charge in the articles of impeachment that President Clinton had obstructed justice.

When the truth came to light, Judge Wright held Mr. Clinton in contempt of court for lying, fined him $90,000, and made him pay her expenses for traveling to Washington to preside over his "tainted" deposition.[148] The Arkansas Supreme Court suspended Mr. Clinton's license to practice law for five years, and fined him $25,000 for giving misleading testimony in the Paula Jones case. Mr. Clinton settled the sexual harassment by paying Paula Jones $850,000, most of which was paid by insurance.[149]

4. Judicial Power

The federal courts are provided for in Article III of the Constitution. It would be more accurate to say that the Supreme Court is provided for, as becomes clear from the first sentence of clause 1:

> The judicial Power of the United States, shall be vested in one supreme Court, and in such inferior Courts as the Congress may from time to time ordain and establish.

Thus, the Constitution does not require the Congress to establish inferior federal courts; but, of course, it has done so, as it is specifically empowered to do.[150] Nor, for that matter, must Congress confer on the inferior

---

[148] Jones v. Clinton, 36 F.Supp.2d 1118 (E.D. Ark. 1999); Rotunda at n. 14.
[149] Pittsburgh Post-Gazette, national section, May 23, 2000; Toobin 395.
[150] See also Art. I, § 8, cl. 9.

courts jurisdiction to decide all matters within the federal judicial power.[151]

Federal judges are appointed by the president, and confirmed by the Senate (called the "advice and consent" procedure).[152] The Constitution specifies no particular qualifications for appointment, nor standards for confirmation, and the Senate occasionally refuses to confirm presidential appointments.[153] The last nomination to be rejected was Republican President Reagan's nomination of Robert Bork, whom the Democratic Senate considered too conservative.[154]

As provided in the Constitution, all federal "Article III" judges "hold their Offices during good Behaviour, and shall, at stated Times, receive for their Services, a Compensation, which shall not be diminished during their Continuance in Office."[155] This means that federal judges' salaries cannot be reduced, and federal judges cannot be forced to retire or leave office. The only avenue available to remove them is by impeachment, as with the president, but whereas no president has been removed by the impeachment process, five judges have been.

The Constitution does not prescribe the size of the Supreme Court, and in the early years, the size fluctuated. The number of judges (called "Justices") was set by law at nine in 1869.[156]

The Supreme Court has a great deal of discretion in deciding which cases it wants to hear. This discretion results principally from the employment by the Congress if its authority under Article III, section 2 to regulate the Supreme Court's appellate jurisdiction. Congress has by statute established two avenues of appellate review. The first, called "appeal," is mandatory. However, this avenue is extremely limited, for an appeal only lies from a decision of a three-judge district court panel (which is a rare animal in itself) that grants or denies injunctive relief.[157] All other review by the Supreme Court is by writ of certiorari, which is discretionary. For example, a party in any civil or criminal case that has been decided by a federal court of appeals can petition for certiorari whether or not constitutional issues are involved.[158] However, the Supreme Court will not grant the petition, and hear the case, unless it involves "special and important reasons,"[159] such as a conflict in the decisions of the various appellate courts, or when an important federal issue has not yet been decided.

---

[151] Sheldon v. Sill, 49 U.S. 441 (1850).
[152] Art. II, § 2, cl. 2.
[153] Massey.
[154] Ross at p. 993.
[155] Art. III. § 1.
[156] Act of March 3, 1863, chap. C, § 1, 12 Stat. 794.
[157] 28 U.S.C. § 1253.
[158] 28 U.S.C. § 1254.
[159] U.S. Sup. Ct. Rule 17.

a. Express Grants of (and Limitations on) Judicial Power

Article III of the Constitution provides not only for the establishment of the Supreme Court and inferior courts, it also specifies what matters these courts may decide. A three-step procedure is warranted in judging whether federal courts have jurisdiction to decide any particular dispute. The first issue to address is the nature of the dispute, that is, whether it falls with the subject matter jurisdiction of the federal court. Thereafter, one must consider whether the dispute meets the "case or controversy" requirement of Article III. Third, it must be asked whether the dispute, though federal and otherwise justiciable under the "case or controversy" clause, is nonetheless beyond the purview of the courts because its resolution is constitutionally committed to the "political" branches of government (the "political question" doctrine).

i. Heads of Federal Judicial Power (Subject Matter Jurisdiction)

Unlike states, which have courts of general jurisdiction, the federal judiciary, like the federal government as a whole, enjoys jurisdiction only in cases enumerated in the Constitution. By definition these are cases in which the federal government has some particular interest. For ease of discussion, these instances of federal judicial jurisdiction are gathered under two heads: diversity jurisdiction and federal question jurisdiction.

The federal courts possess federal question jurisdiction over cases or controversies:[160]

- "arising under this Constitution, the Laws of the United States, and Treaties made, or which shall be made, under their authority [28 U.S.C. § 1331]; ...
- affecting Ambassadors, other public Ministers and Counsels [original, "trial" jurisdiction in the Supreme Court pursuant to Art. III, § 2, cl. 2]; ...
- [involving] admiralty and maritime Jurisdiction [exclusive federal jurisdiction, 28 U.S.C. § 1333]; ...
- to which the United States shall be a Party [28 U.S.C. § 1345]; ...
- between two or more States [original jurisdiction with the Supreme Court, 28 U.S.C. § 1251]."

The federal courts exercise diversity of citizenship jurisdiction (where the amount in controversy must generally exceed $50,000) over cases or controversies:[161]

---

[160] Art. III, § 2, cl. 1.
[161] Art. III, § 2, cl. 1.

- "between Citizens of different States [28 U.S.C. § 1332(a)(1), which includes permanent foreign residents];
- between Citizens of the same State claiming Lands under Grants of different States, and between a State, or the Citizens thereof, and foreign States [28 U.S.C. §§ 1330 and 1332(a)(4)]."

Cases that do not fall under one of these heads of jurisdiction are not justiciable in the federal courts, but they may well be in the state courts. The courts of the states are not limited by the constraints of Article III.

There are very few cases that can be brought only in the federal, and not in the state, courts. These cases of exclusive federal judicial jurisdiction include admiralty, bankruptcy, patent and copyright, claims arising under the securities exchange laws, and antitrust.[162] In all other cases the federal and state courts have concurrent jurisdiction.

The common law tradition of judicial law-making is considered to be "policy-making" and therefore in part legislative.[163] Since, according to the Constitution, *all* legislative power is vested in Congress, does that mean that there can be no federal common law?[164]

ii. Limitation of Jurisdiction to "Cases or Controversies"

Article III, section 2 limits the jurisdiction of the federal court to "cases" or "controversies." The terms, which mean the same thing, have been construed to require that the matter in controversy be "definite and concrete, touching the legal relations of parties having adverse legal interests. It must be a real and substantial controversy admitting of specific relief through a decree of a conclusive character."[165]

The "case or controversy" requirement has spawned a host of sometimes sophisticated doctrines and distinctions, the most important of which—advisory opinions, ripeness, mootness, and standing—are sketched here.

The requirement that there be a "real and substantial controversy" has come to mean, most fundamentally, that neither the Supreme Court nor the federal courts will render advisory opinions on statutory interpretation, constitutionality of proposed legislation, or any other matter. This restraint tells the Congress in effect that it should not enact legislation if it harbors doubts about its constitutionality. Whether this makes for better government or not is open to debate. For the same reason the federal

---

[162] 28 U.S.C. §§ 1333, 1334 1338, 78aa, 1337 and 18 U.S.C. § 3231.
[163] See Gregory v. Ashcroft, 501 U.S. 452 (1991).
[164] See Kramer.
[165] Aetna Life Insurance Co. v. Haworth, 300 U.S. 227 (1937).

courts will not hear collusive or "friendly" suits, that is, where one side finances and controls the whole litigation.[166]

Ripeness, as its name suggests, refers to the temporal readiness of the matter for judicial determination. In large part, the reticence of the federal courts to decide matters that are not yet ripe is due to "prudential principles of judicial self-restraint."[167] A brewing controversy is not enough to invoke federal judicial relief. The threatened harm must be real and immediate, not hypothetical. For example, in one case the Supreme Court refused to rule on the constitutionality of a statute that outlawed contraceptives where the law had been on the books for 80 years but had not been enforced despite "ubiquitous, open, public sales" of contraceptives.[168]

If ripeness is the locomotive on the train of time, then mootness is the temporal caboose. The federal courts will not review cases that have been resolved, for there is no longer a case or controversy.[169] However, having served one's criminal sentence does not end collateral legal consequences, such as loss of voting rights.[170] By the same token, if a claim, although ostensibly moot, is "capable of repetition, yet evading review," the case or controversy requirement will not be a bar to review. Examples of the latter exception include pregnancy and voting.[171]

The requirement of "standing" has produced a large number of decisions, and a tremendous literature. In standing cases, there is seldom a problem with ripeness or mootness or even of advisory opinions; rather, the particular plaintiff is perceived not to possess "such a personal stake in the outcome of the controversy as to assure that concrete adverseness which sharpens the presentation of issues."[172] The personal stake need not be particularly large to satisfy the Supreme Court. In *United States* v. *SCRAP*,[173] a group of law students was held to have standing to challenge a policy of the Interstate Commerce Commission which discouraged recycling and therefore, it was alleged, diminished the quality of the students' physical environment. One major exception to the standing requirement has been created for taxpayer challenges to federal spending programs that are alleged to exceed specific constitutional limitations, such as the Establishment Clause of the First Amendment.[174]

---

[166] Chicago & Grand Trunk Railway v. Wellman, 143 U.S. 339 (1892).
[167] Rescue Army v. Municipal Court, 331 U.S. 549 (1949).
[168] Poe v. Ullman, 367 U.S. 497 (1961).
[169] Liner v. Jafco, Inc., 375 U.S. 301 (1964).
[170] Sibron v. New York, 392 U.S. 40 (1968).
[171] Moore v. Ogilvie, 394 U.S. 814 (1969).
[172] Baker v. Carr, 369 U.S. 186 (1962).
[173] 412 U.S. 669 (1973).
[174] Flast v. Cohen, 392 U.S. 83 (1968).

The case or controversy requirement is imposed by the Constitution, not by statutory law. Therefore it cannot be ameliorated by a statute which purports to allow any person, regardless of interest or injury, to challenge alleged statutory violations.[175]

b. Implied Grants of (and Limitations on) Judicial Power

The Constitution does not specifically provide for the judicial review of the constitutionality of governmental acts, whether they be legislative, executive, or administrative. In this way the American Constitution differs textually from those of, for example, Austria, Germany, and Spain, that specifically provide for constitutional courts. Efforts to create a Council of Revision to review with the authority to judge the constitutionality of legislative and executive acts of Congress before they went into effect were rejected at the Constitutional Convention.[176]

With the authority to judge the constitutionality of legislative and executive acts comes the corresponding responsibility not to usurp legislative and constitutional authority. This responsibility, founded upon the principle of separation of powers, is termed the "political question" doctrine. Discussion of this doctrine follows an exposition of the institution of judicial review.

i. Judicial Review of Constitutionality

The catalogue of the Supreme Court's judicial province, discussed above, speaks only of cases "arising under this Constitution."[177] The closest textual suggestion of a judicial power to rule on the constitutionality of legislation is the Supremacy Clause, Article IV, section 2, which reads:

> This Constitution, and the Laws of the United States which shall be made in Pursuance thereof; and all Treaties made, or which shall be made, under the Authority of the United States, shall be the supreme Law of the Land; and the Judges in every State shall be bound thereby, any Thing in the Constitution or Laws of any State to the Contrary notwithstanding.

Admittedly, this clause does not stipulate what body should determine whether the laws are made "in Pursuance" of the Constitution. The final clause might also be read to indicate that the courts were only supposed to consider the conformity of state law with federal law.

---

[175] Lujan v. Defenders of Wildlife, 504 U.S. 555 (1992).
[176] Farrand at p. 21.
[177] Art. III, § 2, cl. 1.

In England, courts had occasionally refused to enforce acts of Parliament. Lord Coke, in *Dr. Bonham's Case*,[178] stated that "the common law will controul acts of Parliament, adjudge them to be utterly void [when they are] against common right and reason."[179] But this was not descriptive of British practice in the 18th century. The Privy Council had employed the principle of *ultra vires* to invalidate colonial acts, and state courts had set aside acts of state legislatures for incompatibility with their constitutions. Legal historians have searched in vain for evidence that the Framers of the Constitution did not expect the courts to rule on constitutionality. Professor Bickel writes[180] that the Framers "tacitly" intended such a power. Still, it is curious from a historical standpoint that the power was first confirmed in a case where the Supreme Court concluded that it had no jurisdiction. That case, perhaps the most famous in American constitutional jurisprudence, follows.

By way of background, after suffering defeat in the elections of 1800, the outgoing Congress created 42 new positions as justices of the peace in the District of Columbia. President John Adams, who had been defeated in the election by Thomas Jefferson, wanted to fill all vacant judicial positions with federally minded judges before he left office. He appointed his Secretary of State, John Marshall, the man who wrote the following opinion, to the vacant seat as Chief Justice at the United States Supreme Court. After the Senate confirmed Marshall's appointment, President Adams signed Marshall's commission (formal document evidencing the appointment) and Marshall, as outgoing secretary of state, affixed the seal of the United States to the commission, and took delivery of it himself. The Senate confirmed President Adams' appointments of William Marbury, the petitioner in the following case, and a number of other judges on the day before Jefferson took office. The outgoing president signed the commissions, and the seal of the United States was affixed to them, but the commissions were left undelivered.

When Jefferson's secretary of state, respondent Madison, refused to deliver the commissions, William Marbury filed suit directly in the United States Supreme Court seeking a writ of mandamus, a species of court order, to compel Madison to deliver his commission and, thus, allow him to begin sitting as a justice of the peace. Marbury premised his petition on section 13 of the Judiciary Act of 1789. This legislation bestowed on the Supreme Court jurisdiction to issue writs of mandamus "to persons holding office under the authority of the United States." In doing so, the Judiciary Act purported to enlarge the so-called original jurisdiction of the Supreme Court beyond that provided in Article III of the Constitution,

---

[178] 8 Rep. 118a (C.P. 1610).
[179] Gunther & Sullivan at p. 14.
[180] At p. 15.

which mentions only cases and controversies "affecting Ambassadors, other public Ministers and Counsels, and those in which a State shall be a Party."

Was this enlargement of the jurisdiction of the Supreme Court consistent with the Constitution? Was it appropriate for the Court even to address the issue?

CASE: **Marbury v. Madison**
5 U.S. 137 (1803)

Opinion of the court [by Chief Justice Marshall]

At the last term, on the affidavits then read and filed with the clerk, a rule was granted in this case, requiring the secretary of state to show cause why a mandamus should not issue, directing him to deliver to William Marbury his commission as a justice of the peace for the county of Washington, in the district of Columbia.

No cause has been shown, and the present motion is for a mandamus. The peculiar delicacy of this case, the novelty of some of its circumstances, and the real difficulty attending the points which occur in it, require a complete exposition of the principles on which the opinion to be given by the court is founded.

In the order in which the court has viewed this subject, the following questions have been considered and decided.

1st. Has the applicant a right to the commission he demands?

2dly. If he has a right, and that right has been violated, do the laws of his country afford him a remedy?

3dly. If they do afford him a remedy, is it a mandamus issuing from this court?

The first object of inquiry is,

1st. Has the applicant a right to the commission he demands?

His right originates in an act of congress passed in February 1801, concerning the district of Columbia ....

The last act to be done by the president, is the signature of the commission. He has then acted on the advice and consent of the senate to his own nomination. The time for deliberation has then passed ....

It is therefore decidedly the opinion of the court, that when a commission has been signed by the president, the appointment is made; and that the commission is complete when the seal of the United States has been affixed to it by the secretary of state.

...

2. This brings us to the second inquiry; which is: If he has a right, and that right has been violated, do the laws of his country afford him a remedy? The very essence of civil liberty certainly consists in the right of every individual to claim the protection of the laws, whenever he receives an injury. One of the first duties of government is to afford that protection. In Great Britain the king himself is sued in the respectful form of a petition, and he never fails to comply with the judgment of his court.

The government of the United States has been emphatically termed a government of laws, and not of men. It will certainly cease to deserve this high appellation, if the laws furnish no remedy for the violation of a vested legal right. If this obloquy is to be cast on the jurisprudence of our country, it must arise from the peculiar character of the case.

...

It is then the opinion of the court: 1st. That by signing the commission of Mr. Marbury, the president of the United States appointed him a justice of peace for the county of Washington in the district of Columbia; and that the seal of the United States, affixed thereto by the secretary of state, is conclusive testimony of the verity of the signature, and of the completion of the appointment; and that the appointment conferred on him a legal right to the office for the space of five years. 2d. That, having this legal title to the office, he has a consequent right to the commission; a refusal to deliver which is a plain violation of that right, for which the laws of his country afford him a remedy.

3. It remains to be inquired whether he is entitled to the remedy for which he applies?

...

The act to establish the judicial courts of the United States authorizes the supreme court 'to issue writs of mandamus, in cases warranted by the principles and usages of law, to any courts appointed, or persons holding office, under the authority of the United States.'

The secretary of state, being a person, holding an office under the authority of the United States, is precisely within the letter of the description; and if this court is not authorized to issue a writ of mandamus to such an officer, it must be because the law is unconstitutional, and therefore absolutely incapable of conferring the authority, and assigning the duties which its words purport to confer and assign.

The constitution vests the whole judicial power of the United States in one supreme court, and such inferior courts as congress shall, from time to time, ordain and establish....

In the distribution of this power it is declared that 'the supreme court shall have original jurisdiction in all cases affecting ambassadors, other public ministers and consuls, and those in which a state shall be a party. In all other cases, the supreme court shall have appellate jurisdiction.'

...

When an instrument organizing fundamentally a judicial system, divides it into one supreme, and so many inferior courts as the legislature may ordain and establish; then enumerates its powers, and proceeds so far to distribute them, as to define the jurisdiction of the supreme court by declaring the cases in which it shall take original jurisdiction, and that in others it shall take appellate jurisdiction, the plain import of the words seems to be, that in one class of cases its jurisdiction is original, and not appellate; in the other it is appellate, and not original. If any other construction would render the clause inoperative, that is an additional reason for rejecting such other construction, and for adhering to the obvious meaning.

To enable this court then to issue a mandamus, it must be shown to be an exercise of appellate jurisdiction, or to be necessary to enable them to exercise appellate jurisdiction.

...

It is the essential criterion of appellate jurisdiction, that it revises and corrects the proceedings in a cause already instituted, and does not create that case ....

The authority, therefore, given to the supreme court, by the act establishing the judicial courts of the United States, to issue writs of mandamus to public officers, appears not to be warranted by the constitution; and it becomes necessary to inquire whether a jurisdiction, so conferred, can be exercised.

The question, whether an act, repugnant to the constitution, can become the law of the land, is a question deeply interesting to the United States; but, happily, not of an intricacy proportioned to its interest. It seems only necessary to recognize certain principles, supposed to have been long and well established, to decide it.

That the people have an original right to establish, for their future government, such principles as, in their opinion, shall most conduce to their own happiness, is the basis on which the whole American fabric has been erected. The exercise of this original right is a very great exertion; nor can it nor ought it to be frequently repeated. The principles, therefore, so established are deemed fundamental. And as the authority, from which they proceed, is supreme, and can seldom act, they are designed to be permanent.

This original and supreme will organizes the government, and assigns to different departments their respective powers. It may either stop here; or establish certain limits not to be transcended by those departments.

The government of the United States is of the latter description. The powers of the legislature are defined and limited; and that those limits may not be mistaken or forgotten, the constitution is written. To what purpose are powers limited, and to what purpose is that limitation committed to writing; if these limits may, at any time, be passed by those intended to be restrained? The distinction between a government with limited and unlimited powers is abolished, if those limits do not confine the persons on whom they are imposed, and if acts prohibited and acts allowed are of equal obligation. It is a proposition too plain to be contested, that the constitution controls any legislative act repugnant to it; or, that the legislature may alter the constitution by an ordinary act.

Between these alternatives there is no middle ground. The constitution is either a superior, paramount law, unchangeable by ordinary means, or it is on a level with ordinary legislative acts, and like other acts, is alterable when the legislature shall please to alter it.

If the former part of the alternative be true, then a legislative act contrary to the constitution is not law: if the latter part be true, then written constitutions are absurd attempts, on the part of the people, to limit a power in its own nature illimitable.

Certainly all those who have framed written constitutions contemplate them as forming the fundamental and paramount law of the nation, and consequently the theory of every such government must be, that an act of the legislature repugnant to the constitution is void.

This theory is essentially attached to a written constitution, and is consequently to be considered by this court as one of the fundamental principles of our society. It is not therefore to be lost sight of in the further consideration of this subject.

If an act of the legislature, repugnant to the constitution, is void, does it, notwithstanding its invalidity, bind the courts and oblige them to give it effect? Or, in other words, though it be not law, does it constitute a rule as operative as if it was a law? This would be to overthrow in fact what was established in theory; and would seem, at first view, an absurdity too gross to be insisted on. It shall, however, receive a more attentive consideration.

It is emphatically the province and duty of the judicial department to say what the law is. Those who apply the rule to particular cases, must of necessity expound and interpret that rule.

If two laws conflict with each other, the courts must decide on the operation of each.

So if a law be in opposition to the constitution: if both the law and the constitution apply to a particular case, so that the court must either decide that case conformably to the law, disregarding the constitution; or conformably to the constitution, disregarding the law: the court must determine which of these conflicting rules governs the case. This is of the very essence of judicial duty. If then the courts are to regard the constitution; and he constitution is superior to any ordinary act of the legislature; the constitution, and not such ordinary act, must govern the case to which they both apply.

...

The judicial power of the United States is extended to all cases arising under the constitution.

Could it be the intention of those who gave this power, to say that, in using it, the constitution should not be looked into? That a case arising under the constitution should be decided without examining the instrument under which it arises?

This is too extravagant to be maintained.

...

Thus, the particular phraseology of the constitution of the United States confirms and strengthens the principle, supposed to be essential to all written constitutions, that a law repugnant to the constitution is void, and that courts, as well as other departments, are bound by that instrument.

The rule must be discharged.

To recapitulate, all the judges of the U.S. Supreme Court (there were five at the time) ruled that Madison was acting unlawfully in withholding Marbury's commission, but they refused to order Madison to comply with the law because, they held in the narrow sense, the Constitution did not give them the jurisdiction to decide the case, at least not in the first instance (original jurisdiction). Congress's attempt to enlarge that jurisdiction was "repugnant to the constitution [and] void. Accordingly, the "courts, as well as other departments, are bound by" the Constitution first, and statutes second. In result, then, the Supreme Court held section 13 of the Judiciary Act of 1789 unconstitutional.

Politically, Chief Justice Marshall's opinion was brilliant. Although Marbury was left without a judicial remedy, had Marshall ruled in his favor, the Jefferson administration would surely have ignored the order.[181]

---

[181] Chemerinsky, Constitutional Law at p. 46.

In addition, there was a real risk that Jefferson might seek the impeachment of more Federalist judges. One, an insane drunkard, had been impeached in early 1802 for "Treason, Bribery, or other high Crimes and Misdemeanors" under Article II, section 4, of the Constitution, and was removed from office on his conviction by the Senate in March 1804.[182] One day later the House impeached Supreme Court Justice Samuel Chase for political activity incompatible with his office, but the Senate failed to convict him.

A few years after *Marbury* v. *Madison*, the Supreme Court confirmed its constitutional power to judge the constitutionality of state legislation.[183] Shortly thereafter it was confronted with the question of whether the Constitution conferred upon it the power to review the judgments of state courts in cases that fall within the jurisdiction of the federal courts. At issue was the forerunner of section 1257(a) of title 28 of the United States Code:

> Final judgments or decrees rendered by the highest court of a State in which a decision could be had, may be reviewed by the Supreme Court by writ of certiorari where the validity of a treaty or statute of the United States is drawn in question or where the validity of a statute of any State is drawn in question on the ground of its being repugnant to the Constitution, treaties, or laws of the United States ....

By way of background, the Commonwealth of Virginia confiscated land owned by the plaintiff Martin's uncle, a British subject, in 1782 and granted it to Hunter in 1789. Martin filed suit in the Virginia court against Hunter and his lessee, contending that the confiscation violated a 1783 treaty between the United States and Great Britain. The Virginia Court of Appeals ruled for the defendant on the ground that the confiscation had preceded the treaties. Martin then sought review by the United States Supreme Court under section 25 of the Judiciary Act. That court reversed, holding that the Commonwealth of Virginia had not perfected its title before the treaty took effect. The Virginia court refused to acknowledge the reversal, claiming that Congress had no power to extend the jurisdiction of the Supreme Court to review judgments of state courts.

---

[182] Gunther & Sullivan at p. 12.
[183] Fletcher v. Peck, 10 U.S. 87 (1810).

CASE: **Martin v. Hunter's Lessee**
14 U.S. 304 (1816)

STORY, J., delivered the opinion of the court ....
[The] appellate power is not limited by the terms of the third article to any particular courts. The words are, 'the judicial power (which includes appellate power) shall extend to *all cases,*' &c., and 'in all other cases before mentioned the supreme court shall have appellate jurisdiction.' It is the *case,* then, and not the *court,* that gives the jurisdiction. If the judicial power extends to the case, it will be in vain to search in the letter of the constitution for any qualification as to the tribunal where it depends. [If] the text be clear and distinct, no restriction upon its plain and obvious import ought to be admitted, unless the inference be irresistible.

If the constitution meant to limit the appellate jurisdiction to cases pending in the courts of the United States, it would necessarily follow that the jurisdiction of these courts would, in all the cases enumerated in the constitution, be exclusive of state tribunals. How otherwise could the jurisdiction extend to *all* cases arising under the constitution, laws, and treaties of the United States, or to all cases of admiralty and maritime jurisdiction? If some of these cases might be entertained by state tribunals, and no appellate jurisdiction as to them should exist, then the appellate power would not extend to *all,* but to *some,* cases. If state tribunals might exercise concurrent jurisdiction over all or some of the other classes of cases in the constitution without control, then the appellate jurisdiction of the United States might, as to such cases, have no real existence, contrary to the manifest intent of the constitution. [This] construction would abridge the jurisdiction of such court far more than has been ever contemplated in any act of congress ....

[It] is plain that the framers of the constitution did contemplate that cases within the judicial cognizance of the United States not only might but would arise in the state courts, in the exercise of their ordinary jurisdiction. With this view the sixth article declares, that 'this constitution, and the laws of the United States which shall be made in pursuance thereof, and all treaties made, or which shall be made, under the authority of the United States, shall be the supreme law of the land, and the judges in every state shall be bound thereby, any thing in the constitution or laws of any state to the contrary notwithstanding.' It is obvious that this obligation is imperative upon the state judges in their official, and not merely in their private, capacities. From the very nature of their judicial duties they would be called upon to pronounce the law applicable to the case in judgment. They were not to decide merely according to the laws or constitution of the state, but according to the constitution, laws and treaties of the United States—'the supreme law of the land.'

...

It has been argued that such an appellate jurisdiction over state courts is inconsistent with the genius of our governments, and the spirit of the constitution. That the latter was never designed to act upon state sovereignties, but only upon the people, and that if the power exists, it will materially impair the sovereignty of the states, and the independence of their courts ....

It is a mistake that the constitution was not designed to operate upon states, in their corporate capacities. It is crowded with provisions which restrain or annul the sovereignty of the states in some of the highest branches of their prerogatives. The tenth section of the first article contains a long list of disabilities and prohibitions imposed upon the states. Surely, when such essential portions of state sovereignty are taken away, or prohibited to be exercised, it cannot be correctly asserted that the constitution does not act upon the states. The language of the constitution is also imperative upon the states as to the performance of many duties. It is imperative upon the state legislatures to make laws prescribing the time, places, and manner of holding elections for senators and representatives, and for electors of president and vice-president. And in these, as well as some other cases, congress have a right to revise, amend, or supercede the laws which may be passed by state legislatures. When, therefore, the states are stripped of some of the highest attributes of sovereignty, and the same are given to the United States; when the legislatures of the states are, in some respects, under the control of congress, and in every case are, under the constitution, bound by the paramount authority of the United States; it is certainly difficult to support the argument that the appellate power over the decisions of state courts is contrary to the genius of our institutions. The courts of the United States can, without question, revise the proceedings of the executive and legislative authorities of the states, and if they are found to be contrary to the constitution, may declare them to be of no legal validity. Surely the exercise of the same right over judicial tribunals is not a higher or more dangerous act of sovereign power.

Nor can such a right be deemed to impair the independence of state judges. It is assuming the very ground in controversy to assert that they possess an absolute independence of the United States. In respect to the powers granted to the United States, they are not independent; they are expressly bound to obedience by the letter of the constitution; and if they should unintentionally transcend their authority, or misconstrue the constitution, there is no more reason for giving their judgments an absolute and irresistible force, than for giving it to the acts of the other co-ordinate departments of state sovereignty.

...

This is not all. A motive of another kind, perfectly compatible with the most sincere respect for state tribunals, might induce the grant of appellate power over their decisions. That motive is the importance, and even necessity of *uniformity* of decisions throughout the whole United States, upon all subjects within the purview of the constitution. Judges of equal learning and integrity, in different states, might differently interpret a statute, or a treaty of the United States, or even the constitution itself: If there were no revising authority to control these jarring and discordant judgments, and harmonize them into uniformity, the laws, the treaties, and the constitution of the United States would be different in different states, and might, perhaps, never have precisely the same construction, obligation, or efficacy, in any two states. The public mischiefs that would attend such a state of things would be truly deplorable; and it cannot be believed that they could have escaped the enlightened convention which formed the constitution. What, indeed, might then have been only prophecy, has now become fact; and the appellate jurisdiction must continue to be the only adequate remedy for such evils.

...

On the whole, the court are of opinion, that the appellate power of the United States does extend to cases pending in the state courts; and that the 25th section of the judiciary act, which authorizes the exercise of this jurisdiction in the specified cases, by a writ of error, is supported by the letter and spirit of the constitution. We find no clause in that instrument which limits this power; and we dare not interpose a limitation where the people have not been disposed to create one ....

[Reversed.]

Does it follow from these cases and from the institution of judicial review that inferior federal courts have the authority to decide that statutes are unconstitutional?[184] What about the authority of federal courts to rule on the constitutionality of state and local governmental actions?[185] Finally, should state judges be able to invalidate their own state's legislation under the federal constitution?[186]

ii. The "Political Question" Doctrine

The Supreme Court's discretion, discussed above, to select by writ of certiorari what cases to hear must be distinguished from another doctrine that seems to function like discretion, but is actually based on the theory and conviction that the Supreme Court lacks discretion to decide certain cases even though they arise under the Constitution and involve real controversies. The doctrine is referred to, somewhat misleadingly, as the political question doctrine. It holds that the Supreme Court is prohibited by principles of separation of powers from interfering in the fundamental workings of the other two "political" branches of government.

Because the political question doctrine works at a high level of abstraction, it is difficult to describe and predict its impact on everyday disputes. To help guide itself in deciding which cases it shall not decide, the Supreme Court has articulated four questions.[187] These are:

- Does the Constitution exhibit a "textually demonstrable" commitment of the issue to one of the political branches, that is, to the Congress or the president?
- Is there a lack of judicially manageable standards for resolving the issue?
- Is there a need for finality in the action of the political branch? Is it difficult or impossible to devise effective judicial remedies?

Applying the separation of powers policies embedded in these questions, the Supreme Court has refused to review procedures concerning constitutional amendments,[188] election to the Congress,[189] and impeachment,[190]

---

[184] See 16 Am. Jur. 2d, Constitutional Law § 116.
[185] See Chemerinsky, *Parity*.
[186] E.g., Jackman v. Bodine, 43 N.J. 453(1964); see U.S. Const. Art. VI, § 2 and Williams.
[187] Baker v. Carr, 369 U.S. 186 (1962).
[188] Coleman v. Miller, 307 U.S. 422 (1939).
[189] Roudebush v. Hartke, 405 U.S. 15 (1972).
[190] Nixon v. United States, 506 U.S. 224 (1993).

although in the last case it suggested that "political" matters are reviewable if they exceed the textual limits of the Constitution. The area of foreign relations has also been one in which the Supreme Court has indicated that the Constitution forbids it from second-guessing the president, Senate, and Congress.[191]

---

[191] E.g., Martin v. Mott, 25 U.S. 19 (1827), considering what the recognized government of a country is, and Goldwater v. Carter, 444 U.S. 996 (1979), where four justices opined that the question whether the president may unilaterally terminate a treaty is political and thus unreviewable.

SUBPART B
THE GOVERNMENTS OF THE STATES

TODAY, IT IS SOMETIMES DIFFICULT TO COMPREHEND THAT THIRTEEN OF THE STATES WERE in existence before the federal government, that the new federal government has eventually replaced them in major areas, that it has come to dominate them financially, but that it has still not subjugated them or relegated them to the status of federal agencies.

Federalism functions haphazardly in the United States. It shields state legislatures from most direct interference by the federal government, but does not protect them against federal preemption of traditional state matters, or allow them to violate federal constitutional rights or regulate interstate or foreign commerce.[192] While state executive branches cannot be forced to enforce federal law, they are subject to some federal control, such as when they are acting as employers, or when affecting federal constitutional rights. State judiciaries, unlike state executive officers, must enforce federal law directly.

Various prudential reasons have been advanced for federal structures like the one in the United States. The most frequent justification is roughly the same as the policy underlying the principle of separation of powers: division of the monopoly on governmental power to avoid tyranny, caprice, and oppression.

A second reason advanced is experimentation. According to Justice Brandeis in dissent in *New State Ice Co.* v. *Liebman*:

> To stay experimentation in things social and economic is a grave responsibility. Denial of the right to experiment might be fraught with serious consequences to the Nation. It is one of the happy incidents of the federal system that a single courageous State may, if its citizens choose, serve as a laboratory; and try novel social and economic experiments without risk to the rest of the country.[193]

A third justification for federalism is plurality for its own sake, an appreciation for differing regional legislation that reflects various social, political,

---

[192] This text does not treat the so-called "negative" or "dormant" commerce clause, that is, the implied prohibition against regulation by the states of interstate and international commerce.
[193] 285 U.S. 262, 322 (1932).

and other phenomena. A fourth argument is democratic involvement, which is more practical at the local or even state level than on the federal level. The chances for citizen involvement, and the sense of responsibility felt by elected officials, are greater when geographic and other distances are reduced. Finally, overlapping jurisdictions are thought to encourage competition between federal and state officials for the approval of the populace.

In order to help the reader sense the tension between the federal and state governments, the two positions—federal power vs. "states rights"—are polarized under two provisions of the Constitution, the Supremacy Clause[194] and the Tenth Amendment. This part begins by looking at the text of the Constitution. It then sketches the historical rise of federal dominance and presents the present state of the law on "states rights." The part concludes with thoughts on whether or not the state governments should not be federalized, or if there continued existence does not serve public interests that might be collected under the term "subsidiarity" or "localism."

1. THE SUPREMACY CLAUSE

> This Constitution, and the Laws of the United States which shall be made in Pursuance thereof; and all Treaties made, or which shall be made, under the Authority of the United States, shall be the supreme Law of the Land; and the Judges in every State shall be bound thereby, any Thing in the Constitution or Laws of any State to the Contrary notwithstanding.[195]

Unlike the federal government, the states enjoy general governmental powers, including what is generally referred to as the "police power," that is, the power to promote the health, morals, safety, and general welfare. The police power allows the states and their subdivisions to enact any law that is not repugnant to constitutional law. As a review of the catalogue of federal powers will reveal, the federal government enjoys no comparable power.

a. Concurrent Jurisdiction

In light of the expansive powers of the states, it is perhaps surprising that the states receive so little mention in the Constitution. This is undoubtedly

---

[194] Art. VI, cl. 2.
[195] Art. VI, § 2.

because the Framers were confronted with designing a new federal government, not with designing state governments, which were already in existence and governed by their own constitutions.

As foreseen by the Constitution, the major role to be played by the states in influencing the affairs of the federal government, and in protecting state autonomy, was in the Senate. Regardless of the geographic size or population of a state, each state is entitled to two senators.[196] Originally, the senators were chosen by the state legislature, much as representatives are appointed to the *Bundesrat* in Germany. This practice came to mean that political parties, which are not mentioned in the Constitution, exerted substantial, indirect control on the federal government, for no law can take effect unless both houses of Congress approve. The practice of appointing senators in this fashion was abolished in 1913 on the ratification of the Seventeenth Amendment. Ever since, senators, like members of the House of Representatives, are elected directly by the people. The senators' "district" is coincidental with the geographic boundaries of the state. Election and reelection to the Senate no longer mean responding to the political interests of an identifiable institution, but rather to diffuse popular interests and concerns. Thus, in a very real sense, the states as institutions were disenfranchised by the Seventeenth Amendment.

The role of the states in the election of the president and vice-president is equally indirect. As mentioned above, these offices are filled via the Electoral College. The Electoral College, in turn, consists of electors in a number equal to the combined number of senators and representatives in the state. The electors are chosen by the legislature. However, they are ordinarily bound to vote for the candidates who received the highest numbers of votes in the popular election.

The only direct control that the states as institutions possess over the federal government is that exercised on amending the Constitution. According to Article V, in order for the Constitution to be amended, the amendment must be proposed by two-thirds of both houses of Congress and ratified by three-fourths of the legislatures of the states. (No use has yet been made of the alternative procedure provided for in Article V, the constitutional convention.) The paucity of amendments to the Constitution testifies to the difficulty of this process, and to the corresponding insipidity of the states as institutions in directing federal policy.

On the other hand, the Constitution does significantly circumscribe the states. Beginning in the first Article, the Constitution forbids the states, among other things, to enter into treaties, coin money, and grant any title of nobility.[197] The states are also forbidden, without the consent

---

[196] Art. I, § 3.
[197] Art. I, § 10, cl. 1.

of the Congress, to tax imports or exports, except to the extent absolutely necessary to enforce their inspection laws.[198] Nor may states, without the consent of Congress, keep troops in time of peace, or engage in war unless actually invaded or in imminent danger of being invaded.[199] Further, each state must accord "Full Faith and Credit ... to the public Acts, Records, and judicial Proceedings of every other State."[200] Each state has an obligation to extradite persons charged with crimes in another state.[201] And, more importantly, each state must accord citizens of other states the same "Privileges and Immunities" that automatically are accorded its own citizens.[202]

The most important limitations on the powers of the states are found in the amendments to the Constitution. Thus, slavery was abolished in the states which had it.[203] Former slaves were given the same rights as others to vote in federal and state elections.[204] The manufacture, sale, and transportation of intoxicating beverages were prohibited.[205] Women and 18-year-olds were given the franchise in all federal and state elections.[206] (Women's suffrage was begun on a limited level by Kentucky in 1838 and accorded on an equal basis with men in the Wyoming Territory in 1869.) But the most profound limitations on the powers of the states are found in section 1 of the Fourteenth Amendment:

> All persons born or naturalized in the United States and subject to the jurisdiction thereof, are citizens of the United States and of the State wherein they reside. No State shall make or enforce any law which shall abridge the privileges or immunities of citizens of the United States; nor shall any State deprive any person of life, liberty, or property, without due process of law; nor deny any person within its jurisdiction the equal protection of the laws.

As discussed in the second part of this book, the "due process" and "equal protection" clauses are the two most important fonts of constitutional rights in the U.S. today. The "due process clause" of the Fourteenth Amendment has been interpreted by the federal courts to forbid the states to violate most of the rights protected by the Bill of Rights, which were

---

[198] Art. I, § 10, cl. 2.
[199] Art. I, § 10, cl. 3.
[200] Art. IV, § 1.
[201] Art. IV, § 2, cl. 2.
[202] Art. IV, § 2, cl. 1.
[203] Amend. 13.
[204] Amend. 15.
[205] Amend. 18, repealed by Amend. 21.
[206] Amends. 19 and 26.

originally directed to the federal government alone.[207] This interpretation automatically brings disputes between people who feel their rights are being violated by the governments of the states within the "federal question" jurisdiction of the federal courts. The impact of this federalization of rights has been felt most acutely in the criminal arena, where the vast majority of prosecutions are for violations of state law. But few areas of public life have not been affected. And, of course, the status of the states has waned in the wake of the recognition and enforcement of federal rights.

In summary, the Constitution is not a document that defines the goals and institutions of American government. There are no catalogues, as there are in the German Basic Law, that divide governmental powers between the state and federal governments. Rather, the U.S. Constitution confines itself, with few exceptions, to delineating the powers of the federal government, on the one hand, and the rights of the citizens on the other. The governments of the states are sandwiched somewhere in between.

Nonetheless, it is useful to think in terms of three groups of governmental powers: those granted exclusively to the federal government or expressly denied to the states, those exercised concurrently with the states, and those reserved to the states exclusively, basically because they not fall within the enumerated powers of the Congress. As we saw above, exclusive federal powers are very few in number. They include the powers over foreign affairs (e.g., naturalization and citizenship, declaration of war, national defense, treaties) and over the federal government's political agenda, budget, officials, institutions, and property. At the other end are those powers, also very few in number, that are reserved exclusively to the states. These are discussed below, after the discussion of preemption.

b. Preemption

With the exception of those few cases in which exclusive legislative power has been bestowed on the federal government, and assuming the federal government has not legislated on the same subject, state governments are free to legislate on any subject they choose, providing, of course, that they do not contravene some particular constitutional impediment, for example, by violating the privileges and immunities clause[208] or by discriminating against interstate commerce.[209] Thus, it was held in any early case that states could enact bankruptcy laws because Congress had not made use of its authority to regulate bankruptcies.[210]

---

[207] Duncan v. Louisiana, 391 U.S. 145 (1968).
[208] Edwards v. California, 314 U.S. 160 (1941).
[209] Welton v. Missouri, 91 U.S. 275 (1876).
[210] Sturges v. Crowninshield, 17 U.S. 122 (1819).

The complexion changes when Congress has legislated on the subject, whether or not the state legislation preceded or succeeded the federal. If Congress has legislated, the state law is not automatically void. Rather, it is void only if Congress clearly intended to preempt state law. The Supreme Court has described the inquiry in *Gade* v. *National Solid Waste Management Association*:

> Preemption may be either express or implied, and is compelled whether Congress' command is explicitly stated in the statute's language or implicitly contained in its structure and purpose. Absent explicit preemptive language, we have recognized at least two types of implied preemption: field preemption, where the scheme of federal regulation is so pervasive as to make reasonable the inference that Congress left no room for the States to supplement it, and conflict preemption, where compliance with both federal and state regulations is a physical impossibility, or where state law stands as an obstacle to the accomplishment and execution of the full purposes and objectives of Congress.[211]

The Supreme Court frequently states that, where preemption is not express, it should not likely be implied. As stated in *Medtronic, Inc.* v. *Lohr*:

> [B]ecause the States are independent sovereigns in our federal system, we have long presumed that Congress does not cavalierly preempt state-law causes of action. In all preemption cases, and particularly in those in which Congress has legislated in a field which the States have traditionally occupied, we 'start with the presumption' that 'the historic police powers of the States were not to be superseded by the Federal Act unless that was the clear and manifest purpose of Congress.'[212]

Returning to our example of bankruptcy laws, the Supreme Court has invalidated a state law that denied a drivers license to one who had failed to satisfy a judgment arising out of an automobile accident, even if the debt had been discharged in bankruptcy. The court concluded that the purpose of the federal bankruptcy law was to provide uniform standards for determining when a debt was discharged, and that to allow states to regulate in this fashion would undermine this purpose.[213]

---

[211] 505 U.S. 88, 98 (1992).
[212] 518 U.S. 470 (1996).
[213] Perez v. Campbell, 402 U.S. 637 (1971).

2. THE TENTH AMENDMENT

> The powers not delegated to the United States by the Constitution, nor prohibited by it to the States, are reserved to the States respectively, or to the people.

In Subpart A of Part One of this book, we saw that, although the federal government is textually a government of limited, enumerated powers, in fact, these powers have been very widely construed, by the Congress and by the federal courts, to stretch those powers to envelop almost every conceivable field of human endeavor. In the foregoing subpart we saw that there is no need for a correspondingly wide interpretation of the original powers of the states, for these powers are considered plenary unless, which rarely happens, the Constitution expressly or impliedly confers exclusive jurisdiction on the federal government or unless, which quite often happens, the Congress legislates on a matters that are concurrently regulated by one or more states, and the congressional legislation expressly or impliedly preempts the state legislation.

In this subpart, we consider what residual exclusive powers, if any, persist only with the states. This question is traditionally addressed in the context of the Tenth Amendment, but it could also be addressed under the "guarantee clause"[214] or under the doctrine that the federal government is one of enumerated powers. In other words, the Tenth Amendment is tautological.[215] In upholding sections of the Fair Labor Standards Acts as within the scope of regulation of interstate commerce, Justice Stone, delivering the opinion of the court in *United States v. Darby* wrote:

> Our conclusion is unaffected by the Tenth Amendment .... The amendment states but a truism that all is retained which has not been surrendered. There is nothing in the history of its adoption to suggest that it was more than declaratory of the relationship between the national and state governments as it had been established by the Constitution before the amendment or that its purpose was other than to allay fears that the new national government might seek to exercise powers not granted, and that the states might not be able to exercise fully their reserved powers.[216]

---

[214] Art. IV, § 4.
[215] New York v. United States, 505 U.S. 144, 157 (1992) (O'Connor, J., concurring).
[216] 312 U.S. 100, 123–124 (1940).

a. The Tenth Amendment in the Courts

We concluded in the preceding subpart that the federal government had exclusive jurisdiction over its political agenda, budget, officials, institutions, and property. The same cannot quite be said for state governments. The federal government may regulate conditions of state governmental employment, which, at least indirectly, regulates state budgets,[217] but may not create a cause of action for damages against states or their subdivisions.[218] Concerning property, the Supreme Court has never held that Congress may regulate land in state ownership. Two cases, however, explicitly recognize congressional power under the commerce clause to regulate some economic uses of private land.[219]

In the areas of state political agendas and institutions the states fare better. Congress may not force the states to enact or enforce a federal regulatory program. In *New York* v. *United States*,[220] the Supreme Court considered the constitutionality of the Low-Level Radioactive Waste Policy Amendments Act of 1985, by which Congress sought to require the states to provide for the safe disposal of radioactive wastes generated within their borders. The act even went so far as to provide that the states would "take title" to any wastes within their borders that were not properly disposed of by a certain date, and that they then would be liable for "all damages directly or indirectly incurred." The Supreme Court ruled the provision unconstitutional. If the federal government could "commandeer" the states, the court reasoned, it would undermine government accountability because Congress could make a decision, but the states would bear the political responsibility for a decision that was not theirs. The only direct encroachment on the political agenda of the states that has been upheld by the courts is the questionable decision upholding a federal law that compelled state utility commissions to consider adopting federal standards, but stopped short of trying to require them to adopt those standards.[221] In short, there is no American equivalent to German "framework laws,"

---

[217] See United States v. Darby, 312 U.S. 100 (1941) (minimum wage and maximum hours), Garcia v. San Antonio Metropolitan Transit Authority, 469 U.S. 528 (1985), United Transportation Union v. Long Island R.R. Co, 455 U.S. 678 (1982) (Railway Labor Act), Equal Opportunity Employment Commission v. Wyoming, 460 U.S. 226 (1983), and Gregory v. Ashcroft, 501 U.S. 452 (1991) (Age Discrimination in Employment Act.).

[218] See Alabama v. Garrett, 531 U.S. 356 (2001) (Americans with Disabilities Act) and Kimel v. Florida Board of Regents, 528 U.S. 62 (2000) (Age Discrimination in Employment Act).

[219] See Hodel v. Virginia Surface Mining & Reclamation Association, 452 U.S. 264 (1981), discussed above, and Wickard v. Filburn, 317 U.S. 111 (1942), involving home-grown wheat on 23 acres—9 hectares—of land.

[220] 505 U.S. 157 (1992).

[221] Federal Energy Regulatory Commission v. Mississippi, 456 U.S. 742 (1982).

by which the federal government requires the German states (Länder) to legislate.[222]

In light of these cases, and the one that follows, how can state judges be required to enforce federal laws?[223]

The case that follows concerns the constitutionality of the Brady Handgun Violence Prevention Act.

CASE: **Printz v. United States**
521 U.S. 98 (1997)

JUSTICE SCALIA delivered the opinion of the Court.

[The Brady Handgun Violence Prevention Act requires the Attorney General to establish a national system for instantly checking prospective handgun purchasers' backgrounds and commands the "chief law enforcement officer" (CLEO) of each local jurisdiction to conduct such checks and perform related tasks on an interim basis until the national system becomes operative. Petitioners, the CLEOs for counties in Montana and Arizona, filed separate actions challenging the interim provisions' constitutionality.. . .

The question presented in these cases is whether certain interim provisions of the Brady Handgun Violence Prevention Act . . . commanding state and local law enforcement officers to conduct background checks on prospective handgun purchasers and to perform certain related tasks, violate the Constitution.

. . .

From the description set forth above, it is apparent that the Brady Act purports to direct state law enforcement officers to participate, albeit only temporarily, in the administration of a federally enacted regulatory scheme. . . .

The petitioners here object to being pressed into federal service, and contend that congressional action compelling state officers to execute federal laws is unconstitutional. Because there is no constitutional text speaking to this precise question, the answer to the CLEOs' challenge must be sought in historical understanding and practice, in the structure of the Constitution, and in the jurisprudence of this Court. We treat those three sources, in that order, in this and the next two sections of this opinion.

---

[222] Currie at pp. 50–52.
[223] See also Testa v. Klatt, 330 U.S. 386 (1947).

Petitioners contend that compelled enlistment of state executive officers for the administration of federal programs is, until very recent years at least, unprecedented. The Government contends, to the contrary, that the earliest Congresses enacted statutes that required the participation of state officials in the implementation of federal laws. ... The Government's contention demands our careful consideration, since early congressional enactments "provid[e] 'contemporaneous and weighty evidence' of the Constitution's meaning. ..." Indeed, such "contemporaneous legislative exposition of the Constitution ..., acquiesced in for a long term of years, fixes the construction to be given its provisions. "... Conversely if, as petitioners contend, earlier Congresses avoided use of this highly attractive power, we would have reason to believe that the power was thought not to exist.

The Government observes that statutes enacted by the first Congresses required state courts to record applications for citizenship..., transmit abstracts of citizenship applications and other naturalization records to the Secretary of State..., and to register aliens seeking naturalization and issue certificates of registry. ... It may well be, however, that these requirements applied only in States that authorized their courts to conduct naturalization proceedings. See... *Holmgren* v. *United States*[224] (explaining that the Act of March 26, 1790 "conferred authority upon state courts to admit aliens to citizenship" and refraining from addressing the question "whether the States can be required to enforce such naturalization laws against their consent"); *United States* v. *Jones*[225] (stating that these obligations were imposed "with the consent of the States" and—could not be enforced against the consent of the States"). Other statutes of that era apparently or at least arguably required state courts to perform functions unrelated to naturalization, such as resolving controversies between a captain and the crew of his ship concerning the seaworthiness of the vessel..., hearing the claims of slave owners who had apprehended fugitive slaves and issuing certificates authorizing the slave's forced removal to the State from which he had fled..., taking proof of the claims of Canadian refugees who had assisted the United States during the Revolutionary War..., and ordering the deportation of alien enemies in times of war....

These early laws establish, at most, that the Constitution was originally understood to permit imposition of an obligation on

---

[224] 217 U.S. 509, 516–517 (1910).
[225] 109 U.S. 513, 519–520 (1883).

state judges to enforce federal prescriptions, insofar as those prescriptions related to matters appropriate for the judicial power. That assumption was perhaps implicit in one of the provisions of the Constitution, and was explicit in another. In accord with the so called Madisonian Compromise, Article III, §1, established only a Supreme Court, and made the creation of lower federal courts optional with the Congress—even though it was obvious that the Supreme Court alone could not hear all federal cases throughout the United States.... And the Supremacy Clause, Art. VI, cl. 2, announced that "the Laws of the United States ... shall be the supreme Law of the Land; and the Judges in every State shall be bound thereby." It is understandable why courts should have been viewed distinctively in this regard; unlike legislatures and executives, they applied the law of other sovereigns all the time....

... The only early federal law the Government has brought to our attention that imposed duties on state executive officers is the Extradition Act of 1793, which required the "executive authority" of a State to cause the arrest and delivery of a fugitive from justice upon the request of the executive authority of the State from which the fugitive had fled.... That was in direct implementation, however, of the Extradition Clause of the Constitution itself, see Art. IV, §2.

Not only do the enactments of the early Congresses, as far as we are aware, contain no evidence of an assumption that the Federal Government may command the States' executive power in the absence of a particularized constitutional authorization, they contain some indication of precisely the opposite assumption. On September 23, 1789—the day before its proposal of the Bill of Rights...—the First Congress enacted a law aimed at obtaining state assistance of the most rudimentary and necessary sort for the enforcement of the new Government's laws: the holding of federal prisoners in state jails at federal expense. Significantly, the law issued not a command to the States' executive, but a recommendation to their legislatures. Congress "recommended to the legislatures of the several States to pass laws, making it expressly the duty of the keepers of their gaols, to receive and safe keep therein all prisoners committed under the authority of the United States," and offered to pay 50 cents per month for each prisoner.... Moreover, when Georgia refused to comply with the request..., Congress's only reaction was a law authorizing the marshal in any State that failed to comply with the Recommendation of September 23, 1789, to rent a temporary jail until provision for a permanent one could be made....

...

To complete the historical record, we must note that there is not only an absence of executive commandeering statutes in the early Congresses, but there is an absence of them in our later history as well, at least until very recent years. ...

...

The constitutional practice we have examined above tends to negate the existence of the congressional power asserted here, but is not conclusive. We turn next to consideration of the structure of the Constitution, to see if we can discern among its "essential postulate[s]"... a principle that controls the present cases.

...

The Framers' experience under the Articles of Confederation had persuaded them that using the States as the instruments of federal governance was both ineffectual and provocative of federal state conflict.... Preservation of the States as independent political entities being the price of union, and "[t]he practicality of making laws, with coercive sanctions, for the States as political bodies" having been, in Madison's words, "exploded on all hands," . . . the Framers rejected the concept of a central government that would act upon and through the States, and instead designed a system in which the state and federal governments would exercise concurrent authority over the people—who were, in Hamilton's words, "the only proper objects of government"....

...

Finally, and most conclusively in the present litigation, we turn to the prior jurisprudence of this Court. Federal commandeering of state governments is such a novel phenomenon that this Court's first experience with it did not occur until the 1970's, when the Environmental Protection Agency promulgated regulations requiring States to prescribe auto emissions testing, monitoring and retrofit programs, and to designate preferential bus and carpool lanes. The Courts of Appeals for the Fourth and Ninth Circuits invalidated the regulations on statutory grounds in order to avoid what they perceived to be grave constitutional issues...; and the District of Columbia Circuit invalidated the regulations on both constitutional and statutory grounds.... After we granted certiorari to review the statutory and constitutional validity of the regulations, the Government declined even to defend them, and instead rescinded some and conceded the invalidity of those that remained, leading us to vacate the opinions below and remand for consideration of mootness....

...

We held in *New York* [v. *United States*] that Congress cannot compel the States to enact or enforce a federal regulatory program. Today we hold that Congress cannot circumvent that prohibition by conscripting the State's officers directly. The Federal Government may neither issue directives requiring the States to address particular problems, nor command the States' officers, or those of their political subdivisions, to administer or enforce a federal regulatory program. It matters not whether policymaking is involved, and no case by case weighing of the burdens or benefits is necessary; such commands are fundamentally incompatible with our constitutional system of dual sovereignty. ...

[Concurring and dissenting opinions omitted.]

---

b. A Principle of Localism or Subsidiarity?

The political and judicial struggle regarding states' rights in the United States seems destined, at least in the near future, to be dominated by the concepts and precepts of the commerce and the spending clauses. This is unfortunate, because the tradition, thinking, and terminology of commerce, spending, and economics do not lend themselves well to the present-day debate on federalism. For instance, the reason why schoolground guns do not seem to many to be an appropriate subject for federal regulation has nothing to do with commerce or the economy or federal spending but rather with the tradition of local supervision of education and with the conviction that local governance of education is democratically preferable to national government.

Some commentators argue that education, land-use, law enforcement, courts, and private law, especially family law, should remain "localized" or that the federal concurrent powers, even that over interstate commerce, ought to be exercisable only where there is special justification.[226] Uniform federal environmental standards, for example, might be easy to justify, whereas uniform family law, educational, land-use, and law enforcement standards might not be. These and similar concerns could be subsumed under something akin to the European principle of subsidiarity, which enjoins institutions of the European Union to act in areas of concurrent jurisdiction only when local measures are inadequate:

> The Community shall act within the limits of the powers conferred upon it by this Treaty and of the objectives assigned to it therein.

---

[226] See Lundmark, *Guns* at p. 204.

In areas which do not fall within its exclusive competence, the Community shall take action, in accordance with the principle of subsidiarity, only if and in so far as the objectives of the proposed action cannot be sufficiently achieved by the Member States and can therefore, by reason of the scale or effects of the proposed action, be better achieved by the Community.[227]

One potential constitutional anchor for a principle of localism or subsidiarity is the Tenth Amendment. Alternatively, the "necessary and proper" clause[228] might be read to embody subsidiarity. Or subsidiarity might be held to belong to penumbral states' rights à la the privacy rights of individuals.[229] Or perhaps the Constitution will be amended, or the congressional mentality will so change in favor of local, democratic self-determination, accountability, and flexibility that no amendment will be necessary.

---

[227] Maastricht Treaty on European Union, Art. 3b.
[228] Art. I, § 8, cl. 18.
[229] See Griswold v. Connecticut, 381 U.S. 479 (1965): The "specific guarantees in the Bill of Rights have penumbras, formed by emanations from those guarantees that help give them life and substance."

PART TWO

Constitutional Rights

THE REMAINDER OF THIS BOOK CENTERS ON CORE PRINCIPLES OF CONSTITUTIONAL RIGHTS. Sometimes constitutional rights are referred to by the term "civil" rights, but that term is avoided in this text because it can include statutorily as well as constitutionally based rights. "Right," as used in this text, means "constitutional right."

The coverage must necessarily be selective. This book gives scant mention to state and federal statutory rights, even though these rights may be far more important to citizens and non-citizens alike than the constitutional variety. The Age Discrimination in Employment Act,[230] the Americans with Disabilities Act of 1990,[231] and the Civil Rights Act of 1964, including Title VII,[232] are just three of the myriad federal statutes that protect individuals against governmental (and often private) actors. Rights recognized by the laws and constitutions of the states and their subdivisions are also beyond the purview of this book. For example, in *Robins v. Pruneyard Shopping Center*,[233] the California Supreme Court refused to follow the United States Supreme Court's decision in *Lloyd v. Tanner*[234] on the ground that the California Constitution is more protective of free speech than the First Amendment.[235] To cite an example from statutory law, where more examples of divergencies from federal norms can be found: the Unruh Civil Rights Act in California[236] prohibits discrimination in housing against families with children.[237] In the equal protection area, courts have construed state constitutions to require the reform of school funding.[238] On the whole, however, state constitutional protection of rights is virtually identical to that of the federal constitution.[239]

Three major categories of constitutional rights are not covered by this book, although they are sometimes mentioned in passing. The first categorical exception from coverage is procedure. Procedural rights are

---

[230] 29 U.S.C. §§ 621-634, ruled unconstitutional to the extent it allows state employees to sue for damages in Kimel v. Florida Board of Regents, 528 U.S. 62 (2000).

[231] 42 U.S.C. § 12101 *et seq.*, ruled unconstitutional to the extent it allows state employees to sue for damages in Board of Trustees of the University of Alabama v. Garrett, 531 U.S. 356 (2001).

[232] 42 U.S.C. § 2000 *et seq.*

[233] 23 Cal. 3d 889, aff'd 447 U.S. 74 (1980).

[234] 407 U.S. 551 (1972).

[235] See generally Kahn.

[236] California Civil Code § 51.

[237] Marina Point, Ltd. v. Wolfson, 30 Cal. 3d 721 (1982); see generally Singer and 30 A.L.R.4th 1187 (1998).

[238] E.g., Serrano v. Priest, 5 Cal. 3d 584 (1971), which the United States Supreme Court declined to follow in San Antonio Independent School District v. Rodriguez, 411 U.S. 1 (1973).

[239] See Solimine & Walker at p. 1467 and nn. 68–70.

generally the province of administrative law and civil procedure. The second exception covers all substantive and procedural rights that belong to the domain of criminal procedure. Property rights, the third exception, enjoy a unique status among liberty rights; but their constitutional protection heeds principles somewhat at odds with those of other liberty rights, making a brief summary for purposes of this volume infeasible. One significant issue shared by property and other liberty rights, but which is not treated in this book, is the extent to which corporations and associations are entitled to invoke constitutional protection, and whether or not the equal treatment of natural and legal persons does not harm or dilute the rights of the former.

Finally, with few exceptions, the brevity of this book does not allow the handling of constitutional, statutory, and common law rights in purely private transactions, for that would mean treating virtually all private law topics, including the law of obligations (tort, contract, and unjust enrichment), property, and family law. Few areas of private law have escaped examination for constitutionality in recent decades under what is sometimes referred to as the "constitutionalization of private law." Some areas of private law, such as defamation and, to a lesser extent, the legitimacy of children, have been more or less co-opted by the Constitution. Their discussion in this book is not just unavoidable; it is indispensable to an appreciation of the role of the United States Constitution and the Supreme Court in American society.

Constitutional rights are viewed as either liberty or equality rights. Liberty rights shield persons as individuals against state action. Equality rights protect the individual as a member of a protected group, which is usually referred to as a "class." In order to accord with the language of the Fifth and Fourteenth Amendments, liberty rights are referred to as "due process" rights. (Sometimes the adjective "substantive" is added to distinguish them from procedural due process rights.) Equality rights are ordinarily referred to as "equal protection" rights, which conforms more closely to the verbiage of the Fourteenth Amendment.

As illuminated in the materials that follow, the boundary between liberty and equality is fluid. Indeed, liberty rights can be linguistically recast as equality rights, and *vice versa*: ultimately, the person claiming a liberty right can style herself a group of one, who is being "discriminated against" on the basis of some individualistic characteristic or behavior. She consequently can employ the jargon of both liberty and equality. If the particular governmental measure affects every person equally, it is said that only due process would be available to challenge the measure. However, examples to illustrate this last proposition are harder to find than might at first be thought. Would a statute requiring the donation of one kidney from each human being only violate due process? What if the statute were attacked by a person who only has one kidney? Similarly, a law that denied everyone the right to travel interstate would not likely be challenged by those who do not intend to travel, or who are physically unable to do so.

Until the 1950s, the equal protection clause remained largely dormant. Thinking in equal-protection terms began to take hold with the Great Society programs of the administration of President Lyndon B. Johnson and with the Civil Rights Movement, which sought to promote the interests of African-Americans as a group. Coincidentally, the Supreme Court had become shy of protecting due process rights because of the intense criticism it had suffered due to the unpopular recognition of economic rights. It was hoped that the methodology of equality would offer a value-neutral, or at least less conservative, way of protecting constitutional rights.

The expansion of the role of the federal and state legislatures as distributors of statutory privileges and benefits necessitated the "discrimination" between the groups or "classes" of persons to be benefited, and those who would not be. The equal protection clause also offered a conceptual advantage in that it lent itself readily to thinking in terms of groups, rather than of individuals, that were benefited by, or excluded from, the privileges accorded under the growing number of government programs. Thus, in large measure, the growth in equal protection analysis has coincided with the expansion of the state.

The interplay between liberty and equality rights gives rise to any number of additional topics treated below in more detail. One such topic is the perceived conflict between liberty and equality, where the bestowal of more equality is said necessarily to reduce individual liberty. Perhaps a better way to express this presumed conflict is to say that one man's liberty is another man's equality. For instance, extending the franchise to women in effect halved the voting rights (liberty) of each man and distributed his half to a woman, leaving the aggregate of societal liberty arguably the same. This image assumes that liberty is a zero-sum game. It does not admit of the possibility that a redistribution of rights can augment societal liberty.

Another topic is the emotional root of rights. Liberty respects greed and sloth, whereas equality legitimizes envy.[240] We find ourselves using the language of liberty when seeking respect, and that of equality when seeking pity. Yet another topic is the vertical, corrective quality of liberty and the horizontal, distributive justice of equality.

The themes of Part One of this book—separation of powers and federalism—reincarnate themselves in Part Two in the guise of rights. For the recognition of judicially enforceable rights does more or less directly what separation of powers and federalism do mediately: protect

---

[240] Holmes at p. 942; see Plato at p. 301, discussed in Lundmark, *Forms* at p. 649.

individual liberty. The tension between the legislative and judicial powers is experienced most intensely when a court invalidates a properly enacted law because it violates a constitutional right. Federalism accounts for the phenomena that not quite all of the federal rights listed in the Bill of Rights can be asserted against the state and local governments[241] and that not all of the rights that protect people from the state and local governments bind the federal government.[242]

The coverage begins with two matters of primary concern to the judicial protection of constitutional rights. First is the question of the governmental nature of the impingement on constitutional rights, for constitutional rights generally accord protection only against acts of governmental actors, so-called "state action." Second is the methodology of striking a just balance between democratic, majoritarian interests on the one hand, and individual rights on the other. This methodology is discussed under the rubric "levels of scrutiny."

1. "STATE ACTION"

The "state action" doctrine is summarized at this juncture because of its primacy to the recognition and enforcement of all constitutional rights. The word "state" in "state action" is used in the sense of "governmental." Ordinarily this means that the person or persons who caused the alleged infringement of constitutional rights must have been acting on behalf of a public entity. For, according to the state action doctrine, federal constitutional rights do not protect against action by private people or organizations, but rather only against action by public actors.

The term "public actors" in this context embraces all local, state, and federal agencies, including some private-law businesses and organizations, and their agents and employees. For example, in *Lebron v. National Railroad Passenger Corporation*,[243] the Supreme Court held the railway corporation Amtrak to be a public entity for purposes of the state action doctrine. In reaching its conclusion, the Supreme Court relied on the fact that the President of the United States appoints members to the Board of Directors of Amtrak. It was of no moment that the authorizing legislation specifically denied that Amtrak was a governmental agency.

---

[241] E.g., Apodaca v. Oregon, 406 U.S. 404 (1972), jury protection of the 6th Amendment, and Minneapolis & St. Louis R.R. Co. v. Bombolis, 241 U.S. 211 (1916), civil jury right of the 7th Amendment.
[242] E.g., Hampton v. Mow Sun Wong, 426 U.S. 88 (1976), equal protection of the 14th Amendment; Ogden v. Saunders, 25 U.S. 213 (1827), contract clause of Art. I, § 10.
[243] 513 U.S. 374 (1995).

The reasons, or at least the explanations, for the doctrine of state action are historical, prudential, and textual. Historically, the U.S. Constitution was a product of Enlightenment thinking about natural law and liberalism, which was in large measure inspired by the felt irrationality and capriciousness of monarchial rule. The Founding Fathers were preoccupied with potential threats from the government they were creating, and not with wider social and moral affairs. Further, it was thought that the common law adequately protected individual rights from other individuals so that constitutional protection was unnecessary.[244] Through the centuries, as legislative law replaced, attenuated, and complemented the common law, this private-law protective task has passed more to the legislatures, or to cooperative efforts by judges and legislators.

The prudential justification for the state action requirement is basically that the federal judicial (and perhaps legislative) restraint encapsulated in the doctrine means, alternatively, more sovereignty for the states (federalism) or more freedom from regulation (liberty). Most Americans would probably agree with the aphorism attributed to Jefferson: "That government is best that governs least." And the Supreme Court has held that the Constitution does not impose a general obligation on state, federal, or local government to protect people from each other.[245]

The textual explanation for the state action doctrine is the clearest and strongest: All of the rights articulated in the text of the Constitution (see Attach. D) and in the amendments are addressed to either the federal or to the state governments. For example, freedom of speech is enshrined in the First Amendment, which begins, "Congress shall make no law ..." Equality receives specific mention only in the second sentence of the Fourteenth Amendment, which reads in part, "nor shall any State ... deny to any person within its jurisdiction the equal protection of the laws."

The Thirteenth Amendment is somewhat of an anomaly, for it is directed both at public and private conduct. It reads, "Neither slavery nor involuntary servitude, except as a punishment for crime whereof the party shall have been duly convicted, shall exist within the United States, or any place subject to their jurisdiction." While the Thirteenth Amendment was intended to destroy private-law rights, it also binds the government.[246]

The state action doctrine is sometimes misunderstood to mean that private law is beyond the purview of the constitution. This is most certainly not true. In the United States, private law, that is, the law that governs relationships between private persons, falls traditionally and basically

---

[244] Chemerinsky, Constitutional Law at p. 511.
[245] See DeShaney v. Winnebago County Department of Social Services, 489 U.S. 189 (1989).
[246] See Bailey v. Alabama, 219 U.S. 219 (1911), holding imprisonment for failure to pay a debt unconstitutional.

within the law-making province of the states. Private law consists either of statutory law, of common law (judge-made law), or of a mixture of the two. In enacting statutes to regulate private transactions, or even public ones for that matter, state legislators engage in "state action" *per se* and are subject to constitutional restraints. State-court judges, in developing their common law and in interpreting legislation, fall squarely within the supremacy clause of Article VI, section 2, which states that "the Judges in every State shall be bound" by the Constitution. Accordingly, they are bound not to enforce laws that are incompatible with constitutional rights. This creates a judicial climate that is sensitive to the protection of constitutional values at every state of proceedings.

Does this then mean that the state action doctrine is a sham and that every aspect of human life, however private, is subject to constitutional scrutiny? Not quite. Business entities and commercial transactions are governed by federal, state, and controls which incorporate—and sometimes augment—constitutional rights and extend them to cover otherwise private commercial transactions. For example, legislation routinely broadens the privacy rights of employees by preventing prospective employers from learning about sexual orientation, from demanding genetic testing, and from testing for AIDS. Legislation and the common law also forbid discrimination against customers. But, that being said, there are non-commercial private activities in daily life that do still remain outside the dominion of constitutional, statutory, and common law, where private actors can do things that would not be allowed by businesses and public actors.

Accordingly, you may use race, gender, age, religion, and national origin in choosing your friends; but, if you are a landlord or landlady, you may not consider these criteria in renting an apartment. You may prefer not to shop in a liquor store because it is owned by Arabs; but the Arabian owners may not refuse to sell to you because you are Jewish. You may wish to adopt only Asian children; but the adoption agency may not deny your application because you are Roman Catholic. You may vote for a candidate solely because she is female; but the candidate, once elected, cannot award you a lucrative contract simply because you were born in Berlin.

The Supreme Court has recognized two functional extensions[247] of the state action requirement to embrace certain activities that are not purely private in nature. The first extension, that for public functions, encompasses activities, undertaken by purely private individuals or organizations, that traditionally belonged to the exclusive prerogative of the state. Voting in primary elections is an example. A political party, which is a private organization, cannot exclude blacks from voting in party primary or

---

[247] Also referred to as "exceptions." See Chemerinsky, Constitutional Law at p. 517.

pre-primary elections that select the party's candidate for public office.[248] Another case illustrating the public function exception from the state action requirement concerned a "company town" whose streets and sidewalks, while privately owned, were the functional equivalent of public streets.[249]

The other extension of the state action doctrine covers private action with significant state involvement. Adjudicated cases include the following: administration by the public administrator of a will containing a racially discriminatory condition;[250] joint public/private action to seize a debtor's assets in execution of a judgment;[251] judicial enforcement of a race-based restrictive covenant in a deed;[252] use of race-based peremptory challenges in a civil trial;[253] and operating a restaurant on publicly owned property.[254]

2. LEVELS OF SCRUTINY

Every case concerning alleged violations of constitutional rights presents certain common questions of pedigree and magnitude of the intrusion, and of weightiness of the private right and countervailing public interest. The questions of pedigree include whether the action is based on a law, and whether that law is in turn based on the state or federal constitution. These questions arise in the subjects covered in Part One of this book. Questions of magnitude of the intrusion arise when an otherwise constitutional law comes into conflict with a constitutional right. More extensive incursions can be conceptually justified if the public interest is urgent, or the private right less weighty.

Following the practice of the Supreme Court, this book systemizes the methodology of judicial review ("scrutiny") of rights to a unitary hierarchy of tests that amalgamate questions of pedigree, intensity, and weight into three tests. In doing so, it attempts to reduce, but not completely avoid, discussions of the nuances or "glosses" placed on the various tests by the Justices of the Supreme Court when they are considering specific constitutional rights. Conceptually, at least, alleged violations of constitutional rights are judged within the formalized structure, which employs a different constitutional yardstick depending on the perceived level of importance of

---

[248] Smith v. Allwright, 321 U.S. 649 (1944); Terry v. Adams, 345 U.S. 461 (1953).
[249] Marsh v. Alabama, 326 U.S. 501 (1946).
[250] Evans v. Abney, 396 U.S. 435 (1970).
[251] Lugar v. Edmondson Oil Co., 457 U.S. 922 (1982).
[252] Shelley v. Kraemer, 334 U.S. 1 (1948).
[253] Edmonson v. Leesville Concrete Co., 500 U.S. 614 (1991).
[254] Burton v. Wilmington Parking Authority, 365 U.S. 715 (1961).

the right. Some commentators hold that this tiered approach is neither desirable nor practically possible.[255]

The first level is employed to judge the constitutionality of the ends and means of every governmental act. The ends of any such act must be lawful or "valid"; and the means chosen must rationally lead to the accomplishment of the ends. In theory, this level of review involves no balancing whatsoever: the ends are either lawful or unlawful; the means chosen are either aimed at reaching the ends, or they are not. The other two tests or "levels of review" do, however, involve balancing. These tests are invoked when the governmental act impinges upon certain constitutional rights.

The levels of review elaborated below are employed to judge the constitutionality of governmental actions "on their face," that is, without considering the particular factual predicament of the challenger. The other style of judicial review, that which considers the particular facts of the case, is called "as applied."

a. "Minimum Scrutiny" (Lawful or "Valid" Ends/Rational Means)

Hearkening back to Part One of this book, all governmental action must be based on a law which in turn is based on the state or federal constitution. Another way of expressing the same thing is that the (federal, state, or local) governmental goal must fall within the powers that the entity enjoys, or else it is *ultra vires* and void. For example, in *Pollock* v. *Farmers' Loan & Trust Co.*,[256] the Supreme Court ruled that Congress lacked power to tax incomes from property, and in *Oregon* v. *Mitchell*,[257] the Supreme Court held that Congress was powerless to set the voting age in state and local elections. Incidentally, these rulings led respectively to the Sixteenth and Twenty-sixth Amendments. The cases *Marbury* v. *Madison* and *United States* v. *Lopez* from Part One of this book are example of cases where Congress was held to lack jurisdiction for the legislation under challenge.

When judging the legitimacy of a statute of the Congress, the legislative goal must fall within the ambit of an enumerated power, such as the interstate commerce clause. As shown in Part One, various tests have been developed to judge the fundamental validity of legislation, depending on its alleged constitutional basis.[258]

When the legislation is obviously within the jurisdiction of the particular legislative body that enacted it, courts will sometimes gloss over this

---

[255] E.g., Shaman; Beal v. Doe, 432 U.S. 438, 461 n. 6 (1977), Marshall, J., dissenting, and advocating a sliding scale.
[256] 157 U.S. 429 (1895).
[257] 400 U.S. 112 (1970).
[258] See, e.g., United States v. Lopez, 514 U.S. 549 (1995).

foundational issue. At other times, this first level of scrutiny will finally resolve the legal dispute.[259]

What happens if the governmental goal is proper, but the means chosen to attain the goal are not calculated, or are poorly designed, to accomplish the goal? Said another way, what if the law is not "rational"? Ordinarily, courts show great deference to legislation, and will not interfere with legislative judgments unless they are "demonstrably arbitrary and irrational."[260] The burden of proof is on the person challenging the state action.[261] This level of review ("scrutiny") is usually termed the "rational basis" test.

The attitude of deference accorded even state legislators by the United States Supreme Court is summarized in *Williamson v. Lee Optical Co.*:

> [T]he Oklahoma law may exact a needless, wasteful requirement in many cases. But it is for the legislature, and not the courts, to balance the advantages and disadvantages of the new requirement.... [T]he law need not be in every respect logically consistent with its aims to be constitutional. It is enough that there is an evil at hand for correction, and that it might be thought that the particular legislative measure was a rational way to correct it. The day is gone when this Court uses the Due Process Clause [to] strike down state laws... because they may be unwise, improvident, or out of harmony with a particular school of [thought].[262]

It is rare that a law employs an irrational, arbitrary, or unreasonable means to accomplish a legitimate goal. One of the few governmental actions ruled unconstitutional by the Supreme Court on this basis was the practice of a county tax assessor in *Allegheny Pittsburgh Coal Co. v. County Commission*[263] not to reassess real property for tax purposes until the property was sold. The court ruled not only that the practice was arbitrary, but also that it was unsupported by state law and therefore *ultra vires*.

The common law is not immune from minimal constitutional scrutiny. Even jury awards of punitive damages in private actions can be challenged on constitutional grounds if they are "grossly excessive," that is, if the award bears no rational relationship to the state's interests in punishment and deterrence.[264]

---

[259] E.g., Williams v. Vermont, 472 U.S. 14 (1985).
[260] Duke Power Co. v. Carolina Environmental Study Group, Inc., 438 U.S. 69 (1978).
[261] United States v. Carolene Products Co., 304 U.S. 144 (1938).
[262] 348 U.S. 483 (1955).
[263] 488 U.S. 336 (1989).
[264] BMW of North America, Inc. v. Gore, 517 U.S. 559 (1996).

b.   "Strict Scrutiny" (Compelling Ends/Necessary Means)

"Rational basis" is the weakest mode of judicial review, where courts accord the most respect to the democratically declared interests of the majority. The highest level of review is termed "strict scrutiny." If a public action, usually a statute, is judged by this standard, it must satisfy two criteria: the ends must be compelling, and the means necessary. These two requirements are discussed in order.

Under strict scrutiny, it is not enough that the goal or purpose sought to be achieved by the government (termed "state interest") is merely lawful, as required for minimum scrutiny. Rather, to satisfy strict scrutiny, the governmental goal must be compelling.[265] Examples of interests judged "compelling" by the courts are difficult to find. Consequently, the late Professor Gerald Gunther at Stanford University once quipped that "strict scrutiny" is "strict in theory fatal in fact."[266] Two of the few cases upholding laws challenged under this test are in the area of voting. The Supreme Court has upheld state requirements that candidates of new political parties demonstrate public support before having their names placed on the ballot. The compelling state interest consisted of preserving the integrity of the electoral process, which would otherwise have become unmanageable and confusing.[267] Voter registration and 30-day residency requirements before voting have similarly been justified by the compelling state interest in preserving the integrity of the electoral process.[268]

The second requirement under the standard of "strict scrutiny" is that the means must be necessary to attain the manifest goal. That is, "the means chosen to accomplish the State's asserted purpose must be specifically and narrowly tailored to accomplish that purpose."[269] Under this prong of strict scrutiny, the government must show (for it has the burden of proof) that the alternative that it has chosen is the least restrictive (due process) or least discriminatory (equal protection).[270] Staying with voting rights (and the right to travel), the Supreme Court has struck down as too restrictive durational residency requirement of one year in state elections and three months in county elections.[271] A similar fate befell residency requirements for public welfare benefits and free non-emergency medical care, since the private need is great and the administrative burden on the state slight.[272]

---

[265] San Antonio Independent School District v. Rodriguez, 411 U.S. 1 (1973).
[266] Gunther, *Foreword* at p. 8.
[267] American Party of Texas v. White, 415 U.S. 767 (1974).
[268] Marston v. Lewis, 410 U.S. 679 (1973).
[269] Wygant v. Jackson Board of Education, 476 U.S. 267, 280 (1986).
[270] Miller v. Johnson, 515 U.S. 900 (1995).
[271] Dunn v. Blumstein, 405 U.S. 330 (1972).
[272] Shapiro v. Thompson, 394 U.S. 618 (1969); Memorial Hospital v. Maricopa County, 415 U.S. 250 (1974).

Strict scrutiny is used both for certain due process and certain equal protection rights. In the context of due process, strict scrutiny is employed for all rights explicitly guaranteed by the Constitution, and for many others which have been held to be implicitly guaranteed. Together, the due process rights entitled to strict scrutiny are called "fundamental rights." Explicitly guaranteed rights include freedom of religion, freedom of speech, freedom of association, freedom to petition the government for a redress of grievances, all traceable to the First Amendment, and the right to vote, which is secured by various constitutional provisions and amendments. Implicit fundamental rights include, among others, the right to travel and the right of privacy. For equal protection purposes, courts utilize strict scrutiny to assess the constitutionality of measures that involve a "suspect class." Suspect classifications are those based on race, national origin, and sometimes foreign citizenship.

c. "Intermediate Scrutiny" (Important Ends/Substantially Related Means)

"Intermediate scrutiny," as one might suspect, is the name given to review that demands more than a lawful goal and minimal rationality but that is not quite rigorous enough to be called strict. Here the governmental purpose must be important, but not necessarily "compelling." And the means chosen must be substantially related to the purpose, but they need not be "necessary." The approach is similar to "proportionality" review in German and European law,[273] although it does not go by that name in the United States. As with strict scrutiny, the government bears the burden of proof under intermediate scrutiny.

An example of a law that failed the "substantially related" test can be found in *Rubin v. Coors Brewing Co.*,[274] which considered the constitutionality of a post-Prohibition federal law that prohibited brewers from reporting alcohol content on beer containers. The goal of the legislation was to discourage breweries from increasing sales by raising alcohol levels. The courts employed intermediate scrutiny because the law regulated commercial speech. They ruled the law unconstitutional because the government could have achieved its goal through less restrictive means.[275]

As with strict scrutiny, intermediate scrutiny is employed both under the due process clause and under the equal protection clause. Under equal

---

[273] See authorities cited in Lundmark, *Systemizing* at p. 33. The Supreme Court uses what it calls "proportionality review" to judge the constitutionality of fines under the 8th Amendment. This has the effect of subjecting fines to intermediate scrutiny. See United States v. Bajakajian, 524 U.S. 321 (1998).
[274] 515 U.S. 618 (1995).
[275] See Lundmark, *Freiheit*.

protection analysis, intermediate scrutiny is exercised over governmental measures that discriminate against or penalize so-called quasi-suspect classes. To date, quasi-suspect classifications have been held to be those based on legitimacy[276] and gender.[277] Under due process, intermediate scrutiny is applied to the regulation of speech in public forums[278] and to commercial speech.[279]

Consider whether, in the following case, the Supreme Court is employing strict or intermediate scrutiny. Why does the court employ equal protection rather than due process analysis?

CASE: Plyler v. Doe
457 U.S. 202 (1982)

JUSTICE BRENNAN delivered the opinion of the Court.

[A Texas statute authorized local school districts to deny free public education to children who had not been "legally admitted" into the United States. Pursuant to this statute, the Tyler Independent School District required "undocumented" children to pay a "tuition fee" in order to enroll.]

[In] applying the Equal Protection Clause to most forms of state action, we thus seek only the assurance that the classification at issue bears some fair relationship to a legitimate public purpose.

But we would not be faithful to our obligations under the Fourteenth Amendment if we applied so deferential a standard to every classification. [With] respect to [some] classifications, it is appropriate to enforce the mandate of equal protection by requiring the State to demonstrate that its classification has been precisely tailored to serve a compelling governmental interest. In addition, we have recognized that certain forms of legislative classification, while not facially invidious, nonetheless give rise to recurring constitutional difficulties; in these limited circumstances we have sought the assurance that the classification reflects a reasoned judgment consistent with the ideal of equal protection by inquiring whether it may fairly be viewed as furthering a substantial interest of the State. We turn to a consideration of the standard appropriate for the evaluation of [the challenged law].

---

[276] Lehr v. Robertson, 463 U.S. 248 (1983).
[277] Craig v. Boren, 429 U.S. 190 (1976).
[278] Ward v. Rock Against Racism, 491 U.S. 781 (1989).
[279] Central Hudson Gas & Electric Corp. v. Public Service Commission of New York, 447 U.S. 557, 566 (1980).

Sheer incapability or lax enforcement of the laws barring entry into this country [has] resulted in the creation of a substantial "shadow population" of illegal migrants—numbering in the millions—within our borders. This situation raises the specter of a permanent caste of undocumented resident aliens, encouraged by some to remain here as a source of cheap labor, but nevertheless denied the benefits that our society makes available to citizens and lawful residents....

Congress has developed a complex scheme governing admission to our Nation and status within our borders. The obvious need for delicate policy judgments has counseled the Judicial Branch to avoid intrusion into this field. But this traditional caution does not persuade us that unusual deference must be shown the [challenged classification]. The States enjoy no power with respect to the classification of aliens. This power is "committed to the political branches of the Federal Government." [And although] the States do have some authority to act with respect to illegal aliens, at least where such action mirrors federal objectives and furthers a legitimate state [goal], there is no indication that the disability imposed [the challenged law]corresponds to any identifiable congressional policy. [We] discern three colorable state interests that might support [the classification].

First, [the State suggests that it may] protect itself from an influx of illegal immigrants. [But there] is no evidence in the record suggesting that illegal entrants impose any significant burden on the State's economy. To the contrary, the available evidence suggests that illegal aliens underutilize public services, while contributing their labor to the local economy and tax money to the state fisc.

Second [the State suggests] that undocumented children are appropriately singled out for exclusion because of the special burdens they impose on the State's ability to provide high-quality public education. But the record in no way supports the claim that exclusion of undocumented children is likely to improve the overall quality of education in the State. [Moreover], even if improvement in the quality of education were a likely result of barring some number of children from the schools of the State, the State must support its selection of this group as the appropriate target for exclusion. In terms of educational cost and need, however, undocumented children are "basically indistinguishable" from legally resident alien children.

Finally, [the State suggests] that undocumented children are appropriately singled out because their unlawful presence within the United States renders them less likely than other children to remain within the boundaries of the State, and to put their education to productive social or political use within the State. Even assuming that such an interest is legitimate, it is an interest that is most difficult to quantify. The State has no assurance that any child, citizen or not, will employ the education provided by the State within the confines of the State's borders. In any event, the record is clear that many of the undocumented children disabled by this classification will remain in this country indefinitely, and that some will become lawful residents or citizens of the United States. It is difficult to understand precisely what the State hopes to achieve by promoting the creation and perpetuation of a subclass of illiterates within our boundaries, surely adding to the problems and costs of unemployment, welfare, and crime. It is thus clear that whatever savings might be achieved by denying these children an education, they are wholly insubstantial in light of the costs involved to these children, the State, and the Nation.

If the State is to deny a discrete group of innocent children the free public education that it offers to other children residing within its borders, that denial must be justified by a showing that it furthers some substantial state interest. No such showing was made here....

[Concurring and dissenting opinions omitted.]

In his dissent in *Plyler*, Chief Justice Burger wrote disparagingly about what he called the "quasi-fundamental rights" analysis introduced by the majority. This terminology is now widely used to refer to due process rights that warrant intermediate scrutiny.

The following case concerns the Virginia Military Institute (VMI), which, at the time, was the sole single-sex school among Virginia's public institutions of higher learning. VMI's distinctive mission is to produce "citizen soldiers." VMI uses an "adversative method" of training not available elsewhere in Virginia to instill physical and mental discipline in its cadets and impart to them a strong moral code. VMI's adversative method features "[p]hysical rigor, mental stress, absolute equality of treatment, absence of privacy, minute regulation of behavior, and indoctrination in desirable values." VMI cadets live in Spartan barracks where surveillance is constant and privacy nonexistent; they wear uniforms, eat together in the mess hall, and regularly participate in drills. Entering students are incessantly exposed to the "rat line," comparable in intensity to Marine Corps boot camp.

The United States sued Virginia and VMI, alleging that VMI's exclusively male admission policy violated the Fourteenth Amendment's Equal

Protection Clause. In response, Virginia proposed a parallel program for women: Virginia Women's Institute for Leadership (VWIL).

CASE: United States v. Virginia
[Virginia Military Institute or "VMI" Case]
518 U.S. 515 (1996)

Justice Ginsburg delivered the opinion of the Court.

...

Without equating gender classifications, for all purposes, to classifications based on race or national origin, the Court... has carefully inspected official action that closes a door or denies opportunity to women (or to men).... To summarize the Court's current directions for cases of official classification based on gender: Focusing on the differential treatment or denial of opportunity for which relief is sought, the reviewing court must determine whether the proffered justification is "exceedingly persuasive. "... The State must show "at least that the [challenged] classification serves 'important governmental objectives and that the discriminatory means employed' are 'substantially related to the achievement of those objectives.'"... The justification must be genuine, not hypothesized or invented post hoc in response to litigation. And it must not rely on overbroad generalizations about the different talents, capacities, or preferences of males and females....

...

Measuring the record in this case against the review standard just described, we conclude that Virginia has shown no "exceedingly persuasive justification" for excluding all women from the citizen soldier training afforded by VMI.

...

Virginia next argues that VMI's adversative method of training provides educational benefits that cannot be made available, unmodified, to women. Alterations to accommodate women would necessarily be "radical," so "drastic," Virginia asserts, as to transform, indeed "destroy," VMI's program.... Neither sex would be favored by the transformation, Virginia maintains: Men would be deprived of the unique opportunity currently available to them; women would not gain that opportunity because their participation would "eliminat[e] the very aspects of [the] program that distinguish [VMI] from ... other institutions of higher education in Virginia. "...

...

The notion that admission of women would downgrade VMI's stature, destroy the adversarial system and, with it, even the school, is a judgment hardly proved, a prediction hardly different from other "self fulfilling prophec[ies]"... once routinely used to deny rights or opportunities. When women first sought admission to the bar and access to legal education, concerns of the same order were expressed. For example, in 1876, the Court of Common Pleas of Hennepin County, Minnesota, explained why women were thought ineligible for the practice of law. Women train and educate the young, the court said, which "forbids that they shall bestow that time (early and late) and labor, so essential in attaining to the eminence to which the true lawyer should ever aspire. It cannot therefore be said that the opposition of courts to the admission of females to practice... is to any extent the outgrowth of... 'old fogyism[.]'... [I]t arises rather from a comprehension of the magnitude of the responsibilities connected with the successful practice of law, and a desire to grade up the profession."...

...

Women's successful entry into the federal military academies, and their participation in the Nation's military forces, indicate that Virginia's fears for the future of VMI may not be solidly grounded. The State's justification for excluding all women from "citizen soldier" training for which some are qualified, in any event, cannot rank as "exceedingly persuasive," as we have explained and applied that standard.

[Justice Ginsberg also concluded that the education and training offered at VWIL were not comparable.]

For the reasons stated, the initial judgment of the Court of Appeals ... is affirmed, the final judgment of the Court of Appeals... is reversed, and the case is remanded for further proceedings consistent with this opinion.

It is so ordered.

[Concurring and dissenting opinions omitted.]

SUBPART A

LIBERTY (DUE PROCESS)

AS SEEN IN ATTACHMENT D, THE ORIGINAL TEXT OF THE CONSTITUTION ONLY sporadically recognized individual rights. There was no list or "bill" of rights, even though most state constitutions that were adopted during the American Revolution contained a clear declaration of rights.[280]

Historians offer a number of explanations for this omission, including that the enumeration of powers was sufficient protection, and that an enumeration of rights would imply that other rights did not exist.[281] Whatever the historic reason for the original omission, ratification of the new Constitution to replace the Articles of Confederation followed in a number of states only after Federalists (those promoting the new constitution) promised to add a bill of rights.

The first Congress convened under the Constitution set to work immediately on the task of adding a bill of rights to the Constitution. James Madison drafted 15 proposed amendments. The Congress accepted 12 of the proposals pursuant to the amendment procedure in Article V. By December 15, 1791, enough states had ratified ten of these to make them a permanent part of the Constitution. (One of the remaining two proposed amendments was finally ratified on May 7, 1992 and became the Twenty-seventh Amendment.) Although technically not part of the original text of the Constitution, the Bill of Rights (the first 10 amendments) has historically been considered part of the Constitution for all intents and purposes.

This subpart emphasizes fundamental constitutional rights, that is, those that are subsumable under the due process clauses of the Fourth and Fourteenth Amendments and that are subject to "strict scrutiny." To be deemed fundamental, the right must be "explicitly or implicitly guaranteed by the Constitution."[282] This distinction between explicit and implicit rights is followed in the following discussion. The question of how fundamental rights become recognized as "implicit" is deferred until those rights are discussed below.

---

[280] E.g., Virginia Declaration of Rights of 1776; see generally Hall.
[281] Chemerinsky, Constitutional Law at p. 5, noting that it was to quiet such fears that the 9th Amendment was added.
[282] San Antonio Independent School District v. Rodriguez, 411 U.S. 1 (1973).

The fundamental rights discussed below must be distinguished from minor, implicit, non-fundamental constitutional rights which find application in judging whether one has been accorded procedural due process. These are lower echelon constitutional rights that exist in addition to the explicit and implicit fundamental rights that are the subject of this subpart. Textually understood, these non-fundamental rights emanate from, or at least can be subsumed under, the triune "life, liberty, or property" of the Fifth and Fourteenth Amendments.

Procedural due process rights play an indispensable role in the criminal arena, which is beyond the scope of this book. In the civil context, if the courts determine that a right or interest enjoyed by an individual is embraced by the term "liberty" or "property," then the individual is constitutionally entitled to procedural safeguards before that right or interest can be impaired or denied. Outside the criminal context, the Supreme Court has recognized a constitutional "liberty interest" in being free from physical restraints,[283] in contracting and engaging in gainful employment,[284] and in continuing a developed parent-child relationship.[285] "Property" has been held to safeguard the following: public education when school attendance is required,[286] welfare benefits,[287] driving privileges,[288] utility service,[289] existing causes of action,[290] and public employment.[291]

1. EXPLICIT FUNDAMENTAL RIGHTS

If one disregards the Ninth and Tenth Amendments, which do not guarantee specific rights, half of the remaining eight amendments catalogue rights that basically are intended to protect those suspected of crimes.[292] One amendment, the Seventh Amendment, recognizes a right to a jury trial in civil cases before the federal courts, and thus creates a procedural, rather than a substantive, right. Of the three remaining amendments,

---

[283] Vitek v. Jones, 445 U.S. 480 (1980).
[284] Board of Regents v. Roth, 408 U.S. 564 (1972).
[285] Lehr v. Robinson, 463 U.S. 248 (1983).
[286] Goss v. Lopez, 419 U.S. 565 (1975).
[287] Goldberg v. Kelly, 397 U.S. 254 (1970).
[288] Bell v. Burson, 402 U.S. 535 (1971).
[289] Memphis Light, Gas & Water Division v. Craft, 436 U.S. 1 (1978).
[290] Logan v. Zimmerman Brush Co., 455 U.S. 422 (1982).
[291] Arnett v. Kennedy, 416 U.S. 134 (1974).
[292] See 4th, 5th (also protecting property), 6th, and 8th Amendments.

two of them[293] are antiquated, having virtually no currency.[294] That leaves the First Amendment:

> Congress shall make no law respecting an establishment of religion, or prohibiting the free exercise thereof; or abridging the freedom of speech, or of the press, or the right of the people peaceably to assemble, and to petition the Government for a redress of grievances.

A review of the amendments that do not belong to the Bill of Rights[295] similarly results in the reduction to a single amendment that has served as the repository of the most expansive constitutional rights. That is the Fourteenth Amendment, section 1 of which reads:

> All persons born or naturalized in the United States and subject to the jurisdiction thereof, are citizens of the United States and of the State wherein they reside. No State shall make or enforce any law which shall abridge the privileges or immunities of citizens of the United States; nor shall any State deprive any person of life, liberty, or property, without due process or law; nor deny to any person within its jurisdiction the equal protection of the laws.

Textually, the Fourteenth Amendment contains three protections of constitutional rights, respectively referred to as the privileges and immunities clause, the due process clause,[296] and the equal protection clause.

The first of these three clauses has remained largely a dead letter in protecting individual rights since the Supreme Court held in 1873, in a questionable opinion, that the fundamental rights protected against federal action by the first eight amendments were not "privileges or immunities of citizens of the United States" so as to be protected from state action under the Fourteenth Amendment.[297]

The due process clause of the Fourteenth Amendment, on the other hand, has been construed to "incorporate" the First Amendment and make it enforceable against the states.[298] The same process of "selective incorporation" has been used to apply almost all protections of the Bill of Rights to the states

---

[293] 2nd and 3rd Amendments.
[294] Most commentators opine that the right to bear arms is not a personal right, but rather a right enjoyed by each state to arm a militia. Lundmark, *Guns* at p. 188. See discussion in Chemerinsky, Constitutional Law at pp. 26–28, 504–505.
[295] 11th through 27th Amendments.
[296] Compare the federal counterpart in the 5th Amendment.
[297] Slaughterhouse Cases, 83 U.S. 36 (1873).
[298] Gitlow v. New York, 268 U.S. 652 (1925).

by finding that they are "implicit in the concept of ordered liberty."[299] The Supreme Court has never ruled on whether the right not to have soldiers quartered in one's home (Third Amend.) or the prohibition against excessive fines (Eighth Amend.) apply against the state and local governments.[300] According to the Supreme Court, the "right to bear arms" (Second Amend.) does not apply to the states.[301] Nor do the right to a grand jury indictment[302] and the right to a jury trial in civil cases.[303] Similarly, but in reverse, the federal due process clause (Fifth Amend.) has been held to incorporate the equal protection clause of the Fourteenth Amendment against the federal government.[304]

Thus, from a textual standpoint, the individual rights protected by the U.S. Constitution can be reduced to or subsumed under two overarching principles: due process and equal protection. Freedom of speech, discussed immediately below, is perhaps the cardinal constitutional liberty or due process right.

a. Speech

Because of the preeminent role played by free speech in the political life and government of the United States, the subject of free speech has been selected for more extensive coverage in this book. The articulated freedoms of press, assembly, and petition are treated peripherally, if at all.

Scholars resort to four major theories to justify freedom of speech.[305] These are that freedom of speech is necessary for self-governance, that speech serves the discovery of truth via the marketplace of ideas, that it protects and promotes individual autonomy, and that it fosters tolerance. Invoking the first two of these justifications, Justice Brandeis defended freedom of speech in his well-known concurring opinion in *Whitney* v. *California*:

> Those who won our independence ... valued liberty both as an end and as a means.... They believed that freedom to think as you will and to speak as you think are means indispensable to the discovery and spread of political truth.... Discussion affords ordinarily adequate protection against the dissemination of

---

[299] Palko v. Connecticut, 302 U.S. 319 (1937).
[300] Chemerinsky, Constitutional Law at p. 505.
[301] Presser v. Illinois, 116 U.S. 252 (1886). See discussion in Chemerinsky, Constitutional Law at pp. 26–28, 504–505.
[302] Hutardo v. California, 110 U.S. 516 (1884).
[303] Minneapolis & St. Louis R.R. Co. v. Bombolis, 241 U.S. 211 (1916).
[304] Bolling v. Sharpe, 347 U.S. 483 (1954).
[305] Chemerinsky, Constitutional Law 925-930.

noxious doctrine.... [T]he remedy to be applied is more speech, not enforced silence.[306]

Although the decisional matrix that structures the protection of all civil liberty rights is identical, the United States Supreme Court has created frequently complex approaches to First Amendment rights in general, and freedom of speech in particular. Ignoring some of the complexity, the following discussion subsumes the free-speech case law of the Supreme Court under four questions: What is speech for constitutional purposes?; What are the categories of unprotected speech, also referred to as "non-speech"?; Is the regulation issue content-based or content-neutral?; and Is the regulation a licensing or other traditionally valid restriction?

i. What is Speech for Constitutional Purposes?

Through the centuries, the Supreme Court and other federal courts, not to mention state courts, have frequently been confronted with deciding what conduct is protected by the First Amendment in general, and by the free speech clause in particular.

The following discussion omits historical developments, and theoretical nuances, in favor of including more factual detail from court decisions over the past 50 years. These decisions show a high degree of protection of speech and related conduct, even extending constitutional protection to fund-raising and to commercial advertising.

Although it probably goes without saying, free speech includes not only the freedom to hold political and other opinions and beliefs, but also to act in accordance with these opinions and beliefs.[307] Speech encompasses far more than the spoken word. Speech also includes writing, even if the writing does not fall within the traditional ambit of freedom of the press, such as wearing a jacket with the inscription "Fuck the Draft" in a courthouse corridor.[308] Freedom of speech embraces conduct. For example, the freedom to hold and disseminate one's views includes the right to solicit and accept funds.[309] Acknowledging that "[i]t is possible to find some kernel of expression in almost every activity a person undertakes," the Supreme Court distinguishes between conduct that is speech for constitutional purposes, and conduct that is nothing more than everyday, non-expressive activity.[310] Accordingly, to enjoy protection under the

---

[306] 274 U.S. 357, 375 (1927).
[307] Dawson v. Delaware, 503 U.S. 159 (1992).
[308] Cohen v. California, 403 U.S. 15 (1971). "Draft" refers to military conscription.
[309] Village of Schaumburg v. Citizens for a Better Environment, 444 U.S. 620 (1980). The Supreme Court upheld laws limiting the amount of money that a person or group can contribute to a political candidate in Buckley v. Valeo, 424 U.S. 1 (1976).
[310] City of Dallas v. Stanglin, 489 U.S. 12, 25 (1989).

First Amendment, the conduct must (1) have been an intent "to convey a particularized message" and (2) "in the surrounding circumstances the likelihood [must have been] great that the message would be understood by those who viewed it."[311] These and other doctrines and cases concerning conduct are usually grouped under the heading "symbolic expression," treated briefly below.

Less obviously, the Supreme Court has ruled that the freedom to speak includes the freedom not to speak. For example, the Supreme Court upheld the right of a car owner in New Hampshire to block out the state's motto "Live Free or Die" on his state-issued license plate. The court wrote, "The right to speak and the right to refrain from speaking are complementary components of the broader concept of 'individual freedom of mind.'"[312] In the same vein, the Supreme Court ruled unconstitutional a compulsory flag salute and compulsory recitation of the "Pledge of Allegiance" in *West Virginia State Board of Education* v. *Barnette*, holding:

> [T]he compulsory flag salute and pledge required affirmation of a belief and an attitude of mind.... If there is any fixed star in our constitutional constellation, it is that no official, high or petty, can prescribe what shall be orthodox in politics, nationalism, religion or other matters of opinion or force citizens to confess by word or act their faith therein.[313]

Perhaps more momentously, in *Talley* v. *California*,[314] the Supreme Court declared a ban on anonymous handbills unconstitutional, saying:

> [The] obnoxious press licensing law of England, which was also enforced on the Colonies was due in part to the knowledge that exposure of the names of printers, writers and distributors would lessen the circulation of literature critical of the government.... Anonymous pamphlets, leaflets, brochures, and even books have played an important role in the progress of mankind.

In *McIntyre* v. *Ohio Elections Commission*,[315] the Supreme Court invalidated a prohibition against the distribution of anonymous campaign literature, and in *DeBartolo Corp.* v. *Florida Gulf Coast Building and Construction Trades Council*,[316] it held that union construction workers enjoyed a constitutional

---

[311] Spence v. Washington, 418 U.S. 405, 410–411 (1974).
[312] Wooley v. Maynard, 430 U.S. 705, 714 (1977).
[313] 319 U.S. 624 (1943).
[314] 362 U.S. 60 (1960).
[315] 514 U.S. 334 (1995).
[316] 485 U.S. 568 (1988).

right to pass out leaflets to customers at a shopping mall, urging them not to shop at any of the stores in the mall until the owner of the mall (who did not own the stores) had reached an agreement with the union on a construction contract.

CASE: **United States v. Eichman**
496 U.S. 310 (1990)

JUSTICE BRENNAN delivered the opinion of the Court.

In these consolidated appeals, we consider whether appellees' prosecution for burning a United States flag in violation of the Flag Protection Act of 1989 is consistent with the First Amendment. Applying our recent decision in *Texas* v. *Johnson*, 491 U. S. 397 (1989), the District Courts held that the Act cannot constitutionally be applied to appellees. We affirm.

I

[T]he United States prosecuted certain appellees for violating the Flag Protection Act of 1989, by knowingly setting fire to several United States flags on the steps of the United States Capitol while protesting various aspects of the Government's domestic and foreign policy. [T]he United States prosecuted other appellees for violating the Act by knowingly setting fire to a United States flag in Seattle while protesting the Act's passage. ....

II

Last term in Johnson, we held a Texas statute criminalizing the desecration of venerated objects, including the United States flag, was unconstitutional as applied to an individual who had set such a flag on fire during a political demonstration....

After our decision in Johnson, Congress passed the Flag Protection Act of 1989. The Act provides in relevant part:

(a) (1) Whoever knowingly mutilates, defaces, physically defiles, burns, maintains on the floor or ground, or tramples upon any flag of the United States shall be fined under this title or imprisoned for not more than one year, or both.

...

The Government contends that the Flag Protection Act is constitutional because, unlike the statute addressed in Johnson, the Act does not target expressive conduct on the basis of the content of its message.... The Act proscribes conduct (other than disposal) that damages or mistreats a flag, without regard to the actor's motive, his intended message, or the likely effects of his conduct on onlookers. By contrast, the Texas statute expressly prohibited only those acts of physical flag desecration "that the actor knows will seriously offend" onlookers ....

...

[T]he precise language of the Act's prohibitions confirms Congress' interest in the communicative impact of flag destruction. The Act criminalizes the conduct of anyone who "knowingly mutilates, defaces, physically defiles, burns, maintains on the floor or ground, or tramples upon any flag."... Each of the specified terms—with the possible exception of "burns"—unmistakably connotes disrespectful treatment of the flag and suggests a focus on those acts likely to damage the flag's symbolic value. ....

...

III

...

We are aware that desecration of the flag is deeply offensive to many. But the same might be said, for example, of virulent ethnic and religious epithets, see *Terminiello v. Chicago...*, vulgar repudiations of the draft, see *Cohen v. California...*, and scurrilous caricatures, see *Hustler Magazine, Inc. v. Falwell....* "If there is a bedrock principle underlying the First Amendment, it is that the Government may not prohibit the expression of an idea simply because society finds the idea itself offensive or disagreeable." Johnson.... Punishing desecration of the flag dilutes the very freedom that makes this emblem so revered, and worth revering. The judgments of the District Courts are
Affirmed.
[Dissenting opinion omitted.]

---

ii. What are the Categories of Unprotected Speech ("non-speech")?

There are four generally recognized categories of speech and expression that are not protected by the First Amendment, which are also referred to as "non-speech." In the order treated below, these are (1) crimes involving speech, (2) defamation and other torts, (3) fighting words, and (4) obscenity.

aa. Crimes Involving Speech

The notion that, when speech forms part of an independent crime, it enjoys no constitutional protection, is perhaps so obvious that it need not be elaborated upon. Examples include an illegal transaction, such as an agreement to monopolize in contravention of the antitrust laws,[317] telling a bank teller to hand over all the money in his cash drawer, and lying when one is under oath (the crime of perjury).

A number of decisions of the United States Supreme Court involve alleged conspiracies to overthrow the government.[318] The Supreme Court has distinguished between urging people to believe in the need for violent overthrow, on the one hand, and urging them to act on their belief, on the other. The former is absolutely protected by the First Amendment, but the latter can be made punishable.[319] However, advocacy of the use of force, or the violation of law, cannot constitutionally be punished unless it is "directed to inciting or producing imminent lawless action and is likely to incite or produce such action." See the following case.

CASE: **Brandenburg v. Ohio** 395 U.S. 444 (1969)

PER CURIAM.

The appellant, a leader of a Ku Klux Klan group, was convicted under the Ohio Criminal Syndicalism statute for "advocat[ing]... the duty, necessity, or propriety of crime, sabotage, violence, or unlawful methods of terrorism as a means of accomplishing industrial or political reform" and for "voluntarily assembl[ing] with any society, group, or assemblage of persons formed to teach or advocate the doctrines of criminal syndicalism.".... He was fined $1,000 and sentenced to one to 10 years' imprisonment....

The record shows that a man, identified at trial as the appellant, telephoned an announcer-reporter on the staff of a Cincinnati television station and invited him to come to a Ku Klux Klan "rally" to be held at a farm in Hamilton County. With the cooperation of the organizers, the reporter and a cameraman attended the meeting and filmed the events. Portions of the films were later broadcast on the local station and on a national network.

The prosecution's case rested on the films and on testimony identifying the appellant as the person who communicated with the reporter and who spoke at the rally. The State also introduced into evidence several articles appearing in the film, including a

---

[317] But calls for political boycotts are protected. See Lundmark, Free Speech.
[318] E.g., Gitlow v. New York, 268 U.S. 652 (1925); Dennis v. United States, 341 U.S. 494 (1951).
[319] Yates v. United States, 354 U.S. 298 (1957).

pistol, a rifle, a shotgun, ammunition, a Bible, and a red hood worn by the speaker in the films.

One film showed 12 hooded figures, some of whom carried firearms. They were gathered around a large wooden cross, which they burned. No one was present other than the participants and the newsmen who made the film. Most of the words uttered during the scene were incomprehensible when the film was projected, but scattered phrases could be understood that were derogatory of Negroes and, in one instance, of Jews. Another scene on the same film showed the appellant, in Klan regalia, making a speech. The speech, in full, was as follows:

This is an organizers' meeting. We have had quite a few members here today which are—we have hundreds, hundreds of members throughout the State of Ohio. I can quote from a newspaper clipping from the Columbus, Ohio Dispatch, five weeks ago Sunday morning. The Klan has more members in the State of Ohio than does any other organization. We're not a revengent organization, but if our President, our Congress, our Supreme Court, continues to suppress the white, Caucasian race, it's possible that there might have to be some revengeance taken.

We are marching on Congress July the Fourth, four hundred thousand strong. From there we are dividing into two groups, one group to march on St. Augustine, Florida, the other group to march into Mississippi. Thank you.

The second film showed six hooded figures one of whom, later identified as the appellant, repeated a speech very similar to that recorded on the first film. The reference to the possibility of "revengence" was omitted, and one sentence was added: "Personally, I believe the nigger should be returned to Africa, the Jew returned to Israel." Though some of the figures in the films carried weapons, the speaker did not.

[T]he constitutional guarantees of free speech and free press do not permit a State to forbid or proscribe advocacy of the use of force or of law violation except where such advocacy is directed to inciting or producing imminent lawless action and is likely to incite or produce such action. As we said in *Noto* v. *United States*,[320] "the mere abstract teaching... of the moral propriety or even moral necessity for a resort to force and violence, is not the same as preparing a group for violent action and steeling it to such action."... A statute which fails to draw this distinction impermissibly intrudes upon the freedoms guaranteed by the First and

---

[320] 367 U.S. 290, 297–298 (1961).

Fourteenth Amendments. It sweeps within its condemnation speech which our Constitution has immunized from governmental control....

...

Reversed.
[Concurring opinions omitted.]

In 1950, Joseph Beauharnais passed out leaflets in Chicago charging the black population with destroying white neighborhoods, and calling upon the mayor and city council of Chicago to "Preserve and Protect White Neighborhoods! From the constant and continuous invasion, harrassment and encroachment by the negroes." This leaflet continued: "[I]f persuasion and the need to prevent the white race from becoming mongrelized by the Negroes will not unite us, then the aggressions, rapes, robberies, knives, guns and marijuana of the negro, surely will."

Beauharnais was convicted and fined $200 under a state statute that made it a crime to defame a class of people.[321] Should his conviction have been upheld, as it was, by the United States Supreme Court?[322]

bb. Defamation and Other Torts

Defamation is a tort, generally belonging to the uncodified common law of the state, that entitles one to damages (and sometimes an injunction) for the injury done to one's reputation by untruthful statements. According to the Supreme Court, state laws on defamation and other torts, such as violation of copyright[323] and infliction of emotional distress,[324] must meet certain minimal standards to ensure that First Amendment rights are not impinged upon.

These minimal standards are that the defendant must at least have been negligent (no strict or "no-fault" liability); that the factual misstatement must have warned a reasonably prudent editor or broadcaster of its defamatory potential; that damages be limited to compensation for actual injury (including injury to reputation, personal humiliation, and mental suffering); that punitive damages be awarded only in matters of public concern and where the defendant acted with knowledge of falsity or reckless disregard for truth; and that, in matters of public concern, and contrary

---

[321] Beauharnais v. Illinois, 353 U.S. 250 (1952). The statute, which has since been replaced, prohibited any publication that portrayed "depravity, criminality, unchastity, or lack of virtue of a class of citizens, of any race, color, creed or religion... which exposes the citizens of any race, color, creed or religion to contempt, derision, or obloquy."
[322] See comments in Collin v. Smith, 578 F.2d 1197, 1204–1205 (7th Cir. 1978).
[323] Harper & Row v. Nation Enterprises, 471 U.S. 539 (1985).
[324] See Lundmark, Common Law at pp. 10–14, 65–68.

to the common law rule, the plaintiff must bear the burden of proving that the statements are false.[325]

The constitutional significance of defamation increases dramatically when one moves from the private into the public arena and one is dealing with matters of public interest. Here the courts and legislatures must resolve the conflict between the need to protect the reputation and privacy of individuals on the one hand and the public's want, need, or right to know on the other. This conflict has been resolved rather crudely in the United States by decisions of the United States Supreme Court beginning with *New York Times* v. *Sullivan*.[326]

Sullivan concerned a large civil libel (a form of defamation) judgment awarded in the Alabama courts in favor of a local elected official against certain African American clergymen and the New York Times for an advertisement in that newspaper that contained false statements about the official. The Supreme Court reversed the judgment. In doing so it held that,[327] before a public official can recover damages, she must prove by clear and convincing evidence that the statement was false and that the defendant had acted with actual malice, that is, that the defendant knew the statement to be false or else had acted with reckless disregard for the truth.

"Public official" has been expanded to include a candidate for public office.[328] *New York Times* v. *Sullivan* has also been extended to "public figures." One can become a public figure in two ways. One can achieve "general fame or notoriety in the community and pervasive involvement in the affairs of society" and become a public figure for all purposes, or one may "voluntarily inject himself or be drawn into a particular controversy, thus becoming a public figure for a limited range of issues."[329]

cc. Fighting Words

The Supreme Court ruled in 1942 that "fighting words" are not protected by the Constitution because their slight personal social value is outweighed by the public interest in preserving order.[330] In *Chaplinsky*, the Court wrote:

> [A]llowing the broadest scope to the language and purpose of the Fourteenth Amendment [that incorporates the First Amendment

---

[325] Philadelphia Newspaper, Inc. v. Hepps, 475 U.S. 767 (1986); Dun & Bradstreet, Inc. v. Greenmoss Builders, Inc., 472 U.S. 749 (1985); Gertz v. Robert Welch, Inc., 418 U.S. 323 (1974).
[326] 376 U.S. 254 (1964).
[327] "Clear and convincing evidence" is a standard of proof requiring more convincing proof than merely the "weight of the evidence" employed in most civil cases, but it need not rise to the level of proof required by the "beyond a reasonable doubt" standard of the criminal law.
[328] Rosenblatt v. Baer, 383 U.S. 75 (1966).
[329] Gertz v. Robert Welch, Inc., 418 U.S. 323 (1974).
[330] Chaplinsky v. New Hampshire, 315 U.S. 568 (1942).

against the states], it is well understood that the right of free speech is not absolute at all times and under all circumstances. There are certain well-defined and narrowly limited classes of speech, the prevention and punishment of which have never been thought to raise any constitutional problem. These include the lewd and obscene, the profane, the libelous, and the insulting or fighting words—those which by their very utterance inflict injury or tend to incite an immediate breach of the peace.... [S]uch utterances are no essential part of any exposition of ideas, and are of such slight social value as a step to truth that any benefit that may be derived from them is clearly outweighed by the social interest in order and morality. "Resort to epithets or personal abuse is not in any proper sense communication of information or opinion safeguarded by the Constitution."[331]

Chaplinsky ends its list of exceptions to constitutional protection of speech with two different classes: "insulting ... words ... which by their very utterance inflict injury" and "fighting words ... which by their very utterance ... tend to incite an immediate breach of the peace." It is unclear whether the former class (insulting words) exists as an exception to the constitutional protection of speech, for the Supreme Court has yet to review a conviction for uttering "insulting words" as such. While "insult" may give rise to a cause of action for damages,[332] in general it is not a crime by itself, as it is in Germany.[333]

Convictions that reach the Supreme Court for review have been for violation of statutes and ordinances criminalizing "breach of the peace" or "disorderly conduct." For example, the defendant in *Gooding* v. *Wilson*[334] said to a police officer, "White son of a bitch, I'll kill you," and "You son of a bitch, I'll choke you to death." He was convicted under a Georgia statute that made it criminal to "use to or of another, and in his presence, opprobrious words or abusive language, tending to cause a breach of the peace." The Supreme Court found the statute overbroad, and emphasized that the Georgia courts (and presumably police and prosecutors) had a constitutional obligation to construe the statute narrowly so as only to prohibit unprotected fighting words.

In one case, the Supreme Court overturned the conviction of a parent who had repeatedly referred to teachers and members of the school board as "mother-fuckers" at a school board meeting.[335] In another case, a woman

---

[331] At pp. 571-572.
[332] See, e.g., Cal. Civ. Code § 43.
[333] § 192 Strafgesetzbuch (Beleidigung); see Eberle at p. 862.
[334] 405 U.S. 518 (1972).
[335] Rosenfeld v. New Jersey, 409 U.S. 901 (1972).

told the police who were arresting her son that they were "god-damn-motherfucker police." Her conviction for using "opprobrious language" was reversed.[336] In yet another case, an individual holding a speech referred to police officers as "mother-fucking fascist pig cops" and singled out one officer whom he labeled a "black mother-fucking pig." This speaker's conviction was also reversed.[337]

One of the reasons for the reversals in the above cases was the conviction by the Supreme Court that the right of uninhibited debate on public issues is an essential ingredient of the American political system. Thinking back to the reasoning of *New York Times* v. *Sullivan*, one might argue that insults directed at police and other public officers and officials are protected by the Constitution because of the democratic need for uninhibited debate. In *New York Times* v. *Sullivan*, Justice Brennan identified a "profound national commitment to the principle that debate on public issues should be uninhibited, robust, and wide-open, and that it may well include vehement, caustic, and sometimes unpleasantly sharp attacks."[338]

Another conviction that was reversed by the Supreme Court was that of a man who had said, protesting military conscription, "If they ever make me carry a rifle the first man I want to get in my sights is L.B.J. [then president Johnson]. They are not going to make me kill my black brothers." The Supreme Court ruled that the man's statement was "political hyperbole," and thus could not be punished under a law making it a crime "knowingly and willfully [to threaten] to take the life of or to inflict bodily harm upon the President."[339]

dd. Obscenity

Obscene material is not protected by the First Amendment because, according to the Supreme Court, it is "utterly without social importance."[340] "Obscene material," the *Roth* court continued, "is material which deals with sex in a manner appealing to the prurient interest." Said another way it is "material having a tendency to excite lustful thoughts."

On several occasions after *Roth*, the Supreme Court decided what material "had a tendency to excite lustful thoughts" and what did not. After a few years, frustrated by not having been able to articulate standards by which to identify obscenity, Justice Stewart wrote, "I shall not today attempt further to define the kinds of material I understand to be embraced within

---

[336] Lewis v. City of New Orleans, 408 U.S. 913 (1972).
[337] Brown v. Oklahoma, 408 U.S. 914 (1972).
[338] New York Times Co. v. Sullivan, 376 U.S. 254, 270 (1964).
[339] Watts v. United States, 394 U.S. 705 (1969).
[340] Roth v. United States, 354 U.S. 476, 484 (1957).

that shorthand description; and perhaps I could never succeed in intelligibly doing so. But I know it when I see it."[341]

A more or less workable test for determining what is obscene and what is not was announced in 1973 in *Miller v. California*:

> [T]he basic guidelines for the trier of fact must be: (a) whether 'the average person, applying contemporary community standards' would find that the work, taken as a whole, appeals to the prurient interest; (b) whether the work depicts or describes, in a patently offensive way, sexual conduct specifically defined by the applicable state's law; and (c) whether the work, taken as a whole, lacks serious literary, artistic, political or scientific value.[342]

Child pornography can constitutionally be prohibited in the interest of protecting children even if it does not meet the *Miller* criteria.[343]

Even if sale and distribution of obscene material may be criminally prohibited, possession in one's home may not be penalized because doing so would violate one's constitutional right of personal privacy.[344]

CASE: Jenkins v. Georgia
418 U.S. 153 (1974)

Mr. Justice REHNQUIST delivered the opinion of the Court.

Appellant was convicted in Georgia ... for showing the film 'Carnal Knowledge' in a movie theater in Albany, Georgia. The jury that found appellant guilty was instructed on obscenity pursuant to the Georgia statute, which defines obscene material in language similar to that of the definition of obscenity set forth in this Court's plurality opinion in *Memoirs v. Massachusetts*[345]:

> 'Material is obscene if considered as a whole, applying community standards, its predominant appeal is to prurient interest, that is, a shameful or morbid interest in nudity, sex or excretion, and utterly without redeeming social value and if, in addition, it goes substantially beyond customary limits of candor in describing or representing such matters.'....

---

[341] Jacobellis v. Ohio, 378 U.S. 184, 197 (1964).
[342] 413 U.S. 15, 36 (1973).
[343] New York v. Ferber, 456 U.S. 942 (1982).
[344] Stanley v. Georgia, 394 U.S. 351 (1969).
[345] 383 U.S. 413, 418 (1966).

.... After his trial in the Superior Court of Dougherty County, the jury, having seen the film and heard testimony, returned a general verdict of guilty on March 23, 1972. Appellant was fined $750 and sentenced to 12 months' probation. He appealed to the Supreme Court of Georgia, which by a divided vote affirmed the judgment of conviction on July 2, 1973. ...

There is little to be found in the record about the film 'Carnal Knowledge' other than the film itself. However, appellant has supplied a variety of information and critical commentary, the authenticity of which appellee does not dispute. The film appeared on many 'Ten Best' lists for 1971, the year in which it was released. Many but not all of the reviews were favorable....

Appellee contends essentially that under *Miller* the obscenity vel non of the film 'Carnal Knowledge' was a question for the jury, and that the jury having resolved the question against appellant, and there being some evidence to support its findings, the judgment of conviction should be affirmed. We turn to the language of *Miller* to evaluate appellee's contention.

Miller states that the questions of what appeals to the 'prurient interest' and what is 'patently offensive' under the obscenity test which it formulates are 'essentially questions of fact.' ... We held in Paris Adult Theatre I v. Slaton,[346] decided on the same day, that expert testimony as to obscenity is not necessary when the films at issue are themselves placed in evidence. ...

But all of this does not lead us to agree with the Supreme Court of Georgia's apparent conclusion that the jury's verdict against appellant virtually precluded all further appellate review of appellant's assertion that his exhibition of the film was protected by the First and Fourteenth Amendments. Even though questions of appeal to the 'prurient interest' or of patent offensiveness are 'essentially questions of fact,' it would be a serious misreading of *Miller* to conclude that juries have unbridled discretion in determining what is 'patently offensive.' Not only did we there say that 'the First Amendment values applicable to the States through the Fourteenth Amendment are adequately protected by the ultimate power of appellate courts to conduct an independent review of constitutional claims when necessary,' ... but we made it plain that under that holding 'no one will be subject to prosecution for the sale or exposure of obscene materials unless these materials depict or describe patently offensive 'hard core' sexual conduct....' ...

---

[346] 413 U.S. 49 (1973).

We also took pains in *Miller* to 'give a few plain examples of what a state statute could define for regulation under part (b) of the standard announced,' that is, the requirement of patent offensiveness. ... While this did not purport to be an exhaustive catalog of what juries might find patently offensive, it was certainly intended to fix substantive constitutional limitations, deriving from the First Amendment, on the type of material subject to such a determination. It would be wholly at odds with this aspect of *Miller* to uphold an obscenity conviction based upon a defendant's depiction of a woman with a bare midriff, even though a properly charged jury unanimously agreed on a verdict of guilty.

Our own viewing of the film satisfies us that 'Carnal Knowledge' could not be found under the Miller standards to depict sexual conduct in a patently offensive way. Nothing in the movie falls within either of the two examples given in Miller of material which may constitutionally be found to meet the 'patently offensive' element of those standards, nor is there anything sufficiently similar to such material to justify similar treatment. While the subject matter of the picture is, in a broader sense, sex, and there are scenes in which sexual conduct including 'ultimate sexual acts' is to be understood to be taking place, the camera does not focus on the bodies of the actors at such times. There is no exhibition whatever of the actors' genitals, lewd or otherwise, during these scenes. There are occasional scenes of nudity, but nudity alone is not enough to make material legally obscene under the *Miller* standards.

Appellant's showing of the film 'Carnal Knowledge' is simply not the 'public portrayal of hard core sexual conduct for its own sake, and for the ensuing commercial gain' which we said was punishable in *Miller.* ... We hold that the film could not, as a matter of constitutional law, be found to depict sexual conduct in a patently offensive way, and that it is therefore not outside the protection of the First and Fourteenth Amendments because it is obscene. No other basis appearing in the record upon which the judgment of conviction can be sustained, we reverse the judgment of the Supreme Court of Georgia.

[Concurring opinions omitted. There was no dissent.]

Since the *Jenkins* decision, the courts, which have had numerous opportunities to apply the obscenity test to all kinds of arguably obscene depictions of sex and the like, have been hesitant to find something as being obscene and, thus, outside the protection of the First Amendment. Thus, magazines such as *Playboy* and *Penthouse* fall well outside the scope of obscenity.[347] Pornographic material and nude dancing are not considered obscene by the courts.[348]

iii. Is the Regulation Content-Based or Content-Neutral?

Questions of whether something is or is not protected speech generally arise in the context of government regulation. In cases of regulation, constitutionality often hinges on whether the regulation is content-based or content-neutral. Put another way, is the government seeking to regulate speech based upon what the speaker is saying, or is the regulation aimed generally at expression regardless of the particular message?

Cox v. New Hampshire,[349] one of the earliest Supreme Court decisions to distinguish between content-based and content-neutral regulations, involved a Manchester, New Hampshire, city ordinance that required organizers of parades or public demonstrations to obtain a license from the city. A religious group, convicted of violating the ordinance for holding a march without first obtaining a license, challenged the ordinance on constitutional grounds, arguing that the ordinance violated freedom of speech by placing restrictions upon when and where one could speak. The Supreme Court upheld the ordinance because it struck a proper balance between the government's interest in keeping order and the free speech rights of the public. Significantly, the Court stated that it would have decided differently if the city were administering its licensing requirement in a "discriminatory" manner, preferring some groups to others. While the Supreme Court has upheld content-neutral regulations of speech, such as parade permit ordinances, it has consistently struck down attempts to regulate speech based upon content in this context.[350] Some of the invalid ordinances targeted speech with a particular message, others gave government officials unlimited authority to choose what speech would be allowed on public streets.

aa. Content-Based Restrictions on Speech

Because of the constitutional prestige of First Amendment rights, it should come as no surprise that laws or actions impinging, or potentially impinging, upon constitutionally protected free speech based upon the content of that speech are judged by the exacting standards of strict scrutiny. What may be surprising is that the strict scrutiny test is also employed to judge the abstract constitutionality of laws that impinge upon rights given intermediate protection (commercial speech, for example). As illustrated

---

[347] Penthouse International Ltd. v. McAuliffe, 610 F.2d 1353, 1373 (5th Cir.)
[348] California v. LaRue, 409 U.S. 109 (1972)
[349] 312 U.S. 569, 576 (1941).
[350] Lovell v. Griffin, 303 U.S. 444 (1938); Hague v. Committee for Industrial Organization, 307 U.S. 496 (1939); Schneider v. State of New Jersey, 308 U.S. 147 (1939); Cantwell v. Connecticut, 310 U.S. 296 (1940).

in the following case, even laws directed at the lowest echelon of non-protected speech must survive strict scrutiny analysis. Notice the court's use of equal protection discourse. And ask yourselves what other crimes the young man might have been charged with committing.

By way of background to the following case, a teenager had allegedly erected and set fire to a cross on a black family's lawn. He was charged under the St. Paul, Minnesota, Bias-Motivated Crime Ordinance. This ordinance prohibited the display of a burning cross, a swastika, or other symbol that one knows or has reason to know "arouses anger, alarm or resentment in others" on the basis of race, color, creed, religion, or gender. The state supreme court had construed the phrase "arouses anger, alarm or resentment in others" to limit the ordinance's reach to fighting words within the meaning of *Chaplinsky*. It upheld the ordinance because it was narrowly tailored to serve a compelling governmental interest.

CASE: **R.A.V.**[351] **v. City of St. Paul**
505 U.S. 377 (1992)

JUSTICE SCALIA delivered the opinion of the Court.

[We] accept the Minnesota Supreme Court's authoritative statement that the ordinance reaches only those expressions that constitute "fighting words" within the meaning of Chaplinsky. Petitioner [urges] us to modify the scope of the *Chaplinsky* formulation, thereby invalidating the ordinance as "substantially overbroad." We find it unnecessary to consider this issue. Assuming, arguendo, that all of the expression reached by the ordinance is proscribable under the "fighting words" doctrine, we nonetheless conclude that the ordinance is facially unconstitutional in that it [prohibits] speech solely on the basis of the subjects the speech addresses.

I

...

The First Amendment generally prevents government from proscribing speech [because] of disapproval of the ideas expressed. Content-based regulations are presumptively invalid. From 1791 to the present, however, our society [has] permitted restrictions upon the content of speech in a few limited areas, which are "of such slight social value as a step to truth that any benefit that may

---

[351] The petitioner's initials are used instead of his name because the petitioner was a minor.

be derived from them is clearly outweighed by the social interest in order and morality." [*Chaplinsky.*] [We] have sometimes said that these categories of expression are "not within the area of constitutionally protected speech." [Such] statements must be taken in context, however. [What] they mean is that these areas of speech can, consistently with the First Amendment, be regulated because of their constitutionally proscribable content (obscenity, defamation, etc.)—not that they are categories of speech entirely invisible to the Constitution, so that they may be made the vehicles for content discrimination unrelated to their distinctively proscribable content. Thus, the government may proscribe libel; but it may not make the further content discrimination of proscribing only libel critical of the government, [and although a city may proscribe obscenity, it may not prohibit] only those legally obscene works that contain criticism of the city government....

...

II

Applying these principles to the St. Paul ordinance, we conclude that, even as narrowly construed by the Minnesota Supreme Court, the ordinance is facially unconstitutional. Although the phrase in the ordinance, "arouses anger, alarm or resentment in others," has been limited by the Minnesota Supreme Court's construction to reach only those symbols or displays that amount to "fighting words," the remaining, unmodified terms make clear that the ordinance applies only to "fighting words" that insult, or provoke violence, "on the basis of race, color, creed, religion or gender." Displays containing abusive invective, no matter how vicious or severe, are permissible unless they are addressed to one of the specified disfavored topics. Those who wish to use "fighting words" in connection with other ideas—to express hostility, for example, on the basis of political affiliation, union membership, or homosexuality—are not covered. The First Amendment does not permit St. Paul to impose special prohibitions on those speakers who express views on disfavored subjects.

...

.... St. Paul's brief asserts that a general "fighting words" law would not meet the city's needs, because only a content-specific measure can communicate to minority groups that the "group hatred" aspect of such speech "is not condoned by the majority." The point of the First Amendment is that majority preferences must be expressed in some fashion other than silencing speech on the basis of its content.

...

Finally, St. Paul [argues] that, even if the ordinance regulates expression based on hostility towards its protected ideological content, this discrimination is nonetheless justified because it is narrowly tailored to serve compelling state interests. Specifically, [it asserts] that the ordinance helps to ensure the basic human rights of members of groups that have historically been subjected to discrimination, including the right of such group members to live in peace where they wish. We do not doubt that these interests are compelling, and that the ordinance can be said to promote them. But the "danger of censorship" presented by a facially content-based statute, requires that that weapon be employed only where it is "necessary to serve the asserted [compelling] interest." The existence of adequate content-neutral alternatives thus "undercut[s] significantly" any defense of such a statute, casting considerable doubt on the government's protestations that "the asserted justification is in fact an accurate description of the purpose and effect of the law." The dispositive question in this case, therefore, is whether content discrimination is reasonably necessary to achieve St. Paul's compelling interests; it plainly is not. An ordinance not limited to the favored topics, for example, would have precisely the same beneficial effect. In fact, the only interest distinctively served by the content limitation is that of displaying the city council's special hostility towards the particular biases thus singled out. That is precisely what the First Amendment forbids ....

Let there be no mistake about our belief that burning a cross in someone's front yard is reprehensible. But St. Paul has sufficient means at its disposal to prevent such behavior without adding the First Amendment to the fire.

The judgment of the Minnesota Supreme Court is reversed....

[Concurring opinions omitted.]

Lower courts continue to struggle with the issue of cross-burning. In 2003, the Supreme Court upheld a Virginia statute that prohibited the burning of a cross with the intent to intimidate another.[352] The Supreme Court reasoned that the burning of a cross was so closely associated with impending violence that, when done to intimidate a person, the burning lost its constitutional protection and amounted to a form of "non-speech" like fighting words.

---

[352] Virginia v. Black, 538 U.S. 343 (2003).

bb. Content-Neutral, Time, Place, and Manner Restrictions on Speech

By using a form of intermediate scrutiny to judge content-neutral regulations on speech, the Supreme Court has made it somewhat easier for the government to justify its regulations. According to *Heffron v. International Society for Krishna Consciousness*, a measure may constitutionally impose reasonable limitations on the time, place, and manner of exercising free speech rights if four criteria are satisfied:

- The measure must be content-neutral;
- It must be narrowly tailored;
- It must serve a significant governmental interest; and
- It must leave ample alternative forums or channels of communication of protected expression.[353]

A violation of the first criterion (content-neutrality) might independently invalidate the law under the equal protection clause.[354] "Narrowly tailored," the second criterion, means that the law must be neither overbroad nor vague. A law is overbroad when it regulates substantially more speech than is necessary to further the significant governmental interest.[355] The vagueness doctrine "requires that a penal statute define the criminal offense with sufficient definiteness that ordinary people can understand what conduct is prohibited and in a manner that does not encourage arbitrary and discriminatory enforcement."[356]

By requiring in the third criterion that the public interests be "significant," the courts are saying that not just any public interest will do. Public safety, specifically, the orderly and safe movement of crowds at a state fair, has been held sufficiently significant to justify a requirement that the distribution of literature and solicitation of funds be restricted to booths available on a first-come, first-served basis.[357] Public safety and personal privacy are sufficiently significant to require that door-to-door solicitors and canvassers first identify themselves to local authorities.[358] Traffic safety and aesthetics may support restrictions on billboards.[359] Personal privacy, aesthetics, and orderly land-use planning can also warrant restrictions on noise[360] and on the siting of "adult" movie theaters.[361] But the aesthetic

---

[353] Heffron v. International Society for Krishna Consciousness, 452 U.S. 640 (1981).
[354] Chicago Police Department v. Mosley, 408 U.S. 92 (1972).
[355] Schad v. Borough of Mt. Ephraim, 452 U.S. 61 (1981).
[356] Kolender v. Lawson, 461 U.S. 352, 357 (1983).
[357] Heffron v. International Society for Krishna Consciousness, 452 U.S. 640 (1981).
[358] See Hynes v. Mayor of Oradell, 425 U.S. 610 (1976), where the ordinance was nonetheless ruled void for vagueness.
[359] Metromedia, Inc. v. City of San Diego, 453 U.S. 490 (1981).
[360] Kovacs v. Cooper, 336 U.S. 77 (1949).
[361] City of Renton v. Playtime Theatres, Inc., 475 U.S. 41 (1986).

interest in avoiding litter does not warrant requiring that handbills carry the name and address of their author.[362] Nor can it justify a near-total ban on residential signs.[363]

Concerning the fourth criterion, ample alternative forums, some public property is so historically associated with the exercise of First Amendment rights that it cannot be totally closed to protected speech, such as speeches, meetings, parades, and demonstrations. Examples of such "public forums" include streets, sidewalks, and parks,[364] including the public sidewalks abutting the Supreme Court's building and grounds,[365] the grounds around a statehouse,[366] and the sidewalks outside foreign embassies.[367] Further, other public property that is not historically associated with the exercise of First Amendment rights may be deemed a public forum if the state opens it "by policy or by practice" as a place for expressive activity.[368]

iv. *Licensing and Other Traditionally Valid Restrictions on Speech*

aa. *Licensing and Prior Restraints*

Licensing ordinances are often the medium through which First Amendment rights come into conflict with alleged "significant public interests" such as public safety, personal privacy, traffic safety, aesthetics, and orderly land-use planning. Because licensing ordinances restrict the "time, place, and manner" of exercising free speech rights, they are judged by the *Heffron* criteria of content-neutrality, narrowly tailored, significant governmental interest, and ample alternatives.

Licensing of public property for expressive uses is common, and generally constitutional. The Supreme Court has ruled that permit fees can be charged to cover the administrative costs of the permitting and of the event itself.[369] However, remembering the *Heffron* criteria (content-neutrality, narrowly tailored, significant governmental interest, and ample alternatives), any attempt to employ content-based criteria in the granting of the license (as opposed to imposing a condition on the license) will fail unless the distinction in content is "necessary to serve a compelling state interest and [the ordinance] is narrowly drawn to achieve that end."[370] The courts

---

[362] Schneider v. State, 308 U.S. 147 (1939).
[363] City of Ladue v. Gilleo, 512 U.S. 43 (1994).
[364] Hague v. CIO, 307 U.S. 496 (1939).
[365] United States v. Grace, 461 U.S. 171 (1983).
[366] Edwards v. South Carolina, 372 U.S. 229 (1963).
[367] See Boos v. Barry, 485 U.S. 312 (1988).
[368] Perry Education Association v. Perry Local Educators' Association, 460 U.S. 37 (1983), concerning the internal mail system of a public school.
[369] Cox v. New Hampshire, 312 U.S. 569 (1941).
[370] Perry Education Association v. Perry Local Educators' Association, 460 U.S. 37 (1983); e.g., Erznoznik v. City of Jacksonville, 422 U.S. 205 (1975), unsuccessfully

are laxer when it comes to certain types of public property that is not describable as a public forum. For example, in *Cornelius* v. *NAACP Legal Defense & Education Fund*,[371] the Supreme Court allowed organizers of a charity drive for government employees to limit participation to traditional health and welfare charities.

Licensing ordinances which do not directly relate to the use of public property are extremely difficult to justify under the *Heffron* criteria, even if they relate to unprotected speech. The seminal case on this topic of "prior restraints" is *Near* v. *Minnesota*,[372] in which the Supreme Court reversed an injunction, granted pursuant to a state statute, against a newspaper that had published a series of articles that made defamatory and anti-Semitic accusations, preventing it from publishing any malicious, scandalous, or defamatory material. The court wrote:

> [I]t has been generally, if not universally, considered that it is the chief purpose of the guaranty to prevent previous restraints upon publication....
>
> ...
>
> The fact that for approximately one hundred and fifty years there has been almost an entire absence of attempts to impose previous restraints upon publications... is significant of the deep-seated conviction that such restraints would violate constitutional right.
>
> ...
>
> [The] fact that liberty of the press may be abused by miscreant purveyors of scandal does not make any the less necessary the immunity of the press from previous restraint in dealing with official misconduct. Subsequent punishment for such abuses as may exist is the appropriate remedy.[373]

Following *Near*, the Supreme Court in *Lovell* v. *City of Griffin*,[374] invalidated an ordinance that prohibited the distribution of "literature of any kind" without first obtaining a license. In *Freeman* v. *Maryland*,[375] the court invalidated a similar ordinance that applied to motion pictures. Licensing of motion pictures has largely, if not totally, disappeared in the United States. Indeed, the well-advertised ratings of films as "G," "R," etc. are

---

attempting to single out nudity in regulating films shown by drive-in theaters whose screens are visible from highways.
[371] 473 U.S. 788 (1985).
[372] 283 U.S. 697 (1931).
[373] At pp. 713, 718, and 720.
[374] 303 U.S. 444 (1938).
[375] 380 U.S. 51 (1965).

entirely voluntary for film makers and theaters.[376] If there is still a film-licensing ordinance on the books, it would have to meet the procedural safeguards announced in *Freeman* to be valid. Specifically, the standards for denial of a license under the ordinance would have to be "narrowly drawn, reasonable, and definite," the ordinance would have to provide that the censoring agency (and not the applicant) must promptly seek a judicial injunction in case of controversy, the censoring agency would have to bear the burden of demonstrating that the speech is not protected, and the judicial determination would have to be prompt. Criteria similar to these are used for government seizures of allegedly obscene materials. The government may not seize such materials unless there is a prior judicial determination in an adversary hearing that the materials are not protected by the First Amendment.[377]

Near recognized that prior restraints could be constitutional in exceptional cases, such as to prevent the publication of obscenity, the sailing dates of ships in wartime, and incitements to acts of violence and the overthrow by force of orderly governments.[378] The reference to the sailing dates of ships was cited unsuccessfully to prevent the publication of excerpts from the "Pentagon Papers," a top secret, 47-volume report on the Vietnam war prepared by the Department of Defense.[379] Each of the nine justices who heard the case wrote an opinion. The per curiam opinion, signed by the six who voted to lift the injunction granted by the court of appeals, concluded that the government had failed to prove that any of the materials must be kept secret to protect national security.

bb. Restricting "Symbolic Expression"

Although the symbolic communication of an idea is basically protected by the First Amendment, the communication will not be protected if the method of communication has been made illegal for reasons that are independent of the speech. The issue in many cases involving symbolic communication concerns what is actually being targeted by the government regulation. Generally, "when 'speech' and 'nonspeech' elements are combined in the same course of conduct, a sufficiently important governmental interest in regulating the nonspeech element can justify incidental limits on First Amendment freedoms." Thus, while protesting the draft (military conscription) is constitutionally protected, burning or mutilating a man's draft card can constitutionally be prohibited for the independent

---

[376] Mosk at p. 137.
[377] Marcus v. Search Warrant, 367 U.S. 717 (1961).
[378] 283 U.S. at p. 716.
[379] New York Times v. United States, 403 U.S. 713 (1971).

reason that the card facilitates the smooth functioning of the selective service system, and there is no less restrictive alternative.[380]

cc. Restricting Commercial Speech

In 1976, the Supreme Court held that pharmacists have a constitutional right to advertise the prices of prescription drugs,[381] because advertising is commercial speech that is protected by the Constitution. Commercial speech is defined as speech whose dominant theme simply proposes a commercial transaction.[382]

Over the years, the Supreme Court has held that the government can prohibit false and misleading advertising as well as advertising of illegal activities. The government may also regulate true advertising that risks becoming false or deceptive.[383] For instance, the Court upheld a law that barred attorneys from soliciting potential clients in-person because there was a high risk of deception and coercion.[384] Interestingly, the Court stuck down a similar law barring accountants from face-to-face solicitation of prospective clients. It distinguished accountants from lawyers by saying that the latter are "professionals trained in the art of persuasion" and thus, presumably, inherently more coercive.[385]

Most cases in this area involve truthful, non-deceptive commercial speech. Beginning with *Central Hudson Gas & Electric Corp.* v. *Public Service Commission of New York*, the Supreme Court has formulated and refined a test to judge when the government may constitutionally regulate commercial speech. This test, which essentially amounts to intermediate scrutiny, looks at the following factors in addition to the factors above concerning false, deceptive and potentially misleading speech: (1) is there a substantial government interest for regulating the speech; (2) does the regulation directly advance this interest; and (3) is the regulation more extensive than necessary to serve that interest.[386] Using this test, the Court has ruled that lawyers may advertise for their services as long as it's not via face-to-face solicitations.[387] The Court has also ruled that government may not prohibit advertising of abortion services or contraception.[388] In addition,

---

[380] United States v. O'Brien, 391 U.S. 367, 376 (1968).
[381] Virginia State Board of Pharmacy v. Virginia Citizens Consumer Council, Inc., 425 U.S. 748 (1976).
[382] Bolger v. Youngs Drug Products Corp., 463 U.S. 60 (1983). Commercial speech first received protection by the Supreme Court under the First Amendment in Bigelow v. Virginia, 421 U.S. 809 (1975).
[383] See Chemerinsky, Constitutional Law at pp. 1089.
[384] Ohralik v. Ohio, 436 U.S. 447 (1978).
[385] Edenfield v. Fane, 507 U.S. 761, 775 (1993).
[386] 447 U.S. 557, 563 (1980).
[387] Bates v. State Bar of Arizona, 433 U.S. 350 (1977)
[388] Bigelow v. Virginia, 421 U.S. 809 (1975); Carey v. Population Services International, 431 U.S. 678 (1977).

the Court has struck down an attempt to outlaw the display of "For Sale" signs in front of private homes, a law aimed at restricting tobacco ads near schools and parks, and a restriction on the publishing of alcohol prices.[389]

dd. Free Speech Rights of Government Employees

Although it probably goes without saying, free speech includes the freedom to hold political and other opinions and beliefs.[390] Consequently, the Supreme Court has decided a number of cases brought by employees of federal, state, and local governments alleging violations of their First Amendment rights. Some representative cases are mentioned in the following paragraph.

While the government may require employees to take an oath to support the federal and state constitutions,[391] it may not demand that they pledge to "promote respect for the flag and... reverence for law and order."[392] The speech and association protections of the First Amendment forbid hiring, promotion, transfer, or firing of a public employee for party affiliation unless the hiring authority demonstrates that party affiliation is an appropriate requirement for the effective performance of the public office.[393] They similarly forbid retaliatory termination or non-renewal of a contract with an independent contractor on such grounds.[394] However, the government may constitutionally place some limitations on a public employee's rights of political speech and association if the limits are neutral and they are necessary to preserve efficient, nonpartisan public agencies, and to protect public employees from being forced to work for the election of their superiors.[395] This last protection can be extremely important in light of the fact that over half a million people hold elective office in the United States.[396]

b. Religion

The First Amendment contains two protections of religious rights, the "establishment clause" and the "free exercise [of religion] clause."[397] Some of the most fascinating (and baffling) questions confronted under the

---

[389] Linmark Associates, Inc. v. Township of Willingboro, 431 U.S. 85 (1977); Lorillard Tobacco Co. v. Reilly, 533 U.S. 525 (2001); 44 Liquormart, Inc. v. Rhode Island, 517 U.S. 484 (1996).
[390] Dawson v. Delaware, 503 U.S. 159 (1992).
[391] Connell v. Higginbotham, 403 U.S. 207 (1971).
[392] Baggett v. Bullitt, 377 U.S. 360 (1964).
[393] Rutan v. Republican Party of Illinois, 497 U.S. 62 (1990).
[394] O'Hare Truck Service, Inc. v. City of Northlake, 518 U.S. 712 (1996).
[395] Broadrick v. Oklahoma, 413 U.S. 601 (1973).
[396] U.S. Dept. of Commerce, vol. I, no. II.
[397] Consider also the protection of religious belief inherent in Art. VI, cl. 3.

First Amendment concern the "establishment clause," which holds the honor of being the first clause of the First Amendment, treated in the following section.

i. Establishment of Religion

Professor Tribe identifies three different attitudes among the drafters of the Bill of Rights on the need to cleave religion from the state.[398] The evangelical view feared corruption of the churches by a worldly sovereign. Thomas Jefferson espoused the opposing view, that secular interests must be walled off from ecclesiastical incursions. A third view favored free competition among the various sects.

The Jeffersonian view has come to dominate modern thinking on the subject, although it can also be combined with the first approach under a "strict separation" theory.[399] Professor Chemerinsky also identifies a "neutralist theory" that is quite similar to the third theory recognized by Professor Tribe. According to the neutralist theory, government may not favor religion over secularism or one religion over another. Those adhering to this theory have in recent years advanced the test that the government runs afoul of the establishment clause if it "symbolically endorses" a particular religion or generally endorses either religion or secularism.[400] "Accommodation theorists" arguably subscribe to a fourth attitude. They would have government recognize the importance of religion in society and therefore accommodate its presence in government.[401] Under the accommodation theory violation of the establishment clause would occur only if the state established a religion or coerced religious participation.[402]

Without formally adopting any particular theory, the Supreme Court has developed a three-pronged test to judge challenges under the establishment clause: Is there a secular purpose; Does it have a principal or primary effect that neither advances nor inhibits religion; and Does it not foster excessive government entanglement with religion.[403]

Setting aside a time of silence in public schools for "mediation or voluntary prayer" was held to violate the first prong because it has no secular purpose.[404] The same fate befell a program to post the Ten Commandments on the walls of public school classrooms.[405] However, excusing children from public school to attend religious services does not offend the establishment clause, despite its religious purpose.[406]

---

[398] Tribe Vol. II, Chap. 14.
[399] Chemerinsky, Constitutional Law at pp. 1192–1193.
[400] E.g., Lynch v. Donnelly, 465 U.S. 668, 694 (1984).
[401] Chemerinsky, Constitutional Law at p. 1196.
[402] See Lee v. Weisman, 505 U.S. 577, 587 (1992).
[403] Leon v. Kurtzman, 403 U.S. 602 (1971).
[404] Wallace v. Jaffree, 472 U.S. 38 (1985).
[405] Stone v. Graham, 449 U.S. 39 (1980).
[406] Zorach v. Clauson, 343 U.S. 306 (1952).

Laws requiring businesses or government offices to close on Sundays are valid, even though they originally were enacted to aid religion.[407] Invocation and benediction prayers at meetings of public bodies have been upheld,[408] but the same practice has been ruled unconstitutional at public school graduations.[409] Christmas Nativity scenes on public property have often faced judicial challenge on grounds that they establish religion. A crèche with "Gloria in Excelsis Deo" in a courthouse violates the establishment clause even if paid for by private funds, but a Chanukah menorah displayed with a Christmas tree does not.[410]

CASE: Zelman v. Simmons-Harris
536 U.S. 639 (2002)

CHIEF JUSTICE REHNQUIST delivered the opinion of the Court.

The State of Ohio has established a pilot program designed to provide educational choices to families with children who reside in the Cleveland City School District. The question presented is whether this program offends the Establishment Clause of the United States Constitution. We hold that it does not.

There are more than 75,000 children enrolled in the Cleveland City School District. The majority of these children are from low-income and minority families. Few of these families enjoy the means to send their children to any school other than an inner-city public school. For more than a generation, however, Cleveland's public schools have been among the worst performing public schools in the Nation. [The] state auditor found that Cleveland's public schools were in the midst of a "crisis that is perhaps unprecedented in the history of American education." ...

The [Pilot Project Scholarship Program] provides two basic kinds of assistance to parents of children in a covered district. First, the program provides tuition aid for students ... to attend a participating public or private school of their parent's choosing. Second, the program provides tutorial aid for students who choose to remain enrolled in public school.

---

[407] McGowan v. Maryland, 366 U.S. 420 (1961).
[408] Marsh v. Chambers, 463 U.S. 783 (1983).
[409] Lee v. Weisman, 505 U.S. 830 (1992).
[410] County of Allegheny v. American Civil Liberties Union Greater Pittsburgh Chapter, 492 U.S. 573 (1989).

... Any private school, whether religious or nonreligious, may participate in the program and accept program students so long as the school is located within the boundaries of a covered district and meets statewide educational standards. Participating private schools must agree not to discriminate on the basis of race, religion, or ethnic background, or to "advocate or foster unlawful behavior or teach hatred of any person or group on the basis of race, ethnicity, national origin, or religion."... All participating schools, whether public or private, are required to accept students in accordance with rules and procedures established by the state superintendent.

Tuition aid is distributed to parents according to financial need. Families with incomes below 200% of the poverty line are given priority and are eligible to receive 90% of private school tuition .... [Students from low-income families receive 90% of the amount charged for tutorial aid.]

The program has been in operation within the Cleveland City School District since the 1996–1997 school year. In the 1999–2000 school year, 56 private schools participated in the program, 46 (or 82%) of which had a religious affiliation.... More than 3,700 students participated in the scholarship program, most of whom (96%) enrolled in religiously affiliated schools. Sixty percent of these students were from families at or below the poverty line. In the 1998–1999 school year, approximately 1,400 Cleveland public school students received tutorial aid. This number was expected to double during the 1999–2000 school year.

In 1996, respondents, a group of Ohio taxpayers, challenged the Ohio program in state court on state and federal grounds. The Ohio Supreme Court rejected respondents' federal claims, but held that the enactment of the program violated certain procedural requirements of the Ohio Constitution.... The state legislature immediately cured this defect, leaving the basic provisions discussed above intact.

In July 1999, respondents filed this action in United States District Court, seeking to enjoin the reenacted program on the ground that it violated the Establishment Clause of the United States Constitution. In August 1999, the District Court issued a preliminary injunction barring further implementation of the program [and in December 1999] granted summary judgment for respondents. In December 2000, a divided panel of the Court of Appeals affirmed the judgment of the District Court, finding that the program had the "primary effect" of advancing religion in violation of the Establishment Clause ....

The Establishment Clause of the First Amendment, applied to the States through the Fourteenth Amendment, prevents a State from enacting laws that have the "purpose" or "effect" of advancing or inhibiting religion. *Agostini* v. *Felton*.[411] There is no dispute that the program challenged here was enacted for the valid secular purpose of providing educational assistance to poor children in a demonstrably failing public school system. Thus, the question presented is whether the Ohio program nonetheless has the forbidden "effect" of advancing or inhibiting religion.

To answer that question, our decisions have drawn a consistent distinction between government programs that provide aid directly to religious schools ..., and programs of true private choice, in which government aid reaches religious schools only as a result of the genuine and independent choices of private individuals .... Three times we have confronted Establishment Clause challenges to neutral government programs that provide aid directly to a broad class of individuals, who, in turn, direct the aid to religious schools or institutions of their own choosing. Three times we have rejected such challenges.

In *Mueller*,[412] we rejected an Establishment Clause challenge to a Minnesota program authorizing tax deductions for various educational expenses, including private school tuition costs, even though the great majority of the program's beneficiaries (96%) were parents of children in religious schools. ... That the program was one of true private choice, with no evidence that the State deliberately skewed incentives toward religious schools, was sufficient for the program to survive scrutiny under the Establishment Clause.

In *Witters*,[413] we used identical reasoning to reject an Establishment Clause challenge to a vocational scholarship program that provided tuition aid to a student studying at a religious institution to become a pastor. Looking at the program as a whole, we observed that "[a]ny aid ... that ultimately flows to religious institutions does so only as a result of the genuinely independent and private choices of aid recipients." ...

Finally, in *Zobrest*,[414] we applied *Mueller* and *Witters* to reject an Establishment Clause challenge to a federal program that permitted sign-language interpreters to assist deaf children enrolled in religious schools. Reviewing our earlier decisions, we stated

---

[411] 521 U.S. 203, 222–223 (1997).
[412] Mueller v. Allen, 463 U.S. 388 (1983).
[413] Witters v. Washington Department of Services for the Blind, 474 U.S. 481 (1986).
[414] Zobrest v. Catalina Foothills School District, 509 U.S. 1 (1993).

that "government programs that neutrally provide benefits to a broad class of citizens defined without reference to religion are not readily subject to an Establishment Clause challenge." ... Its "primary beneficiaries," we said, were "disabled children, not sectarian schools."

Mueller, Witters, and *Zobrest* thus make clear that where a government aid program is neutral with respect to religion, and provides assistance directly to a broad class of citizens who, in turn, direct government aid to religious schools wholly as a result of their own genuine and independent private choice, the program is not readily subject to challenge under the Establishment Clause ....

...

In sum, the Ohio program is entirely neutral with respect to religion. It provides benefits directly to a wide spectrum of individuals, defined only by financial need and residence in a particular school district. It permits such individuals to exercise genuine choice among options public and private, secular and religious. The program is therefore a program of true private choice. In keeping with an unbroken line of decisions rejecting challenges to similar programs, we hold that the program does not offend the Establishment Clause.

The judgment of the Court of Appeals is reversed.

It is so ordered.

[Concurring and dissenting opinions omitted.]

---

ii. Free Exercise of Religion

Applying the free exercise (of religion) clause, courts will invalidate public action that singles out religion for adverse treatment, or hinders or discriminates against a particular religion.[415] However, the free exercise clause affords no right to a religious exemption from a neutral law that happens to impose a substantial burden on religious practices.[416]

Controversies surrounding the free exercise clause basically break into two halves: What is a religion, and Which religious practices ("exercises") are entitled to constitutional protection? The closest that the Supreme Court has come to defining "religion" has been in the context of construing the Universal Military Training and Selective Service Act, which exempts those "who by reason of their religious training and belief are

---

[415] Church of the Lukumi Babalu Aye, Inc. v. City of Hialeah, 508 U.S. 520 (1993), declaring unconstitutional a city ordinance that barred ritual sacrifice of animals.
[416] Employment Division v. Smith, 494 U.S. 872 (1990), refusing to recognize a constitutional right to the sacramental use of peyote.

conscientiously opposed to participation in war in any form."[417] The former law defined "religious training and belief" as "an individual's belief in relation to a Supreme Being involving duties superior to those arising from any human relation, [as opposed to] essentially political, sociological, or philosophical views or a merely personal moral code." In *United States* v. *Seeger*,[418] the Supreme Court held that "religious... belief," for purposes of this act, includes non-theistic beliefs: "We believe that... the test of belief 'in a relation to a Supreme Being' is whether a given belief that is sincere and meaningful occupies a place in the life of the possessor parallel to that filled by the orthodox belief in God of one who clearly qualifies for the exemption."[419] The reference to a supreme being in the Selective Service Act was deleted in 1967.

While the following case actually presents the issue as to which religious practices are entitled to constitutional protection, it also contains a fruitful discussion on the issue of what constitutes a religion.

CASE: Wisconsin v. Yoder
406 U.S. 205 (1972)

MR. CHIEF JUSTICE BURGER delivered the opinion of the Court.

...

Respondents Jonas Yoder and Wallace Miller are members of the Old Order Amish religion, and respondent Adin Yutzy is a member of the Conservative Amish Mennonite Church. They and their families are residents of Green County, Wisconsin. Wisconsin's compulsory school-attendance law required them to cause their children to attend public or private school until reaching age 16 but the respondents declined to send their children, ages 14 and 15, to public school after they completed the eighth grade. The children were not enrolled in any private school, or within any recognized exception to the compulsory-attendance law, and they are conceded to be subject to the Wisconsin statute.

On complaint of the school district administrator for the public schools, respondents were charged, tried, and convicted of violating the compulsory-attendance law in Green Country Court

---

[417] 451 U.S.C. app. § 456.
[418] 380 U.S. 163 (1965).
[419] The concurring opinion by Justice Douglas also makes an equal protection argument.

and were fined the sum of $5 each. Respondents defended on the ground that the application of the compulsory-attendance law violated their rights under the First and Fourteenth Amendments. The trial testimony showed that respondents believed, in accordance with the tenets of Old Order Amish communities generally, that their children's attendance at high school, public or private, was contrary to the Amish religion and way of life. They believed that by sending their children to high school, they would not only expose themselves to the danger of the censure of the church community, but, as found by the county court, also endanger their own salvation and that of their children. The State stipulated that respondents' religious beliefs were sincere.

In support of their position, respondents presented as expert witnesses scholars on religion and education whose testimony is uncontradicted. They expressed their opinions on the relationship of the Amish belief concerning school attendance to the more general tenets of their religion, and described the impact that compulsory high school attendance could have on the continued survival of Amish communities as they exist in the United States today. The history of the Amish sect was given in some detail, beginning with the Swiss Anabaptists of the 16th century who rejected institutionalized churches and sought to return to the early, simple, Christian life de-emphasizing material success, rejecting the competitive spirit, and seeking to insulate themselves from the modern world. As a result of their common heritage, Old Order Amish communities today are characterized by a fundamental belief that salvation requires life in a church community separate and apart from the world and worldly influence. This concept of life aloof from the world and its values is central to their faith.

...

I

There is no doubt as to the power of a State, having a high responsibility for education of its citizens, to impose reasonable regulations for the control and duration of basic education. See, e.g., *Pierce v. Society of Sisters.*[420] Providing public schools ranks at the very apex of the function of a State. Yet even this paramount responsibility was, in Pierce, made to yield to the right of parents to provide an equivalent education in a privately operated system. There the Court held that Oregon's statute compelling attendance in a public school from age eight to age 16 unreasonably

---

[420] 268 U.S. 510, 534 (1925).

interfered with the interest of parents in directing the rearing of their offspring, including their education in church-operated schools. As that case suggests, the values of parental direction of the religious upbringing and education of their children in their early and formative years have a high place in our society.... Thus, a State's interest in universal education, however highly we rank it, is not totally free from a balancing process when it impinges on fundamental rights and interests, such as those specifically protected by the Free Exercise Clause of the First Amendment, and the traditional interest of parents with respect to the religious upbringing of their children so long as they, in the words of *Pierce*, "prepare [them] for additional obligations."...

...

II

We come then to the quality of the claims of the respondents concerning the alleged encroachment of Wisconsin's compulsory school-attendance statute on their rights and the rights of their children to the free exercise of the religious beliefs they and their forebears have adhered to for almost three centuries. ... Although a determination of what is a "religious" belief or practice entitled to constitutional protection may present a most delicate question, the very concept of ordered liberty precludes allowing every person to make his own standards on matters of conduct in which society as a whole has important interests. Thus, if the Amish asserted their claims because of their subjective evaluation and rejection of the contemporary secular values accepted by the majority, much as Thoreau rejected the social values of his time and isolated himself at Walden Pond, their claims would not rest on a religious basis. Thoreau's choice was philosophical and personal rather than religious, and such belief does not rise to the demands of the Religion Clauses.

...

In sum, the unchallenged testimony of acknowledged experts in education and religious history, almost 300 years of consistent practice, and strong evidence of a sustained faith pervading and regulating respondents' entire mode of life support the claim that enforcement of the State's requirement of compulsory formal education after the eighth grade would gravely endanger if not destroy the free exercise of respondents' religious beliefs.

...

III

The State advances two primary arguments in support of its system of compulsory education. It notes, as Thomas Jefferson pointed out early in our history, that some degree of education is necessary to prepare citizens to participate effectively and intelligently in our open political system if we are to preserve freedom and independence. Further, education prepares individuals to be self-reliant and self-sufficient participants in society. We accept these propositions.

However, the evidence adduced by the Amish in this case is persuasively to the effect that an additional one or two years of formal high school for Amish children in place of their long-established program of informal vocational education would do little to serve those interests. Respondents' experts testified at trial, without challenge, that the value of all education must be assessed in terms of its capacity to prepare the child for life. It is one thing to say that compulsory education for a year or two beyond the eighth grade may be necessary when its goal is the preparation of the child for life in modern society as the majority live, but it is quite another if the goal of education be viewed as the preparation of the child for life in the separated agrarian community that is the keystone of the Amish faith. See *Meyer v. Nebraska*.[421]

. . .

Affirmed.
[Concurring and dissenting opinions omitted.]

---

2. IMPLICIT FUNDAMENTAL RIGHTS

In addition to the rights of speech, press, religion, etc. that are explicitly recognized in the Constitution and its amendments, courts have recognized a whole host of rights that are not directly traceable to a provision in the Constitution. The right to travel is one such right. Another previously mentioned is the right of children of undocumented (illegal) aliens to an education.[422]

Before addressing the question of which implicit rights have been recognized, the discussion will first address the theoretical questions of how and whether they should be recognized.

---

[421] 262 U.S. 390, 400 (1923).
[422] See Plyler, 457 U.S. 202 (1982), abstracted above.

a.   The Judicial Recognition of Fundamental Rights

The more specific questions of how and whether fundamental rights should be recognized, and more general questions of how the Constitution should be interpreted, have been the subject of an ongoing debate that has spanned the 20th century. These debates are summarized below.[423] Note parallels to the debates surrounding "selective incorporation."

Many theories have been advanced for how the constitution *should* be interpreted in general, and how, if at all, fundamental rights should be inferred in particular. At one pole are the originalists.[424] The originalists voice great respect for separation of powers, for federalism, and for democratic institutions. Accordingly, they are more willing than some to tolerate individual cases of apparent injustice. After all, such cases are necessary to ignite public opinion and mobilize the somewhat cumbersome democratic political processes of legislation and of amendment of state and federal constitutions. Originalists abhor abrupt changes in the law. They tend not to recognize implicit constitutional rights unless these were clearly intended by the Framers of the Constitution.

References to the intentions of the Framers of the Constitution are ridiculed by the anti-originalists. The anti-originalists accuse the originalists of wanting to calibrate the present meaning of the Constitution to conform to the intent of the Framers.[425] They point out that the amendment process is not merely cumbersome but positively anti-progressive. They insinuate that the originalists, by advocating democratic amendment of the Constitution, are really just opting for the conservative *status quo*. Anti-originalists want justice now. They are not content to wait for legislators and constitutional amendments. Justice delayed is justice denied. And, as for separation of powers, doesn't that principle exist to promote liberty? And aren't judges the final interpreters of liberty anyway?

While the anti-originalists reach ready consensus when criticizing the originalists, they are not so reliably harmonious when it comes to describing under what circumstances implicit rights can or should be recognized. Some advocate the importation of natural law principles.[426] Others look to moral consensus.[427] Still another would limit the judicial expansion of rights to the subject matter areas of procedure and equal protection.[428] No one seems willing openly to defend the position at the polar extreme of the originalists', that is, that an implicit fundamental right is anything that a majority of the Supreme Court says it is on any certain day. Consider the

---

[423] See generally Chemerinsky, Constitutional Law at pp. 15–28.
[424] See, e.g., Bork.
[425] See, e.g., Ely at p. 18.
[426] E.g., Jaffa.
[427] E.g., Simon.
[428] See Ely at p. 87.

following statement of Supreme Court Justice Charles Evans Hughes: "We are under a Constitution, but the Constitution is what the judges say it is, and the judiciary is the safeguard of our liberty and of our property under the Constitution."[429]

Despite the protestations and warnings of the originalists, courts have continued to "find" new fundamental rights in the Constitution without having a coherent theory for doing so. These rights are summarized in the following discussion.

b. Privacy and Other Implicit Rights

In the first third of this century, the Supreme Court deemed economic rights, such as the right to contract, to be fundamental. As a consequence, much social welfare legislation was ruled unconstitutional. The most infamous of these rulings is *Lochner v. New York*,[430] which held that a law regulating the working hours of bakers unreasonably interfered with "the freedom of master and employee to contract in relation to their employment." The shift away from protecting economic rights coincided with President Roosevelt's announcement of his "Court Packing Plan."[431] *Lochner* was abandoned in *West Coast Hotel v. Parrish*,[432] which upheld a state minimum wage law for women.

For decades after the demise of *Lochner*, courts took a back seat to the state and federal legislators on economic, social, and personal matters that did not impinge upon explicit constitutional rights. But in the mid 1960s, judges again felt the responsibility to protect implicit constitutional rights. This time, however, they eschewed economic rights for the most part (commercial speech is an exception) and embraced the protection of the rights of the criminally accused (not discussed in this book) and certain "personal" rights.

In *Griswold v. Connecticut*,[433] the Supreme Court recognized a fundamental right to privacy, to date the most expansive of the personal, fundamental rights recognized by the Supreme Court. The Supreme Court's opinion in *Griswold*, which was penned by Justice Douglas, expressly rejected relegation of privacy to the discredited concept of "liberty." Rather, Justice Douglas found that privacy was implicit in the First, Third, Fourth, and Fifth Amendments:

---

[429] Hughes at p. 139.
[430] 198 U.S. 45 (1905).
[431] See United States v. Carolene Products Co., 304 U.S. 144, 152 at n. 4 (1938), which inaugurated the age of multi-level review.
[432] 300 U.S. 379 (1937).
[433] 381 U.S. 479 (1965).

[S]pecific guarantees in the Bill of Rights have penumbras, formed by emanations from those guarantees that help give them life and substance. Various guarantees create zones of privacy.... We have had many controversies over these penumbral rights of privacy and repose. These cases bear witness that the right of privacy which presses for recognition here is a legitimate one.[434]

The list of implicit fundamental due process rights is a fairly long one, and the list appears to be growing. In addition to right of children of undocumented (illegal) aliens to an education,[435] the right of privacy,[436] and the right to travel interstate,[437] the list includes the right to be a candidate for elective office,[438] the right to abort a pregnancy,[439] the right to procreate,[440] the right to purchase and use contraceptives,[441] the right to possess obscene material (not including child pornography),[442] the right to engage in consensual homosexual activity,[443] the right to marry,[444] the right to reject medical treatment,[445] the right to keep one's family together,[446] the right to custody of one's children,[447] the right to educate one's children at a parochial school,[448] including the right to have one's children taught in the German language,[449] and the right of access to courts,[450] although this last right might be subsumed under the explicit First Amendment right to petition government for a redress of grievances.

The above list of implicit fundamental rights is not exhaustive. It should also be augmented by fundamental rights guaranteed to those suspected, accused, and convicted of crimes, although sometimes these find textual support in the Constitution,[451] and, therefore, belong in the list of explicit fundamental rights.

---

[434] At pp. 484–485.
[435] See Plyler, 457 U.S. 202 (1982), abstracted above. But see San Antonia Independent School District v. Rodriguez, 411 U.S. 1 (1973), rejecting the claim that education is a fundamental right.
[436] Griswold v. Connecticut, 381 U.S. 479 (1965).
[437] Saenz v. Roe, 526 U.S. 489 (1999), abstracted below.
[438] Lubin v. Parrish, 415 U.S. 709 (1974).
[439] Roe v. Wade, 410 U.S. 113 (1973).
[440] Skinner v. Oklahoma, 316 U.S. 535 (1942).
[441] Griswold v. Connecticut, 381 U.S. 479 (1965).
[442] Stanley v. Georgia, 394 U.S. 557 (1969).
[443] Lawrence v. Texas, 539 U.S. 558 (2003).
[444] Loving v. Virginia, 388 U.S. 1 (1976).
[445] Cruzan v. Director, 497 U.S. 261 (1990).
[446] Moore v. City of East Cleveland, 431 U.S. 494 (1977).
[447] Santosky v. Kramer, 455 U.S. 745 (1982).
[448] Pierce v. Society of Sisters, 268 U.S. 510 (1925).
[449] Meyer v. Nebraska, 262 U.S. 390 (1923).
[450] Bounds v. Smith, 430 U.S. 817 (1977).
[451] E.g., In re Winship, 397 U.S. 358 (1970), requiring proof beyond a reasonable doubt.

CASE: **Roe v. Wade**
410 U.S. 113 (1973)

MR. JUSTICE BLACKMUN delivered the opinion of the Court.

This [appeal presents] constitutional challenges to state criminal abortion legislation. The Texas statutes under attack here [make procuring an abortion a crime except "by medical advice for the purpose of saving the life of the mother." These statutes] are typical of those that have been in effect in many States for approximately a century....

We forthwith acknowledge our awareness of the sensitive and emotional nature of the abortion controversy, of the vigorous opposing views, even among physicians, and of the deep and seemingly absolute convictions that the subject inspires....

Our task, of course, is to resolve the issue by constitutional measurement, free of emotion and of predilection. We seek earnestly to do this, and, because we do, we have inquired into, and in this opinion place some emphasis upon, medical and medical-legal history and what that history reveals about man's attitudes toward the abortion procedure over the centuries....

[The] restrictive criminal abortion laws in effect in a majority of States today are of relatively recent vintage. [They] derive from statutory changes effected, for the most part, in the latter half of the 19th century.

[Abortion] was practiced in Greek times as well as in the Roman Era. [Most] Greek thinkers [commended] abortion, at least prior to viability. [At] common law, abortion performed *before* "quickening"—the first recognizable movement of the fetus in utero, appearing usually from the 16th to the 18th week of pregnancy— was not an indictable offense. [It] was not until [the] middle and late 19th century [that] the quickening distinction [was abandoned] and the degree of the offense [increased]. [Thus,] at common law, at the time of the adoption of our Constitution, and throughout the major portion of the 19th century, [a] woman enjoyed a substantially broader right to terminate a pregnancy than she does in most States today....

Three reasons have been advanced to explain historically the enactment of criminal abortion laws in the 19th century and to justify their continued existence.

It has been argued occasionally that these laws were [designed] to discourage illicit sexual conduct. Texas, however, does not advance this justification in the present case....

A second reason is concerned with abortion as a medical procedure. When most criminal abortion laws were first enacted, the procedure was [hazardous]. [Today, mortality] rates for women undergoing early abortions, where the procedure is legal, appear to be as low as or lower than the rates for normal childbirth ....

The third reason is the State's interest [in] protecting prenatal life. Some of the argument for this justification rests on the theory that a new human life is present from the moment of conception. [But in] assessing the State's interest, recognition may [also] be given to the less rigid claim that [at] least *potential* life is involved....

The Constitution does not explicitly mention any right of privacy. [But] the Court has recognized that a right of personal privacy, or a guarantee of certain areas or zones of privacy, does exist under the Constitution. In varying contexts, the Court or individual Justices have, indeed, found at least the roots of that right in the First Amendment, Stanley v. Georgia[452]; in the Fourth and Fifth Amendments; in the penumbras of the Bill of Rights, [*Griswold*]; in the Ninth Amendment, id., (Goldberg, J., concurring); or in the concept of liberty guaranteed by the first section of the Fourteenth Amendment, see *Meyer* v. *Nebraska*. These decisions make it clear that only personal rights that can be deemed "fundamental" or "implicit in the concept of ordered liberty," are included in this guarantee of personal privacy. They also make it clear that the right has some extension to activities relating to marriage, Loving v. Virginia[453]; procreation [*Skinner*]; contraception [*Eisenstadt*]; family relationships, *Prince* v. *Massachusetts*[454]; and child rearing and education [*Pierce; Meyer*].

This right of privacy, whether it be founded in the Fourteenth Amendment's concept of personal liberty [as] we feel it is, or [in] the Ninth [Amendment] is broad enough to encompass a woman's decision whether or not to terminate her pregnancy. ...

[Appellant argues] that the woman's right is absolute and that she is entitled to terminate her pregnancy at whatever time, in whatever way, and for whatever reason she alone chooses. With this we do not agree. [The] Court's decisions recognizing a right of privacy also acknowledge that some state regulation in areas protected by that right is appropriate....

Where certain "fundamental rights" are involved, the Court has held that regulation limiting these rights may be justified only by

---

[452] 394 U.S. 557, 564 (1969).
[453] 388 U.S. 1, 12 (1967).
[454] 321 U.S. 158, 166 (1944).

a "compelling state interest," and that legislative enactments must be narrowly drawn to express only the legitimate state interests at stake....

The appellee [argues] that the fetus is a "person" within the language and meaning of the Fourteenth Amendment. [If] this suggestion of personhood is established, the appellant's case, of course, collapses, for the fetus' right to life would then be guaranteed specifically by the Amendment....

The Constitution does not define "person" in so many words. Section 1 of the Fourteenth Amendment contains three references to "person." ["Person" is used in numerous clauses that are omitted here.] None [of the usages] indicates, with any assurance, that it has any possible pre-natal application....

Texas urges that, apart from the Fourteenth Amendment, life begins at conception and is present throughout pregnancy, and that, therefore, the State has a compelling interest in protecting that life from and after conception. We need not resolve the difficult question of when life begins. When those trained [in] medicine, philosophy, and theology are unable to arrive at any consensus, the judiciary, at this point in the development of man's knowledge, is not in a position to speculate as to the answer.

It should be sufficient to note briefly the wide divergence of thinking on this most sensitive and difficult question. There has always been strong support for the view that life does not begin until live birth. This was the belief of the Stoics. It appears to be the predominant, though not the unanimous, attitude of the Jewish faith. It may be taken to represent also the position of a large segment of the Protestant community. [The] common law found greater significance in quickening. Physicians and their scientific colleagues [tended] to focus either upon conception, upon live birth, or upon the interim point at which the fetus becomes "viable," that is, potentially able to live outside the mother's womb, albeit with artificial aid. Viability is usually placed at about seven months (28 weeks) but may occur earlier, even at 24 weeks. [The Catholic church recognizes] the existence of life from the moment of conception....

...

... We repeat, however, that the State does have an important and legitimate interest in preserving and protecting the health of the pregnant woman [and] that it has still *another* important and legitimate interest in protecting the potentiality of human life. These interests are separate and distinct. Each grows in substantiality as the woman approaches term and, at a point during pregnancy, each becomes "compelling."

With respect to [the] interest in the health of the mother, the "compelling" point, in the light of present medical knowledge, is at approximately the end of the first trimester. This is so because of the now-established medical fact [that] until the end of the first trimester mortality in abortion may be less than mortality in normal childbirth. It follows that, from and after this point, a State may regulate the abortion procedure to the extent that the regulation reasonably relates to the preservation and protection of maternal health. ...

This means, on the other hand, that, for the period of pregnancy prior to this "compelling" point, the attending physician, in consultation with his patient, is free to determine, without regulation by the State, that, in his medical judgment, the patient's pregnancy should be terminated. If that decision is reached, the judgment may be effectuated by an abortion free of interference by the State.

With respect to [the] interest in potential life, the "compelling" point is at viability. This is so because the fetus then presumably has the capability of meaningful life outside the mother's womb. State regulation protective of fetal life after viability thus has both logical and biological justifications. If the State is interested in protecting fetal life after viability, it may go so far as to proscribe abortion during that period, except when it is necessary to preserve the life or health of the mother.

Measured against these standards, [the Texas statute] sweeps too broadly [and] therefore, cannot survive the constitutional attack made upon it here....

To summarize and to repeat:...

(a) For the stage prior to approximately the end of the first trimester, the abortion decision and its effectuation must be left to the medical judgment of the pregnant woman's attending physician.

(b) For the stage subsequent to approximately the end of the first trimester, the State, in promoting its interest in the health of the mother, may, if it chooses, regulate the abortion procedure in ways that are reasonably related to maternal health.

(c) For the stage subsequent to viability, the State in promoting its interest in the potentiality of human life may, if it chooses, regulate, and even proscribe, abortion except where it is necessary, in appropriate medical judgment, for the preservation of the life or health of the mother....

...

[Concurring and dissenting opinions omitted.]

May a state constitutionally impose the following requirements on women seeking to terminate their pregnancies?

1. Doctors must first provide women with information about the health risks and possible complications (so-called informed consent) and then, absent an emergency, wait 24 hours before performing an abortion.
2. Married women, with certain exceptions, must sign a statement that they have notified their husbands.
3. Minors must have the consent of one parent, or must follow a judicial bypass procedure.

The Supreme Court upheld the first and third requirements, holding, in a decision signed by only three of the nine justices who heard the case, that these restrictions did not have the purpose or effect of imposing an "undue burden" on a woman's right to terminate her pregnancy. They defined "undue burden" as a "substantial obstacle in the path of a woman seeking an abortion before the fetus attains viability."[455]

---

[455] Planned Parenthood of Southeastern Pennsylvania v. Casey, 505 U.S. 833 (1992). See also Gonzales v. Carhart, 127 S. Ct. 1610 (2007), upholding the federal Partial-Birth Abortion Ban Act of 2003.

SUBPART B

EQUALITY (EQUAL PROTECTION)

LIKE DUE PROCESS, EQUAL PROTECTION IS ABOUT RIGHTS. IN THE CONTEXT OF DUE process, the interests of the state, which represents the majority, are seen as conflicting with the rights of individuals. Under equal protection, on the other hand, the individual claims rights as a member of a group. Both liberty and equality rights are anti-democratic in the sense that they curb what the majority may do.

Equality in a literal sense is not articulated in the original Constitution, nor in the Bill of Rights. Commentators are fond of attributing this apparent inadequacy to the racism and sexism of the Founding Fathers. Yet all those who fathered the Constitution also backed the Declaration of Independence (Attach. A), and this document lauds equality before liberty:

> We hold these truths to be self-evident: That all men are created equal. That they are endowed by their Creator with certain unalienable rights.

Further, while the Constitution and the Bill of Rights do not contain a sweeping declaration of equal protection, it is not true that the original Constitution turns a deaf ear to equality. The privileges and immunities clause, for example, ensures that states will not discriminate against citizens of other states.[456] Article IV, section 2 also contains the now superseded prohibition against depriving the class of slave owners of their property in slaves. The Constitution prevents the anti-egalitarian practice of granting titles of nobility.[457] And there are numerous protections of the equality of the states, including the only provision of the Constitution that, by its terms, cannot be amended without consent: the equal representation of each state in the Senate.[458]

This is not to deny that the social milieu and prejudices of the people had no impact on the Framers. On the contrary, the Framers undoubtedly thought of themselves as a fairly homogeneous lot, joined in their opposition to imperial domination. Their factions were geographical, political, and ecclesiastical. Not surprisingly, rights protecting state citizenship and political and religious beliefs found their way into the Bill of Rights. The Framers would have protested mightily had they been "discriminated against" on the basis of religious beliefs. The American Colonists certainly

---

[456] Art. IV, § 2, cl. 1.
[457] Art. I, § 9, cl. 8 and § 10, cl. 1.
[458] Art. V.

objected that their voting rights were marginalized in the English Parliament ("No taxation without representation"). In other words, if the American society of the 18th century had valued, for example, homosexuality, then homosexuality could, and perhaps would, have been explicitly protected by the Bill of Rights.

The reverse side of the same historical coin is that, had the Bill of Rights contained a guaranty of equality, this guaranty would not automatically have rendered unconstitutional classifications based on race, status, gender, sexual orientation, age, foreign citizenship, place of birth, wealth, intelligence, health, disability, etc. For example, the Constitution makes explicit distinctions based on race,[459] status as slave,[460] national citizenship,[461] place of birth,[462] and age.[463] (There is no comparable textual disability based on gender or sexual orientation.) In addition, statutory, administrative, and common law necessarily make hundreds of thousands of distinctions between people, rewarding some, and burdening or "discriminating against" others. To cite just a few examples, laws allow or require unequal treatment based on wealth (progressive income tax), intelligence, height, and disability (exemption from military conscription), and mental and bodily health (institutionalization and quarantine). Penal and other laws regulating behavior "discriminate" against those who behave contrary to majoritarian will. Even non-volitional behavior can be subject to sanction, as in tort liability for negligence or, more pointedly, for strict liability. In other words, an equal protection clause does not tell politicians, bureaucrats, and judges what factors may, what factors shall, and what factors shall not be considered in making differentiations between people. Even discrimination based on race is not necessarily incompatible with an equal protection clause: the Virginia Declaration of Rights of 1776 contained an equal protection clause, and Virginia was a slave-owning state.[464]

There is probably a fundamental philosophical reason why neither the Bill of Rights nor the Constitution explicitly protects equality under the law. As was seen in Part One of this book, the Framers were concerned with constructing a new superstate. Their leitmotif was to bridle this new state, to check its powers, to limit intrusions into liberty. Separating powers horizontally and vertically serves this goal. So does the explicit recognition of fundamental rights. Equality rights, on the other hand, do not conceptually reduce the power of the state to interfere with liberty. Rather, equality rights act to diffuse the governmental intrusion, to spread it over

---

[459] Art. I, § 2, cl. 3.
[460] Art. I, § 2, cl. 3.
[461] Art. I, § 3, cl. 3.
[462] Art. II, § 1, cl. 5.
[463] Art. I, § 2, cl. 2.
[464] Hall at pp. 69–70.

more people. Said crassly, equality does not demand that government leave us alone. That's the mission of liberty. Equality insists that government leave me alone unless it also picks on you. When the government will not or cannot do this, invalidation results. But invalidation is the incidental effect, not the theoretical purpose, of equality.

This essential dispersing aspect of equality means that equality functions as private law in the sense that it adjusts private rights and obligations *inter se*. The most obvious examples arise out of the direct application of the equal protection clause to private conduct, such as the invalidation of the race-based covenant in *Shelley v. Kraemer*.[465] But examples are by no means confined to this small sphere. If laws impose burdens only on particular groups, the lifting of those burdens through the medium of equal protection restores equilibrium among private rights. Similarly, if a government program denies benefits to particular groups, the judicial extension of the program to include those groups in effect conforms the distribution of those benefits to the expectations of those private actors who consider themselves constitutionally identical (equal) to those who initially received benefits.

Friedrich Hayek[466] championed the recognition that equality and liberty are at odds with each other. The more society insists on equal treatment, the less people are free to do what they want to do.[467] This observation is not as profound as it first might sound, for in effect it is defining "liberty" as the freedom to discriminate, and this is just one small part of liberty. Further, the alleged conflict between liberty and equality does not necessarily make the protection of equality undesirable. Almost every private law diminishes liberty in the sense that Hayek is talking about.[468] Laws that regulate the landlord-tenant relationship diminish landlords' choices. Laws prescribing that certain actions be in writing, such as wills, diminish freedom in the same sense. Traffic laws impose limitations on freedom. To repeat, liberty is not synonymous with "good" any more than equality is. Neither liberty nor equality enjoys a monopoly on justice.[469]

Government has undergone a dramatic change in function in the last half century or more. In earlier times the federal, state, and local governments

---

[465] 334 U.S. 1 (1948).
[466] Hayek at p. 84.
[467] Fletcher at p. 126.
[468] Hayek is championing *laissez faire*, which he terms "liberty." As the beginning of The Constitution of Liberty exclaims: "We are concerned in this book with that condition of men in which coercion of some by others is reduced as much as is possible in society. This state we shall describe throughout as a state of liberty or freedom." Hayek at p. 11.
[469] As developed and illustrated below, all liberty rights can be recast as equality rights; and, as such, their recognition too must, according to Hayek, be reducing liberty.

provided only essential public services. National defense, uniform currency, etc. were guaranteed by the federal government. State governments supplied regional services, such as justice systems, water projects, and highways. Local governments funded schools, streets, and utilities, to name just a few. As the United States grew wealthy, governments assumed the role of redistributing wealth and of bestowing social benefits far and above those historically possible. This expansion of government caused a metamorphosis in the importance of rights, leading to immense growth in the prominence of equal protection. Whereas traditionally the government was an institution which could, for the most part, only take, in recent years it has become an institution which gives more and more. This extraordinary transformation has, more than anything else, accounted for the ascendancy of equality over liberty in the popular and legal mind.

1. DISCRIMINATION

A number of theories have been advanced to help recognize factors relevant to equal protection. These typically attempt to identify what factors cannot constitutionally be considered by law makers, since the opposite approach—the articulation of all factors that might constitutionally be considered—is hopelessly multifarious. Thus, for this very practical reason, equal protection has come to mean the absence of illegal discrimination.

Some theorists build on Justice Stone's famous footnote four in *United States* v. *Carolene Products Co.*[470] that decries "prejudice against discrete and insular minorities ... which tends... to curtail the operation of those political processes ordinarily to be relied upon to protect minorities."[471] Other theorists endorse a nebulous "anti-subjugation principle," also called the "group-disadvantaging principle."[472] This principle holds that governmental rules, policies, and practices are unconstitutional if they perennially reinforce the subordinate status of any group.[473] Poetic support for the anti-subjugation principle is found in Justice Brennan's observation in *Zobel* v. *Williams*[474] that the "citizenship clause of the fourteenth amendment ... does not allow for degrees of citizenship." (Does this mean that mentally retarded citizens must be allowed to vote, sit on juries, procreate, etc. to the same degree as others?)

Equal protection is difficult to distinguish from due process. Part of the confusion is due to the Supreme Court's avoidance of due process

---

[470] 304 U.S. 144, 152–153 (1938).
[471] E.g., Ely.
[472] E.g., Tribe Vol. II, Chap. 16.
[473] Fiss at pp. 148–156.
[474] 457 U.S. 66, 69 (1982).

terminology ("rights talk"), which is perceived as having been discredited since *Lochner*.[475] Perhaps as a consequence of this perception, the Supreme Court employed equal protection in addition to due process in *Loving v. Virginia*[476] to strike down a law prohibiting interracial marriage. Another reason why equality confounds with liberty is that due process rights can be analyzed from an equality standpoint, and *vice versa*. For example, Eichman, who burned an American flag, can be thought to have been "discriminated against" because those who burned flags of other countries were not punished.[477] Brandenburg, who made disparaging remarks about blacks and Jews, was singled out for prosecution, while those who made supportive remarks were not.[478] Yoder was discriminated against, one might say, for not sending his child to school.[479] Conversely, the issue in equal protection cases can be rephrased in terms of rights talk. The J.A. Croson Company enjoyed a right, one could say, to contract with the City of Richmond.[480] Yick Wo can be said to have had a right to exercise his profession as a laundry operator and consequently enjoyed a right to an exemption from the requirement that laundries operate only in brick buildings.[481]

Luckily for lawyers and judges (and students), the Supreme Court employs the same decisional matrix for alleged violations of equal protection as it does for alleged violations of due process rights. Accordingly, almost all "discriminations" are judged by the rational basis standard. As a practical matter, it makes no difference whether the plaintiff's argument is couched in terms of liberty or equality. As a result, challenges to governmental actions are increasingly being brought on both equal protection and due process grounds.[482]

Perhaps a few additional examples are in order to illustrate this point. In *Kelley v. Johnson*,[483] the Supreme Court heard a complaint from a policeman who claimed a right to grow his hair as long as he wanted. He might just as well have argued that he was being discriminated against as a

---

[475] See, e.g., Williamson v. Lee Optical Co., 348 U.S. 483 (1955).
[476] 388 U.S. 1 (1967): "Marriage is one of the 'basic civil rights of man,' fundamental to our very existence and survival. To deny this fundamental freedom on so unsupportable a basis as the racial classifications embodied in these statutes, classifications so directly subversive of the principle of equality at the heart of the Fourteenth Amendment, is surely to deprive all the State's citizens of liberty without due process of law."
[477] United States v. Eichman, 496 U.S. 310 (1990).
[478] Brandenburg v. Ohio, 395 U.S. 444 (1969).
[479] Wisconsin v. Yoder, 406 U.S. 205 (1972).
[480] City of Richmond v. J.A. Croson, Co., 488 U.S. 469 (1989).
[481] Yick Wo v. Hopkins, 118 U.S. 356 (1886).
[482] E.g., Washington v. Glucksberg, 521 U.S. 702 n. 3 (1997), City of Chicago v. Int'l College of Surgeons, 522 U.S. 156 (1997), and Campbell v. Louisiana, 523 U.S. 392 (1998).
[483] 425 U.S. 238 (1976).

member of a group of men who belonged to a long-haired counterculture. Either way the courts would subject his claim to "minimal scrutiny." In *Bowers v. Hardwick*,[484] the petitioner challenged a state law that made sodomy illegal. He claimed that he had a constitutional right to sodomize his boyfriend in the privacy of his home. He might as well have argued, but did not, that the law discriminated against him as a homosexual male because he engaged in this behavior. Either way, minimum scrutiny would be used to judge his challenge. In *Lawrence v. Texas*, the case that overruled *Bowers v. Hardwick*, the appellants raised both the due process and equal protection clauses, but the Supreme Court, noting that the two clauses "are linked in important respects," based is decision solely on the equal protection clause, holding that the statute in issue "furthers no legitimate state interest which can justify its intrusion into the personal and private life of the individual." This sounds, at least from the wording, like an application of minimum scrutiny.[485]

The equal protection clause is found in the last clause of section 1 of the Fourteenth Amendment:

No State shall ... deny any person within its jurisdiction the equal protection of the laws.

The equal protection clause of the Fourteenth Amendment is thus textually directed to the states, not to the federal government. The historical reason for this is that the Fourteenth Amendment, like the other Civil War Amendments (Thirteenth and Fifteenth), was aimed at eradicating the institution of slavery, which only existed in state law. The Thirteenth Amendment specifically abolished slavery. The Fourteenth and Fifteenth Amendments dealt with the anticipated reluctance of the former slave states to submit to the will of the vast majority of Americans. Thus, the Fourteenth Amendment makes "[a]ll persons born in the United States ... citizens of the United States and of the State wherein they reside." The Fifteenth Amendment adds the arguably superfluous provision that "the right of citizens of the United States to vote shall not be denied or abridged by the United States or by any State on account of race, color, or previous condition of servitude."

The Supreme Court has interpreted the due process clause of the Fifth Amendment to contain an equal protection clause directed at the federal government.[486] The content of the federal and state protections are not necessarily identical, however.[487]

---

[484] 478 U.S. 573 (1986).
[485] But see Chemerinsky, Constitutional Law at p. 846.
[486] See Bolling v. Sharpe, 347 U.S. 497 (1954).
[487] Hampton v. Mow Sun Wong, 426 U.S. 88 (1976).

a.   *De jure* Discrimination

The reigning doctrine of the Supreme Court looks not to the discriminatory effect of governmental action, but to its purpose, and asks if the purpose is to discriminate "invidiously."[488] According to the Supreme Court, intentional or "*de jure*" discrimination can be explicit in the governmental action (discriminatory "on its face"), or it may be implicit in the action if its enactment or enforcement is tainted by an invidious purpose. The discussion below follows this distinction.

i. Explicit Discriminations

Explicit discriminations are relatively easy to spot. Consider, for example, the case that follows. On March 21, 1942, Congress enacted legislation making it a crime to violate an order issued by a military commander pursuant to specific authority. Three days later, the military commander of the western defense command ordered imposition of a curfew on all persons of Japanese ancestry living on the West Coast.

On May 3, 1942, the same military commander issued an exclusion order, requiring persons of Japanese descent, whether or not they were United States citizens, to leave their homes on the West Coast and report to "Assembly Centers." While some detainees were released from these centers on condition that they remain outside the prohibited zone, others were shipped to "Relocation Centers," which they were prohibited from leaving without permission of the military commander.

Korematsu, a U.S. citizen of Japanese descent, was tried and convicted of remaining in his home contrary to the exclusion order.

CASE: **Korematsu v. United States**
323 U.S. 214 (1944)

MR. JUSTICE BLACK delivered the opinion of the Court.

It should be noted, to begin with, that all legal restrictions which curtail the civil rights of a single racial group are immediately suspect. That is not to say that all such restrictions are unconstitutional. It is to say that courts must subject them to the most rigid scrutiny. Pressing public necessity may sometimes justify the existence of such restrictions; racial antagonism never can....

In the light of the principles we announced in the *Hirabayashi* case, we are unable to conclude that it was beyond the war power

---

[488] Washington v. Davis, 426 U.S. 229 (1976).

of Congress and the Executive to exclude those of Japanese ancestry from the West Coast war area at the time they did. True, exclusion from the area in which one's home is located is a far greater deprivation than constant confinement to the home from 8 p.m. to 6 a.m. Nothing short of apprehension by the proper military authorities of the gravest imminent danger to the public safety can constitutionally justify either. But exclusion from a threatened area, no less than curfew, has a definite and close relationship to the prevention of espionage and sabotage. The military authorities, charged with the primary responsibility of defending our shores, concluded that curfew provided inadequate protection and ordered exclusion....

Here, as in the *Hirabayashi* case,

> ... we cannot reject as unfounded the judgment of the military authorities and of Congress that there were disloyal members of that population, whose number and strength could not be precisely and quickly ascertained. We cannot say that the war-making branches of the Government did not have ground for believing that in a critical hour such persons could not readily be isolated and separately dealt with, and constituted a menace to the national defense and safety, which demanded that prompt and adequate measures be taken to guard against it.

Like curfew, exclusion of those of Japanese origin was deemed necessary because of the presence of an unascertained number of disloyal members of the group, most of whom we have no doubt were loyal to this country. It was because we could not reject the finding of the military authorities that it was impossible to bring about an immediate segregation of the disloyal from the loyal that we sustained the validity of the curfew order as applying to the whole group. In the instant case, temporary exclusion of the entire group was rested by the military on the same ground. ... That there were members of the group who retained loyalties to Japan has been confirmed by investigations made subsequent to the exclusion. Approximately five thousand American citizens of Japanese ancestry refused to swear unqualified allegiance to the United States and to renounce allegiance to the Japanese Emperor, and several thousand evacuees requested repatriation to Japan.

We uphold the exclusion order as of the time it was made and when the petitioner violated it. [In] doing so, we are not unmindful of the hardships imposed by it upon a large group of American citizens. But hardships are part of war, and war is an aggregation of hardships. All citizens alike, both in and out of uniform, feel the impact of war in greater or lesser measure. Citizenship has its responsibilities as well as its privileges, and in time of war the burden is always heavier. Compulsory exclusion of large groups of citizens from their homes, except under circumstances of direst emergency and peril, is inconsistent with our basic governmental institutions. But when under conditions of modern warfare our shores are threatened by hostile forces, the power to protect must be commensurate with the threatened danger....

It is said that we are dealing here with the case of imprisonment of a citizen in a concentration camp solely because of his ancestry, without evidence or inquiry concerning his loyalty and good disposition towards the United States. Our task would be simple, our duty clear, were this a case involving the imprisonment of a loyal citizen in a concentration camp because of racial prejudice. Regardless of the true nature of the assembly and relocation centers—and we deem it unjustifiable to call them concentration camps with all the ugly connotations that term implies—we are dealing specifically with nothing but an exclusion order. To cast this case into outlines of racial prejudice, without reference to the real military dangers which were presented, merely confuses the issue. Korematsu was not excluded from the Military Area because of hostility to him or his race. He was excluded because we are at war with the Japanese Empire, because the properly constituted military authorities feared an invasion of our West Coast and felt constrained to take proper security measures, because they decided that the military urgency of the situation demanded that all citizens of Japanese ancestry be segregated from the West Coast temporarily, and finally, because Congress, reposing its confidence in this time of war in our military leaders—as inevitably it must—determined that they should have the power to do just this. There was evidence of disloyalty on the part of some, the military authorities considered that the need for action was great, and time was short. We cannot—by availing ourselves of the calm perspective of hindsight—now say that at that time these actions were unjustified.

Mr. Justice Jackson, dissenting....

It would be impracticable and dangerous idealism to expect or insist that each specific military command in an area of probable operations will conform to conventional tests of constitutionality. When an area is so beset that it must be put under military control at all, the paramount consideration is that its measures be successful, rather than legal....

But if we cannot confine military expedients by the Constitution, neither would I distort the Constitution to approve all that the military may deem expedient. This is what the Court appears to be doing, whether consciously or not....

The [limitations] under which courts always will labor in examining the necessity for a military order are illustrated by this case. How does the Court know that these orders have a reasonable basis in necessity? No evidence whatever on that subject has been taken by this or any other court....

Much is said of the danger to liberty from the Army program for deporting and detaining these citizens of Japanese extraction. But a judicial construction of the due process clause that will sustain this order is a farm more subtle blow to liberty than the promulgation of the order itself. A military order, however unconstitutional, is not apt to last longer than the military emergency. Even during that period a succeeding commander may revoke it all. But once a judicial opinion rationalizes such an order to show that it conforms to the Constitution, or rather rationalizes the Constitution to show that the Constitution sanctions such an order, the Court for all time has validated the principle of racial discrimination in criminal procedure and of transplanting American citizens. The principle then lies about like a loaded weapon ready for the hand of any authority that can bring forward a plausible claim of an urgent need. Every repetition imbeds that principle more deeply in our law and thinking and expands it to new purposes....

I should hold that a civil court cannot be made to enforce an order which violates constitutional limitations even if it is a reasonable exercise of military authority. The courts can exercise only the judicial power, can apply only law, and must abide by the Constitution, or they cease to be civil courts and become instruments of military policy.

...

My duties as a justice as I see them do not require me to make a military judgment as to whether General DeWitt's evacuation and detention program was a reasonable military necessity. I do not suggest that the courts should have attempted to interfere with the Army in carrying out its task. But I do not think they may be asked to execute a military expedient that has no place in law under the Constitution I would reverse the judgment and discharge the prisoner.

[A concurring opinion and two dissenting opinions are omitted.]

[Justice Robert Jackson, who wrote the dissent quoted above, was the chief prosecutor for the United States at the Nuremberg trials.]

Both the Japanese evacuation and the decision in *Korematsu* have been roundly criticized.[489] In 1984, a federal judge overturned Korematsu's conviction on the ground that the government had knowingly withheld information from the courts.[490] Four years later Congress acknowledged "the fundamental injustice" of the evacuation and provided restitution.[491] *Korematsu* was the last occasion on which the Supreme Court upheld a measure intentionally disadvantaging a racial group.

To this point the discussion has mostly talked about state action that "penalizes" or "discriminates against" members of groups. But what of legislation that confers benefits? What of government programs that grant scholarships only to good students, confer tax exemptions on parents, and reserve welfare to the truly needy? (Incidentally, these can also be seen as penalizing poor students, non-parents, and the wealthy, respectively.) As should be clear from the discussion so far, each of these governmental actions will be judged under minimum scrutiny. That means, assuming the action is not *ultra vires*, that the program will be upheld if it "reasonably" or "rationally" furthers the relevant governmental goal.

What of programs that benefit only members of suspect classes? How about a state scholarship program limited to African Americans, or a statute exempting Japanese or Roman Catholic Americans from capital punishment, or providing that Jews need only work 20 hour weeks in federal jobs for the same pay? (Incidentally, these can also be seen as penalizing non-African Americans, non-Japanese, non-Roman Catholics, and non-Jews, respectively.) Must they too withstand strict scrutiny? That was the question before the Supreme Court in the following case.

CASE: **City of Richmond v. J.A. Croson Co.**
488 U.S. 469 (1989)

JUSTICE O'CONNOR announced the judgment of the Court and delivered the opinion of the Court with respect to Parts I, III-B, and IV, an opinion with respect to Part II, in which

---

[489] E.g., Daniels.
[490] Korematsu v. United States, 584 F. Supp. 1406 (N.D. Cal. 1984).
[491] 102 Stat. 903 (1988).

THE CHIEF JUSTICE [REHNQUIST] and JUSTICE WHITE join, and an opinion with respect to Parts III-A and V, in which THE CHIEF JUSTICE [REHNQUIST], JUSTICE WHITE, and JUSTICE KENNEDY join....

I

[The Minority Business Enterprise] Plan[492] was adopted by the Richmond City Council after a public hearing.... Seven members of the public spoke to the merits of the ordinance: five were in opposition. two in favor. Proponents of the set-aside provision relied on a study which indicated that, while the general population of Richmond was 50% black, only 0.67% of the city's prime construction contracts had been awarded to minority businesses in the 5-year period from 1978 to 1983. It was also established that a variety of contractors' associations [had] virtually no minority businesses within their membership. The city's legal counsel indicated his view that the ordinance was constitutional under this Court's decision in *Fullilove v. Klutznick*.[493] Councilperson Marsh, a proponent of the ordinance, made the following statement:

> "There is some information, however, that I want to make sure that we put in the record. [I] can say without equivocation, that the general conduct of the construction industry in this area, and the State, and around the nation, is one in which race discrimination and exclusion on the basis of race is widespread."

There was no direct evidence of race discrimination on the part of the city in letting contracts or any evidence that the city's prime contractors had discriminated against minority-owned subcontractors. [The case was brought by a contractor whose low bid on a city project was not accepted because of failure to comply with the Plan's requirements. The District Court upheld the Plan, but

---

[492] The Richmond City Council adopted its program in 1983, modeled on the federal one upheld in Fullilove. It required prime contractors on city projects to subcontract at least 30% of the dollar amount of the contract to one or more Minority Business Enterprises (MBEs). Borrowing the definition used by Congress in Fullilove, the Richmond Plan defined an MBE as "[a] business at least [51%] of which is owned and controlled [by] minority group members" and identified eligible minority groups as "Blacks, Spanish-speaking, Orientals, Indians, Eskimos, or Aleuts." There was no geographic limit to the Plan; an otherwise qualified MBE from anywhere in the nation could avail itself of the 30% set-aside. Regulations under the Plan provided that waivers would be granted "in exceptional circumstances," when "every feasible attempt has been made to comply, and it [has been] demonstrated that sufficient, relevant, qualified [MBEs] are unavailable or unwilling to participate in the contract to enable meeting the 30% MBE goal."

[493] 448 U.S. 448 (1980).

the Court of Appeals struck it down as violating both prongs of equal protection scrutiny.] We affirm....

II
...

[That] Congress may identify and redress the effects of society-wide discrimination does not mean that, a fortiori, the States and their political subdivisions are free to decide that such remedies are appropriate. Section 1 of the Fourteenth Amendment is an explicit constraint on state power, and the States must undertake any remedial efforts in accordance with that provision. To hold otherwise would be to cede control over the content of the Equal Protection Clause to the 50 state legislatures and their myriad political subdivisions. The mere recitation of a benign or compensatory purpose for the use of a racial classification would essentially entitle the States to exercise the full power of Congress under § 5 of the Fourteenth Amendment and insulate any racial classification from judicial scrutiny under § 1. We believe that such a result would be contrary to the intentions of the Framers of the Fourteenth Amendment, who desired to place clear limits on the States' use of race as a criterion for legislative action.... As a matter of state law, the city of Richmond has legislative authority over its procurement policies, and can use its spending powers to remedy private discrimination, if it identifies that discrimination with the particularity required by the Fourteenth Amendment. Thus, if the city could show that it had essentially become a "passive participant" in a system of racial exclusion practiced by elements of the local construction industry, we think it clear that the city could take affirmative steps to dismantle such a system. It is beyond dispute that any public entity, state or federal, has a compelling interest in assuring that public dollars, drawn from the tax contributions of all citizens, do not serve to finance the evil of private prejudice.

III
A

... [T]he purpose of strict scrutiny is to "smoke out" illegitimate uses of race by assuring that the legislative body is pursuing a goal important enough to warrant use of a highly suspect tool. The test also ensures that the means chosen "fit" this compelling goal so closely that there is little or no possibility that the motive for the classification was illegitimate racial prejudice or stereotype. Classification based on race carry a danger of stigmatic harm. Unless they are strictly reserved for remedial settings, they may in fact promote notions of racial inferiority and lead to a politics of racial hostility. We thus reaffirm the view expressed by the plurality in *Wygant* that the standard of review under the Equal Protection Clause is not dependent on the race of those burdened or benefited by a particular classification.... In this case, blacks constitute approximately 50% of the population of the city of Richmond. Five of the nine seats on the city council are held by blacks. The concern that a political majority will more easily act to the disadvantage of a minority based on unwarranted assumptions or incomplete facts would seem to militate for, not against, the application of heightened judicial scrutiny in this case.

B

... While there is no doubt that the sorry history of both private and public discrimination in this country has contributed to a lack of opportunities for black entrepreneurs, this observation, standing alone, cannot justify a rigid racial quota in the awarding of public contracts in Richmond, Virginia. It is sheer speculation how many minority firms there would be in Richmond absent past societal discrimination ... Defining these sorts of injuries as "identified discrimination" would give local governments license to create a patchwork of racial preferences based on statistical generalizations about any particular field of endeavor. These defects are readily apparent in this case. The 30% quota cannot in any realistic sense be tied to any injury suffered by anyone....

...

In sum, none of the evidence presented by the city points to any identified discrimination in the Richmond construction industry. We, therefore, hold that the city has failed to demonstrate a compelling interest in apportioning public contracting opportunities on the basis of race. To accept Richmond's claim that past societal discrimination alone can serve as the basis for rigid racial preferences would be to open the door to competing claims for "remedial relief" for every disadvantaged group. The dream of a Nation of equal citizens in a society where race is irrelevant to personal opportunity and achievement would be lost in a mosaic of shifting preferences based on inherently unmeasurable claims of past wrongs. [See *Bakke* (Powell, J.).] We think such a result would be contrary to both the letter and spirit of [equal protection]. The foregoing analysis applies only to the inclusion of blacks within the Richmond set-aside program. There is absolutely no evidence of past discrimination against Spanish-speaking, Oriental, Indian, Eskimo, or Aleut persons in any aspect of the Richmond construction industry. [It] may well be that Richmond has never had an Aleut or Eskimo citizen. The random inclusion of racial groups that, as a practical matter, may never have suffered from discrimination in the construction industry in Richmond suggests that perhaps the city's purpose was not in fact to remedy past discrimination. If a 30% set-aside was "narrowly tailored" to compensate black contractors for past discrimination, one may legitimately ask why they are forced to share this "remedial relief" with an Aleut citizen who moves to Richmond tomorrow? The gross overinclusiveness of Richmond's racial preference strongly impugns the city's claim of remedial motivation.

...

V

Nothing we say today precludes a state or local entity from taking action to rectify the effects of identified discrimination within its jurisdiction. If the city of Richmond had evidence before it that nonminority contractors were systematically excluding minority businesses from subcontracting opportunities, it could take action to end the discriminatory exclusion. Where there is a significant statistical disparity between the number of qualified minority contractors willing and able to perform a particular service and the number of such contractors actually engaged by the locality or the locality's prime contractors, an inference of discriminatory exclusion could arise. Under such circumstances, the city could act to dismantle the closed business system by taking appropriate measures against those who discriminate on the basis of race or other illegitimate criteria. In the extreme case, some form of narrowly tailored racial preference might be necessary to break down patterns of deliberate exclusion.... The city points to no evidence that qualified minority contractors have been passed over for city contracts or subcontracts, either as a group or in any individual case. Under such circumstances, it is simply impossible to say that the city has demonstrated "a strong basis in evidence for its conclusion that remedial action was necessary." *Wygant*.[494] Proper findings in this regard are necessary to define both the scope of the injury and the extent of the remedy necessary to cure its effects. Such findings also serve to assure all citizens that the deviation from the norm of equal treatment of all racial and ethnic groups is a temporary matter, a measure taken in the service of the goal of equality itself. Absent such findings, there is a danger that a racial classification is merely the product of unthinking stereotypes or a form of racial politics. [Because Richmond] has failed to identify the need for remedial action in the awarding

---

[494] 476 U.S., at 277.

of its public construction contracts, its treatment of its citizens on a racial basis violates the dictates of [equal protection].
[Affirmed.]
[Concurring and dissenting opinions omitted.]

---

ii. Implicit Discriminations

Laws that are racially neutral on their face may, nevertheless, constitute *de jure* discriminations in violation of the equal protection clause if their enactment or enforcement is motivated by racial discrimination. The leading case for the former proposition (discriminatorily motivated enactment) is *Gomillion* v. *Lightfoot*.[495] There city boundaries were changed with the effect that nearly all black voters were removed from the city. Although the challengers found no "smoking gun," the city was unable to offer any constitutional explanation for its suspicious action, and the re-districting was declared unconstitutional.

The leading case for the second proposition (discriminatory enforcement) is *Yick Wo* v. *Hopkins*,[496] where ordinances of the City and County of San Francisco required that, to avoid fire, laundries be located in brick buildings. The ordinances allowed the board of supervisors to grant exemptions. Tellingly, the board granted exemptions to all but one of the non-Chinese applicants, but denied over 200 applications filed by Chinese persons. The Supreme Court unanimously reversed Yick Wo's conviction for operating a laundry without a license, holding:

> [T]he facts shown establish an administration directed so exclusively against a particular class of persons as to warrant and require the conclusion, that, whatever may have been the intent of the ordinances as adopted, they are applied by the public authorities charged with the administration, and thus representing the State itself, with a mind so unequal and oppressive as to amount to a practical denial by the State of equal protection of the laws.[497]

Over the course of the century since *Yick Wo* was decided, the Supreme Court has refined its enquiry somewhat. Nowadays, if a challenger proves a substantial disproportionate racial impact in the administration of a racially neutral law, the burden shifts to the state to show that the impact is due to lawful, constitutional factors.[498] This approach has led to a

---

[495] 364 U.S. 339 (1960).
[496] 118 U.S. 356 (1886).
[497] At p. 373.
[498] Castaneda v. Partida, 430 U.S. 482 (1977).

prohibition against use of peremptory challenges on the basis of race and gender.[499]

b.   *De Facto* Discrimination

What of laws and practices that are racially neutral on their face, in their motivation, and in their administration, but that still have a racially disproportionate impact? For example, what of college admission criteria and height exemptions from military conscription that disfavor a disproportionately large percentage of American blacks?

CASE: **Washington v. Davis**
426 U.S. 229 (1976)

MR. JUSTICE WHITE delivered the opinion of the Court.

This case involves the validity of a qualifying test administered to applicants for positions as police officers in the District of Columbia Metropolitan Police Department. The test was sustained by the District Court but invalidated by the Court of Appeals. We are in agreement with the District Court and hence reverse the judgment of the Court of Appeals....

[Respondents, unsuccessful black applicants for positions on the police force, claimed that a test measuring verbal ability, vocabulary, and reading comprehension unconstitutionally discriminated against them. According to the district court, respondents' evidence supported the conclusion that a higher percentage of blacks than whites failed the test, and that the test, and that the test had not been validated to establish its reliability for measuring subsequent job performance. Respondents made no claim that administration of the test constituted an "intentional" or "purposeful" act of discrimination.]

The central purpose of the Equal Protection Clause of the Fourteenth Amendment is the prevention of official conduct discriminating on the basis of race. It is also true that the Due Process Clause of the Fifth Amendment contains an equal protection component prohibiting the United States from invidiously discriminating between individuals or groups. *Bolling* v. *Sharpe*.[500] But our cases have not embraced the proposition that a law or

---

[499] Batson v. Kentucky, 476 U.S. 79 (1986); J.E.B. v. Alabama, 511 U.S. 127 (1994).
[500] 347 U.S. 497 (1954).

other official act, without regard to whether it reflects a racially discriminatory purpose, is unconstitutional solely because it has a racially disproportionate impact.

Almost 100 years ago, *Strauder* v. *West Virginia*,[501] established that the exclusion of Negroes from grand and petit juries in criminal proceedings violated the Equal Protection Clause, but the fact that a particular jury or a series of juries does not statistically reflect the racial composition of the community does not in itself make out an invidious discrimination forbidden by the Clause....

The rule is the same in other contexts. *Wright* v. *Rockefeller*[502] upheld a New York congressional apportionment statute against claims that district lines had been racially gerrymandered. The challenged districts were made up predominantly of whites or of minority races, and their boundaries were irregularly drawn. The challengers did not prevail because they failed to prove that the New York Legislature "was either motivated by racial considerations or in fact drew the districts on racial lines"; the plaintiffs had not shown that the statute "was the product of a state contrivance to segregate on the basis of race or place of origin."...

The school desegregation cases have also adhered to the basic equal protection principle that the invidious quality of a law claimed to be racially discriminatory must ultimately be traced to a racially discriminatory purpose. That there are both predominantly black and predominantly white schools in a community is not alone violative of the Equal Protection Clause. The essential element of de jure segregation is "a current condition of segregation resulting from intentional state action." *Keyes* v. *School Dist. No. 1*[503]....

This is not to say that the necessary discriminatory racial purpose must be express or appear on the face of the statute, or that a law's disproportionate impact is irrelevant in cases involving Constitution-based claims of racial discrimination. A statute, otherwise neutral on its face, must not be applied so as invidiously to discriminate on the basis of race. *Yick Wo* v. *Hopkins*[504]....

Nor on the facts of the case before us would the disproportionate impact of [the test] warrant the conclusion that it is a purposeful device to discriminate against Negroes and hence an infringement of the constitutional rights of respondents as well as other black applicants. As we have said, the test is neutral on its face and rationally may be said to serve a purpose the Government is

---

[501] 100 U.S. 303 (1880).
[502] 376 U.S. 52 (1964).
[503] 413 U.S. 189, 205 (1973).
[504] 118 U.S. 356 (1886).

constitutionally empowered to pursue. Even agreeing with the District Court that the differential racial effect of [the test] called for further inquiry, we think the District Court correctly held that the affirmative efforts of the Metropolitan Police Department to recruit black officers, the changing racial composition of the recruit classes and of the force in general, and the relationship of the test to the training program negated any inference that the Department discriminated on the basis of race or that "a police officer qualifies on the color of his skin rather than ability."...

A rule that a statute designed to serve neutral ends is nevertheless invalid, absent compelling justification, if in practice it benefits or burdens one race more than another would be far reaching and would raise serious questions about, and perhaps invalidate, a whole range of tax, welfare, public service, regulatory, and licensing statutes that may be more burdensome to the poor and to the average black than to the more affluent white....

[Concurring and dissenting opinions omitted.]

---

2. Protected Groups

Every external act at any level of government might theoretically be challenged by a person who claims unfair, discriminatory, that is, unconstitutional treatment. Providing that the person meets "standing" and other procedural prerequisites, the judicial constitutional enquiry will remain at the level of minimum scrutiny unless the treatment being challenged implicates certain rights that the claimant enjoys as an individual or as a member of a group. Rights enjoyed by persons who do not claim membership in a protected group are treated above under due process. There, as was shown, higher scrutiny can be triggered by the invocation of fundamental rights (strict scrutiny) of certain other, quasi-fundamental rights (intermediate scrutiny).

When group rights are involved, the same matrix of levels of review is employed. Strict scrutiny has been reserved for challenges involving so-called suspect classes. Race, national origin, and non-American citizenship have been held by the Supreme Court to be suspect classes, although, for reasons noted below, non-American citizenship ("alienage") is not employed as a suspect class when judging the constitutionality of federal measures. As detailed in the preceding section, *de jure* classifications (both discrimination and "benign" discrimination) are judged under strict scrutiny.

As with cases involving due process rights, equal protection has its own intermediate review. In the due process context, intermediate review is employed when quasi-fundamental rights are invoked. In the equal protection context, intermediate review is employed to judge the constitutionality of *de jure* classifications pertaining to quasi-suspect groups. Gender and illegitimacy are the only classifications presently entitled to intermediate review under the equal protection clause.

The discussion below begins with suspect classifications before turning to the quasi-suspect variety.

a. Suspect Classifications

The Supreme Court employs strict scrutiny when the government[505] discriminates against a "suspect class." Although the Fourteenth Amendment provides few textual clues as to what classifications or discriminations were intended to be prohibited, the Fifteenth Amendment does: race, color, or previous condition of servitude. As a historical matter, the "race" referred to mean the Negro race. "Color" meant the color of Negroes' skin. Discriminations against African American blacks are therefore particularly suspect from a historical standpoint. Courts have held almost all discriminations based on race or "ethnicity" (the currently preferred term) to be inherently suspect.[506] One of very few exceptions to this practice was made in *Morton* v. *Mancari*,[507] which upheld job preferences for American Indians.

Perhaps the most profound use of strict scrutiny in the equal protection context has been in cases involving education. *Missouri ex rel. Gaines* v. *Canada*[508] redressed the refusal of the University of Missouri for racial reasons to admit Lloyd Gaines to the state's public law school, offering instead to provide for his matriculation in an adjoining state. Missouri tried unsuccessfully to invoke the "separate but equal" doctrine of *Plessy* v. *Ferguson*.[509] That doctrine was expressly overruled in the following decision, which ruled that separate public facilities, especially schools, are inherently unequal.

CASE: Brown v. Board of Education [Brown I]
347 U.S. 483 (1954)

MR. CHIEF JUSTICE WARREN delivered the [unanimous] opinion of the Court.

---

[505] See discussion of "state action" above.
[506] E.g., Hernandez v. Texas, 347 U.S. 475 (1954).
[507] 417 U.S. 535 (1974).
[508] 305 U.S. 337 (1938).
[509] 163 U.S. 537 (1896).

These cases come to us from the States of Kansas, South Carolina, Virginia, and Delaware. [In] each of the cases, minors of the Negro race [seek] the aid of the courts in obtaining admission to the public schools of their community on a nonsegregated basis. In each instance, they had been denied admission to schools attended by white children under laws requiring or permitting segregation according to race. [In most of the cases, the courts below denied relief, relying on] the so-called "separate but equal" doctrine announced by this Court in *Plessy v. Ferguson*.[510] [The] plaintiffs contend that segregated public schools are not "equal" and cannot be made "equal," and that hence they are deprived of the equal protection of the laws....

In the first cases in this Court construing the Fourteenth Amendment, decided shortly after its adoption, the Court interpreted it as proscribing all state-imposed discriminations against the Negro race. The doctrine of "separate but equal" did not make its appearance in this Court until 1896 in [*Plessy*] involving not education but transportation....

In approaching this problem, we cannot turn the clock back to 1868 when the Amendment was adopted, or even to 1896 when *Plessy* was written. We must consider public education in the light of its full development and its present place in American life throughout the Nation. Only in this way can it be determined if segregation in public schools deprives these plaintiffs of [equal protection]. Today, education is perhaps the most important function of state and local governments. Compulsory school attendance laws and the great expenditures for education both demonstrate our recognition of the importance of education to our democratic society. It is required in the performance of our most basic public responsibilities, even service in the armed forces. It is the very foundation of good citizenship. Today it is a principal instrument in awakening the child to cultural values, in preparing him for later professional training, and in helping him to adjust normally to his environment. In these days, it is doubtful that any child may reasonably be expected to succeed in life if he is denied the opportunity of an education. Such an opportunity, where the state has undertaken to provide it, is a right which must be made available to all on equal terms.

We come then to the question presented: Does segregation of children in public schools solely on the basis of race, even though the physical facilities and other "tangible" factors may be

---

[510] 163 U.S. 537.

equal, deprive the children of the minority group of equal educational opportunities? We believe that it does. In [*Sweatt*] this Court relied in large part on "those qualities which are incapable of objective measurement but which make for greatness in a law school." In *McLaurin*, the Court [again] resorted to intangible considerations: "[the] ability to study, to engage in discussions and exchange views with other students, and, in general, to learn [the] profession." Such considerations apply with added force to children in grade and high schools. To separate them from others of similar age and qualifications solely because of their race generates a feeling of inferiority as to their status in the community that may affect their hearts and minds in a way unlikely ever to be undone. The effect of this separation on their educational opportunities was well stated by a finding in the Kansas case by a court which nevertheless felt compelled to rule against the Negro plaintiffs: "Segregation of white and colored children in public schools has a detrimental effect upon the colored children. The impact is greater when it has the sanction of the law; for the policy of separating the races is usually interpreted as denoting the inferiority of the negro group. A sense of inferiority affects the motivation of a child to learn. Segregation with the sanction of law, therefore, has a tendency to [retard] the educational and mental development of negro children and to deprive them of some of the benefits they would receive in a [racially] integrated school system." Whatever may have been the extent of psychological knowledge at the time of [*Plessy*], this finding is amply supported by modern authority. Any language in [*Plessy*] contrary to this finding is rejected.

We conclude that in the field of public education the doctrine of "separate but equal" has no place. Separate educational facilities are inherently unequal. Therefore, we hold that the plaintiffs and others similarly situated for whom the actions have been brought are, by reason of the segregation complained of, deprived of [equal protection]. This disposition makes unnecessary any discussion whether such segregation also violates [due process]. Because these are class actions, because of the wide applicability of this decision, and because of the great variety of local conditions, the formulation of decrees in these cases presents problems of considerable complexity. On reargument, the consideration of appropriate relief was necessarily subordinated to the primary question—the constitutionality of segregation in public education. We have now announced that such segregation is a denial of [equal protection]. In order that we may have the full assistance of the parties in formulating decrees, the cases will be restored to the docket, and the parties are requested to present further argument on Questions 4 and 5 previously propounded by the Court for [reargument]

It is so ordered.

CASE: Brown v. Board of Education [Brown II]
349 U.S. 294 (1955)

MR. CHIEF JUSTICE WARREN delivered the opinion of the Court.

These cases were decided on May 17, 1954. The [unanimous] opinions of that date, declaring the fundamental principle that racial discrimination in public education is unconstitutional, are incorporated herein by reference. All provisions of federal, state, or local law requiring or permitting such discrimination must yield to this principle. There remains for consideration the manner in which relief is to be accorded....

Full implementation of these constitutional principles may require solution of varied local school problems. School authorities have the primary responsibility for elucidating, assessing, and solving these problems; courts will have to consider whether the action of school authorities constitutes good faith implementation of the governing constitutional principles. Because of their proximity to local conditions and the possible need for further hearings, the courts which originally heard these cases can best perform this judicial appraisal. Accordingly, we believe it appropriate to remand the cases to those courts. In fashioning and effectuating the decrees, the courts will be guided by equitable principles. Traditionally, equity has been characterized by a practical flexibility in shaping its remedies and by a facility for adjusting and reconciling public and private needs. These cases call for the exercise of these traditional attributes of equity power. At stake is the personal interest of the plaintiffs in admission to public schools as soon as practicable on a nondiscriminatory basis. To effectuate this interest may call for elimination of a variety of obstacles in making the transition to school systems operated in accordance with the constitutional principles set forth in [Brown I]. Courts of equity may properly take into account the public interest in the elimination of such obstacles in a systematic and effective manner. But it should go without saying that the vitality of these constitutional principles cannot be allowed to yield simply because of disagreement with them.

While giving weight to these public and private considerations, the courts will require that the defendants make a prompt and reasonable start toward full compliance with [*Brown I*]. Once such a start has been made, the courts may find that additional time is necessary to carry out the ruling in an effective manner. The burden rests upon the defendants to establish that such time is necessary in the public interest and is consistent with good faith compliance at the earliest practicable date. To that end, the courts may consider problems related to administration, arising from the physical condition of the school plant, the school transportation system, personnel, revision of school districts and attendance areas into compact units to achieve a system of determining admission to the public schools on a nonracial basis, and revision of local laws and regulations which may be necessary in solving the foregoing problems. They will also consider the adequacy of any plans the defendants may propose to meet these problems and to effectuate a transition to a racially nondiscriminatory school system. During this period of transition, the courts will retain jurisdiction of these cases. The [cases are accordingly remanded to the lower courts to take such proceedings and enter such orders and decrees consistent with this opinion as are necessary and proper to admit to public schools on a racially nondiscriminatory basis with all deliberate speed the parties to these cases]....

In response to *Brown*, school districts launched campaigns to integrate segregated schools. Sometimes desegregation has been voluntarily. More often than not it has been court ordered. As a practical matter, desegregation of public schools has involved the bussing of pupils away from neighborhood schools. The Supreme Court has never ruled that schools have an affirmative duty to remedy *de facto* school segregation. However, the Supreme Court has allowed the lower courts to use certain evidentiary presumptions that make intentional segregation easier to prove.[511]

A mother of a little boy in Kentucky has sued because her son is not allowed to attend his neighborhood school because he is white. Is this

---

[511] See Keyes v. School Dist. No. 1, 413 U.S. 189 (1973). In so doing it has "legislated" guidelines for school administrators and judges. See Swann v. Charlotte-Mecklenburg Board of Education, 402 U.S. 1 (1971).

constitutional? See *Parents Involved in Community Schools* v. *Seattle School District No. 1*.[512]

American citizenship has been recognized as a "suspect class" when employed by the states, but not when employed by the federal government.[513] The reason for this distinction lies in the bestowal of plenary power on the federal government over the admission and exclusion of aliens. According to this reasoning, if the states could penalize ("discriminate against") someone based on her lack of U.S. citizenship, then they could do through the back door what they could not do through the front, that is, regulate immigration.[514]

The recognition of alienage as a suspect class has meant that non-U.S. citizens are automatically eligible for benefits conferred by state and local agencies unless the agencies can prove that the discrimination furthers a compelling state interest. This is virtually impossible to do. Consequently, foreigners enjoy rights equal to American citizens to receive state welfare benefits,[515] to gain admission to professions regulated by the states, including the legal profession,[516] to demand financial assistance from the states for higher education,[517] and to secure employment in most state civil service positions.[518] The only compelling interest that the Supreme Court has recognized to date is the protection of "democratic political institutions" from which aliens have traditionally been excluded. (Ironically, this exclusion is one of the reasons for granting "suspect" status to aliens; see Justice Stone's remark above). Accordingly, non-citizens may be denied the right to vote, to stand for public office, and to serve on juries. The Supreme Court has upheld narrowly drawn exclusions of non-citizens from the professions of police officer and school teacher.[519]

b.   Quasi-Suspect Classifications

Intermediate scrutiny in the equal protection context is employed for discrimination against illegitimate children and discrimination based on gender. Because the interests of the state need only rise to the level of important (not compelling) state interests, and because the "fit" between ends and means need only be substantial (not necessary), the state enjoys

---

[512] 551 U.S.___(2007).
[513] Mathews v. Diaz, 426 U.S. 67 (1976), upholding federal denials of Medicare under the rational basis test.
[514] See Toll v. Moreno, 458 U.S. 1 (1982).
[515] Graham v. Richardson, 403 U.S. 365 (1971).
[516] In re Griffiths, 413 U.S. 717 (1973).
[517] Nyquist v. Mauclet, 432 U.S. 1 (1977).
[518] Sugarman v. Dougall, 413 U.S. 634 (1973).
[519] Foley v. Connelie, 435 U.S. 291 U.S. 291 (1978); Ambach v. Norwick, 441 U.S. 68 (1979).

more discretion under intermediate than under strict scrutiny. Unfortunately, the gradations are difficult to apply. Consequently, the outcomes of controversies judged under intermediate scrutiny are more difficult to predict than under strict scrutiny, where measures are almost always invalidated, and under minimal scrutiny, where measures are almost always upheld as valid.

Very few governmental measures discriminate on the basis of legitimacy. Consequently, there have been relatively few opportunities for courts to rule on the constitutionality of such measures. The Supreme Court has struck down state laws excluding illegitimate children from receiving workers' compensation benefits on the death of their fathers and from maintaining wrongful death actions.[520] The Supreme Court also struck down a state law that provided child support only to legitimate children.[521] On the other hand, a state may deny a right of intestate succession to an illegitimate child if paternity is not formally determined before the father's death.[522] The important state interest was found in the need to promote the expeditious disposition of property at death. (The advent of relatively inexpensive DNA analysis may have rendered this interest moot.) Immigration provisions that exclude illegitimate children (and illegitimate fathers) from receiving preferences have also been upheld.[523] Note, however, that this last example of discrimination was subject to a lower level of review because of Congress's plenary power over immigration.

Statutes routinely declare that a child born to a married woman is irrebutably presumed to be the child of the mother's husband.[524] Yet studies betray that many children in intact families were not sired by their mothers' husbands.[525] Does the statutory declaration of legitimacy unconstitutionally discriminate in favor of illegitimate children? Adopted children sometimes desire to know the identity of their genetic parents for medical reasons. Can the legislature or Supreme Court constitutionally recognize a right of adopted children to such information without simultaneously bestowing that right on legitimate children?

Quite a number of cases charging gender discrimination have reached the courts. These too are judged under intermediate scrutiny. To date, all measures that deny benefits to, or impose extra burdens upon, women

---

[520] Weber v. Aetna Casualty & Surety Co., 406 U.S. 164 (1972); Levy v. Louisiana, 391 U.S. 68 (1968).
[521] Gomez v. Perez, 409 U.S. 535 (1973).
[522] Lallix v. Lallix, 439 U.S. 259 (1978).
[523] Fiallo v. Bell, 430 U.S. 787 (1977).
[524] E.g., California Evidence Code § 7540, upheld in Michael H. v. Gerald D., 491 U.S. 110 (1989), criticized in Hadek.
[525] In some urban areas more than one fourth of the children were sired by someone other than the father of record. Wright, Moral Animal at 70.

have been held unconstitutional.[526] A potential exception to the last statement are laws that exclude pregnancy from state disability benefits.[527] Title VII of the federal Civil Rights Act of 1964 makes it unlawful for an employer "to discriminate against any individual with respect to his compensation, terms, conditions, or privileges of employment, because of such individual's race, color, religion, sex, or national origin."[528] Under Title VII, premiums for employer-sponsored health insurance must be identical for men and women even though claims by women are higher.[529] The state of Montana bans the use of gender in determining premiums for every type of insurance.[530] Are these statutes constitutional?

Laws that confer benefits upon women at the expense of men, such as those just mentioned, have almost always been upheld. Property tax exemptions for widows, but not widowers, have been ruled constitutional,[531] as have more generous mandatory discharge procedures in the military,[532] and more generous Social Security payments to women.[533] Other examples include exempting women from statutory rape laws,[534] from mandatory road construction,[535] and from military conscription.[536]

On occasion laws that confer benefits upon women have been ruled unconstitutional. Laws that prescribe lower drinking ages for women,[537] that exclude former wives from the legal obligation to pay alimony (spousal support), that grant only women a right to refuse consent to adoption,[538] and that limit admission to nursing classes at a state university to women[539] have all been declared unconstitutional.

Because discrimination in favor of females is judged by intermediate scrutiny, but that in favor of particular races is assessed according to strict scrutiny, a program that benefits women is easier to justify from a constitutional standpoint than one that benefits African Americans. Is this constitutionally defensible? African Americans constitute 12 percent of

---

[526] E.g., Reed v. Reed, 404 U.S. 1 (1972), Frontiero v. Richardson, 411 U.S. 677 (1973), and United States v. Virginia, 516 U.S. 515 (1996).
[527] Geduldig v. Aiello, 417 U.S. 484 (1974).
[528] 42 U.S.C. §§ 2000e-2(a)(1).
[529] See Gaulding.
[530] Mont. Code Ann. § 49-2-309.
[531] Kahn v. Shevin, 416 U.S. 351 (1974).
[532] Schlessinger v. Ballard, 419 U.S. 498 (1975).
[533] Califano v. Webster, 430 U.S. 313 (1977).
[534] Michael M. v. Sonoma County Superior Court, 450 U.S. 57 (1981).
[535] Butler v. Perry, 240 U.S. 328 (1916), overruling a challenge under the 13th Amendment, and holding that a state may require all able-bodied men between the ages of 21 and 45 to work on road construction.
[536] Rostker v. Goldberg, 453 U.S. 57 (1981), and according unwed mothers, but not fathers, the right to sue for the child's wrongful death. Parham v. Hughes, 441 U.S. 347 (1979).
[537] Craig v. Boren, 429 U.S. 190 (1976).
[538] Caban v. Mohammed, 441 U.S. 380 (1979).
[539] Mississippi University for Women v. Hogan, 458 U.S. 718 (1982).

the population. They are disproportionately underrepresented among registered voters,[540] and earn disproportionately less than non-blacks. Women (12 percent of whom are black) constitute a majority of the American population, are disproportionately over-represented among registered voters,[541] and control over half of the wealth, according to some reports.[542]

To summarize, laws that intentionally disadvantage illegitimate children are usually judged unconstitutional. There are apparently no laws that give an advantage to illegitimate children at the expense of legitimate, but there are a number of laws that intentionally benefit females at the expense of males. These discriminations are almost upheld. All of the measures reviewed by the Supreme Court that intentionally benefit men to the disadvantage of women, except those directly relating to pregnancy, have been ruled unconstitutional. Would the results of these cases have been any different had strict scrutiny been applied?

Should intermediate scrutiny be extended to other groups, or does doing so lead to "tribalization" of constitutional rights?[543] What about the poor? For example, *Boddie* v. *Connecticut*[544] ruled (under the due process clause) that states may not charge court fees to indigents seeking to dissolve their marriages. But states may charge for abortions.[545] Would extending intermediate scrutiny to the poor jeopardize social programs?

Should heightened scrutiny be extended to the elderly? The Supreme Court has held that age is not a suspect classification.[546] Federal statutory law protects workers over the age of 40, and has virtually eliminated all mandatory retirement.[547]

What about the physically disabled and the mentally retarded? Some commentators maintain that the Americans with Disabilities Act of 1990[548] requires courts to employ strict scrutiny to judge classifications based on a disability.[549] In *Cleburne* v. *Cleburne Living Center, Inc.*,[550] a city ordinance

---

[540] See U.S. Bureau of Labor Statistics and the Census Bureau, Current Population Survey (CPS) Table A-1, Reported Voting and Registration by Race, Hispanic Origin, Sex, and Age Groups: November 1964 to 2004.
[541] See U.S. Bureau of Labor Statistics and the Census Bureau, Current Population Survey (CPS) Table A-1, Reported Voting and Registration by Race, Hispanic Origin, Sex, and Age Groups: November 1964 to 2004.
[542] Deutsche Presse-Agentur, Nov. 24, 1998, Ronnie Polanecszky, Philanthropy and Women, Philadelphia Daily News, March 8, 2004 ("In fact, women own over 60 percent of the wealth in America").
[543] See generally Schlesinger.
[544] 401 U.S. 371 (1971).
[545] Harris v. McRae, 448 U.S. 297 (1980).
[546] Massachusetts Board of Retirement v. Murgia, 427 U.S. 307 (1976).
[547] Age Discrimination in Employment Act, 29 U.S.C. §§ 621-634, criticized in Issacharoff & Harris and in Epstein.
[548] 42 U.S.C. § 12101 *et seq.*
[549] Perlin at p. 949, n. 16.
[550] 470 U.S. 1002 (1985).

required that one obtain a special use permit to establish group homes for the mentally retarded, but not to open a dormitory for university students. The Supreme Court found no rational basis for the distinction and invalidated the ordinance.

The case that follows was chosen to conclude this book because it contains issues from both the first and second parts of the book, and because it illustrates the fluidity of the rhetoric and concepts of the Fourteenth Amendment. In ruling California's statute unconstitutional, does the Supreme Court use due process or equal protection or something else? What level scrutiny is being employed? Notice that Congress apparently considered California's approach to be constitutional. Why might members of Congress from other states find California's approach unobjectionable?

CASE: **Saenz v. Roe**
526 U.S. 489 (1999)

Justice STEVENS delivered the opinion of the Court.

In 1992, California enacted a statute limiting the maximum welfare benefits available to newly arrived residents. The scheme limits the amount payable to a family that has resided in the State for less than 12 months to the amount payable by the State of the family's prior residence. The questions presented by this case are whether the 1992 statute was constitutional when it was enacted and, if not, whether an amendment to the Social Security Act enacted by Congress in 1996 affects that determination.

I

California is not only one of the largest, most populated, and most beautiful States in the Nation; it is also one of the most generous. Like all other States, California has participated in several welfare programs authorized by the Social Security Act and partially funded by the Federal Government. Its programs, however, provide a higher level of benefits and serve more needy citizens than those of most other States. In one year the most expensive of those programs, Aid to Families with Dependent Children (AFDC), which was replaced in 1996 with Temporary Assistance to Needy Families (TANF), provided benefits for an average of 2,645,814 persons per month at an annual cost to the State of $2.9 billion. In California the cash benefit for a family of two—a mother and one child—is $456 a month, but in the neighboring State of Arizona, for example, it is only $275.

In 1992, in order to make a relatively modest reduction in its vast welfare budget, the California Legislature enacted §11450.03 of the state Welfare and Institutions Code. That section sought to change the California AFDC program by limiting new residents, for the first year they live in California, to the benefits they would have received in the State of their prior residence. ...

...

... Congress enacted the Personal Responsibility and Work Opportunity Reconciliation Act (PRWORA) in 1996.

PRWORA replaced the AFDC program with TANF. The new statute expressly authorizes any State that receives a block grant under TANF to "apply to a family the rules (including benefit amounts) of the [TANF] program ... of another State if the family has moved to the State from the other State and has resided in the State for less than 12 months."[551]

...

III

The word "travel" is not found in the text of the Constitution. Yet the "constitutional right to travel from one State to another" is firmly embedded in our jurisprudence. *United States* v. *Guest*.[552] Indeed, as Justice Stewart reminded us in *Shapiro* v. *Thompson*,[553] the right is so important that it is "assertable against private interference as well as governmental action ... a virtually unconditional personal right, guaranteed by the Constitution to us all." ...

In *Shapiro*, we reviewed the constitutionality of three statutory provisions that denied welfare assistance to residents of Connecticut, the District of Columbia, and Pennsylvania, who had resided within those respective jurisdictions less than one year immediately preceding their applications for assistance. ... We squarely held that it was "constitutionally impermissible" for a State to enact durational residency requirements for the purpose of inhibiting the migration by needy persons into the State. We further held that a classification that had the effect of imposing a penalty on the exercise of the right to travel violated the Equal Protection Clause "unless shown to be necessary to promote a *compelling* governmental interest," and that no such showing had been made.

In this case California argues that §11450.03 was not enacted for the impermissible purpose of inhibiting migration by needy persons and that, unlike the legislation reviewed in *Shapiro*, it does not penalize the right to travel because new arrivals are not

---

[551] 42 U.S.C. § 604(c) (1994 ed., Supp. II).
[552] 383 U.S. 745, 757 (1966).
[553] 394 U.S. 618 (1969).

ineligible for benefits during their first year of residence. California submits that, instead of being subjected to the strictest scrutiny, the statute should be upheld if it is supported by a rational basis and that the State's legitimate interest in saving over $10 million a year satisfies that test ....

IV

...

The second component of the right to travel is, however, expressly protected by the text of the Constitution. The first sentence of Article IV, §2, provides:

The Citizens of each State shall be entitled to all Privileges and Immunities of Citizens in the several States.

Thus, by virtue of a person's state citizenship, a citizen of one State who travels in other States, intending to return home at the end of his journey, is entitled to enjoy the "Privileges and Immunities of Citizens in the several States" that he visits. ... There may be a substantial reason for requiring the nonresident to pay more than the resident for a hunting license, see *Baldwin v. Fish and Game Comm'n of Mont.*,[554] or to enroll in the state university, see *Vlandis v. Kline*[555] ....

What is at issue in this case, then, is this third aspect of the right to travel—the right of the newly arrived citizen to the same privileges and immunities enjoyed by other citizens of the same State. That right is protected not only by the new arrival's status as a state citizen, but also by her status as a citizen of the United States. That additional source of protection is plainly identified in the opening words of the Fourteenth Amendment.

All persons born or naturalized in the United States, and subject to the jurisdiction thereof, are citizens of the United States and of the State wherein they reside. No State shall make or enforce any law which shall abridge the privileges or immunities of citizens of the United States; ....

... [O]ne of the privileges conferred by this Clause "is that a citizen of the United States can, of his own volition, become a citizen of any State of the Union by a *bona fide* residence therein, with the same rights as other citizens of that State." ...

That newly arrived citizens "have two political capacities, one state and one federal," adds special force to their claim that they have the same rights as others who share their citizenship. Neither mere rationality nor some intermediate standard of

---

[554] 436 U.S. 371, 390–391 (1978).
[555] 412 U.S. 441, 445 (1973).

review should be used to judge the constitutionality of a state rule that discriminates against some of its citizens because they have been domiciled in the State for less than a year. The appropriate standard may be more categorical than that articulated in *Shapiro*, but it is surely no less strict.

V

... Neither the duration of respondents' California residence, nor the identity of their prior States of residence, has any relevance to their need for benefits. Nor do those factors bear any relationship to the State's interest in making an equitable allocation of the funds to be distributed to its needy citizens. ... In short, the State's legitimate interest in saving money provides no justification for its decision to discriminate among equally eligible citizens.

VI

The question that remains is whether congressional approval of durational residency requirements ... somehow resuscitates the constitutionality of § 11450.03. That question is readily answered, for we have consistently held that Congress may not authorize the States to violate the Fourteenth Amendment. Moreover, the protection afforded to the citizen by the Citizenship Clause of that Amendment is a limitation on the powers of the National Government as well as the States.

... Citizens of the United States, whether rich or poor, have the right to choose to be citizens "of the State wherein they reside." U.S. Const., Amdt. 14, § 1. The States, however, do not have any right to select their citizens. ...

[Dissents by Rehnquist and Thomas omitted.]

Attachments

Attachment A

The Declaration of Independence

Action of Second Continental Congress, July 4, 1776

The unanimous Declaration of the thirteen United States of America

WHEN in the Course of human Events, it becomes necessary for one People to dissolve the Political Bands which have connected them with another, and to assume among the Powers of the Earth, the separate and equal Station to which the Laws of Nature and of Nature's God entitle them, a decent Respect to the Opinions of Mankind requires that they should declare the causes which impel them to the Separation.

WE hold these Truths to be self-evident, that all Men are created equal, that they are endowed by their Creator with certain unalienable Rights, that among these are Life, Liberty and the Pursuit of Happiness—That to secure these Rights, Governments are instituted among Men, deriving their just Powers from the Consent of the Governed, that whenever any Form of Government becomes destructive of these Ends, it is the Right of the People to alter or to abolish it, and to institute new Government, laying its Foundation on such Principles, and organizing its Powers in such Form, as to them shall seem most likely to effect their Safety and Happiness. Prudence, indeed, will dictate that Governments long established should not be changed for light and transient Causes; and accordingly all Experience hath shewn [*sic*], that Mankind are more disposed to suffer, while Evils are sufferable, than to right themselves by abolishing the Forms to which they are accustomed. But when a long Train of Abuses and Usurpations, pursuing invariably the same Object, evinces a Design to reduce them under absolute Despotism, it is their Right, it is their Duty, to throw off such Government, and to provide new Guards for their future Security. Such has been the patient Sufferance of these Colonies; and such is now the Necessity which constrains them to alter their former Systems of Government. The History of the present King of Great-Britain is a History of repeated Injuries and Usurpations, all having in direct Object the Establishment of an absolute Tyranny over these States. To prove this, let Facts be submitted to a candid World.

HE has refused his Assent to Laws, the most wholesome and necessary for the public Good.

HE has forbidden his Governors to pass Laws of immediate and pressing Importance, unless suspended in their Operation till his Assent should be obtained; and when so suspended, he has utterly neglected to attend to them.

HE has refused to pass other Laws for the Accommodation of large Districts of People, unless those People would relinquish the Right of Representation in the Legislature, a Right inestimable to them, and formidable to Tyrants only.

HE has called together Legislative Bodies at Places unusual, uncomfortable, and distant from the Depository of their public Records, for the sole Purpose of fatiguing them into Compliance with his Measures.

HE has dissolved Representative Houses repeatedly, for opposing with manly Firmness his Invasions on the Rights of the People.

HE has refused for a long Time, after such Dissolutions, to cause others to be elected; whereby the Legislative Powers, incapable of the Annihilation, have returned to the People at large for their exercise; the State remaining in the mean time exposed to all the Dangers of Invasion from without, and the Convulsions within.

HE has endeavoured to prevent the Population of these States; for that Purpose obstructing the Laws for Naturalization of Foreigners; refusing to pass others to encourage their Migrations hither, and raising the Conditions of new Appropriations of Lands.

HE has obstructed the Administration of Justice, by refusing his Assent to Laws for establishing Judiciary Powers.

HE has made Judges dependent on his Will alone, for the Tenure of their Offices, and the Amount and Payment of their Salaries.

HE has erected a Multitude of new Offices, and sent hither Swarms of Officers to harrass [*sic*] our People, and eat out their Substance.

HE has kept among us, in Times of Peace, Standing Armies, without the consent of our Legislatures.

HE has affected to render the Military independent of and superior to the Civil Power.

HE has combined with others to subject us to a Jurisdiction foreign to our Constitution, and unacknowledged by our Laws; giving his Assent to their Acts of pretended Legislation:

FOR quartering large Bodies of Armed Troops among us;

FOR protecting them, by a mock Trial, from Punishment for any Murders which they should commit on the Inhabitants of these States:

FOR cutting off our Trade with all Parts of the World:

FOR imposing Taxes on us without our Consent:

FOR depriving us, in many Cases, of the Benefits of Trial by Jury:

FOR transporting us beyond Seas to be tried for pretended Offences:

FOR abolishing the free System of English Laws in a neighbouring Province, establishing therein an arbitrary Government, and enlarging its Boundaries, so as to render it at once an Example and fit Instrument for introducing the same absolute Rules into these Colonies:

FOR taking away our Charters, abolishing our most valuable Laws, and altering fundamentally the Forms of our Governments:

FOR suspending our own Legislatures, and declaring themselves invested with Power to legislate for us in all Cases whatsoever.

HE has abdicated Government here, by declaring us out of his Protection and waging War against us.

HE has plundered our Seas, ravaged our Coasts, burnt our Towns, and destroyed the Lives of our People.

HE is, at this Time, transporting large Armies of foreign Mercenaries to compleat the Works of Death, Desolation, and Tyranny, already begun with circumstances of Cruelty and Perfidy, scarcely paralleled in the most barbarous Ages, and totally unworthy the Head of a civilized Nation.

HE has constrained our fellow Citizens taken Captive on the high Seas to bear Arms against their Country, to become the Executioners of their Friends and Brethren, or to fall themselves by their Hands.

HE has excited domestic Insurrections amongst us, and has endeavoured to bring on the Inhabitants of our Frontiers, the merciless Indian Savages, whose known Rule of Warfare, is an undistinguished Destruction, of all Ages, Sexes and Conditions.

IN every stage of these Oppressions we have Petitioned for Redress in the most humble Terms: Our repeated Petitions have been answered only by repeated Injury. A Prince, whose Character is thus marked by every act which may define a Tyrant, is unfit to be the Ruler of a free People.

NOR have we been wanting in Attentions to our British Brethren. We have warned them from Time to Time of Attempts by their Legislature to extend an unwarrantable Jurisdiction over us. We have reminded them of the Circumstances of our Emigration and Settlement here. We have appealed to their native Justice and Magnanimity, and we have conjured them by the Ties of our common Kindred to disavow these Usurpations, which, would inevitably interrupt our Connections and Correspondence. They too have been deaf to the Voice of Justice and of Consanguinity. We must, therefore, acquiesce in the Necessity, which denounces our Separation, and hold them, as we hold the rest of Mankind, Enemies in War, in Peace, Friends.

WE, therefore, the Representatives of the UNITED STATES OF AMERICA, in GENERAL CONGRESS, Assembled, appealing to the Supreme Judge of the World for the Rectitude of our Intentions, do, in the Name, and by Authority of the good People of these Colonies, solemnly Publish and Declare, That these United Colonies are, and of Right ought to be, FREE AND INDEPENDENT STATES; that they are absolved from all Allegiance to the British Crown, and that all political Connection between them and the State of Great-Britain, is and ought to be totally dissolved; and that as FREE AND INDEPENDENT STATES, they have full Power to levy War, conclude Peace, contract Alliances, establish Commerce, and to do all other Acts and Things which INDEPENDENT STATES may of right do. And for the support of this Declaration, with a firm Reliance on the Protection of divine Providence, we mutually pledge to each other our Lives, our Fortunes, and our sacred Honor.

ATTACHMENT B

The Articles of Confederation

Nov. 15, 1777

To all to whom these Presents shall come, we the undersigned Delegates of the States affixed to our Names send greeting.

Articles of Confederation and perpetual Union between the states of New Hampshire, Massachusetts Bay, Rhode Island and Providence Plantations, Connecticut, New York, New Jersey, Pennsylvania, Delaware, Maryland, Virginia, North Carolina, South Carolina Georgia.

I. The Stile of this Confederacy shall be "The United States of America".

II. Each state retains its sovereignty, freedom, and independence, and every power, jurisdiction, and right, which is not by this Confederation expressly delegated to the United States, in Congress assembled.

III. The said States hereby severally enter into a firm league of friendship with each other, for their common defense, the security of their liberties, and their mutual and general welfare, binding themselves to assist each other, against all force offered to, or attacks made upon them, or any of them, on account of religion, sovereignty, trade, or any other pretense whatever.

IV. The better to secure and perpetuate mutual friendship and intercourse among the people of the different States in this Union, the free inhabitants of each of these States, paupers, vagabonds, and fugitives from justice excepted, shall be entitled to all privileges and immunities of free citizens in the several States; and the people of each State shall free ingress and regress to and from any other State, and shall enjoy therein all the privileges of trade and commerce, subject to the same duties, impositions, and restrictions as the inhabitants thereof respectively, provided that such restrictions shall not extend so far as to prevent the removal of property imported into any State, to any other State, of which the owner is an inhabitant; provided also that no imposition, duties or restriction shall be laid by any State, on the property of the United States, or either of them.

If any person guilty of, or charged with, treason, felony, or other high misdemeanor in any State, shall flee from justice, and be found in any of the United States, he shall, upon demand of the Governor or executive power of the State from which he fled, be delivered up and removed to the State having jurisdiction of his offense.

Full faith and credit shall be given in each of these States to the records, acts, and judicial proceedings of the courts and magistrates of every other State.

V. For the most convenient management of the general interests of the United States, delegates shall be annually appointed in such manner as the legislatures of each State shall direct, to meet in Congress on the first

Monday in November, in every year, with a power reserved to each State to recall its delegates, or any of them, at any time within the year, and to send others in their stead for the remainder of the year.

No State shall be represented in Congress by less than two, nor more than seven members; and no person shall be capable of being a delegate for more than three years in any term of six years; nor shall any person, being a delegate, be capable of holding any office under the United States, for which he, or another for his benefit, receives any salary, fees or emolument of any kind.

Each State shall maintain its own delegates in a meeting of the States, and while they act as members of the committee of the States.

In determining questions in the United States in Congress assembled, each State shall have one vote.

Freedom of speech and debate in Congress shall not be impeached or questioned in any court or place out of Congress, and the members of Congress shall be protected in their persons from arrests or imprisonments, during the time of their going to and from, and attendence on Congress, except for treason, felony, or breach of the peace.

VI. No State, without the consent of the United States in Congress assembled, shall send any embassy to, or receive any embassy from, or enter into any conference, agreement, alliance or treaty with any King, Prince or State; nor shall any person holding any office of profit or trust under the United States, or any of them, accept any present, emolument, office or title of any kind whatever from any King, Prince or foreign State; nor shall the United States in Congress assembled, or any of them, grant any title of nobility.

No two or more States shall enter into any treaty, confederation or alliance whatever between them, without the consent of the United States in Congress assembled, specifying accurately the purposes for which the same is to be entered into, and how long it shall continue.

No State shall lay any imposts or duties, which may interfere with any stipulations in treaties, entered into by the United States in Congress assembled, with any King, Prince or State, in pursuance of any treaties already proposed by Congress, to the courts of France and Spain.

No vessel of war shall be kept up in time of peace by any State, except such number only, as shall be deemed necessary by the United States in Congress assembled, for the defense of such State, or its trade; nor shall any body of forces be kept up by any State in time of peace, except such number only, as in the judgement of the United States in Congress assembled, shall be deemed requisite to garrison the forts necessary for the defense of such State; but every State shall always keep up a well-regulated and disciplined militia, sufficiently armed and accoutered, and shall provide and constantly have ready for use, in public stores, a due number of filed pieces and tents, and a proper quantity of arms, ammunition and camp equipage.

No State shall engage in any war without the consent of the United States in Congress assembled, unless such State be actually invaded by enemies, or shall have received certain advice of a resolution being formed by some nation of Indians to invade such State, and the danger is so imminent as not to admit of a delay till the United States in Congress assembled can be consulted; nor shall any State grant commissions to any ships or vessels of war, nor letters of marque or reprisal, except it be after a declaration of war by the United States in Congress assembled, and then only against the Kingdom or State and the subjects thereof, against which war has been so declared, and under such regulations as shall be established by the United States in Congress assembled, unless such State be infested by pirates, in which case vessels of war may be fitted out for that occasion, and kept so long as the danger shall continue, or until the United States in Congress assembled shall determine otherwise.

VII. When land forces are raised by any State for the common defense, all officers of or under the rank of colonel, shall be appointed by the legislature of each State respectively, by whom such forces shall be raised, or in such manner as such State shall direct, and all vacancies shall be filled up by the State which first made the appointment.

VIII. All charges of war, and all other expenses that shall be incurred for the common defense or general welfare, and allowed by the United States in Congress assembled, shall be defrayed out of a common treasury, which shall be supplied by the several States in proportion to the value of all land within each State, granted or surveyed for any person, as such land and the buildings and improvements thereon shall be estimated according to such mode as the United States in Congress assembled, shall from time to time direct and appoint.

The taxes for paying that proportion shall be laid and levied by the authority and direction of the legislatures of the several States within the time agreed upon by the United States in Congress assembled.

IX. The United States in Congress assembled, shall have the sole and exclusive right and power of determining on peace and war, except in the cases mentioned in the sixth article—of sending and receiving ambassadors—entering into treaties and alliances, provided that no treaty of commerce shall be made whereby the legislative power of the respective States shall be restrained from imposing such imposts and duties on foreigners, as their own people are subjected to, or from prohibiting the exportation or importation of any species of goods or commodities whatsoever—of establishing rules for deciding in all cases, what captures on land or water shall be legal, and in what manner prizes taken by land or naval forces in the service of the United States shall be divided or appropriated—of granting letters of marque and reprisal in times of peace—appointing courts for the trial of piracies and felonies commited [*sic*] on the high seas and establishing courts for receiving and determining finally appeals in all cases of captures, provided that no member of Congress shall be appointed a judge of any of the said courts.

The United States in Congress assembled shall also be the last resort on appeal in all disputes and differences now subsisting or that hereafter may arise between two or more States concerning boundary, jurisdiction or any other causes whatever; which authority shall always be exercised in the manner following. Whenever the legislative or executive authority or lawful agent of any State in controversy with another shall present a petition to Congress stating the matter in question and praying for a hearing, notice thereof shall be given by order of Congress to the legislative or executive authority of the other State in controversy, and a day assigned for the appearance of the parties by their lawful agents, who shall then be directed to appoint by joint consent, commissioners or judges to constitute a court for hearing and determining the matter in question: but if they cannot agree, Congress shall name three persons out of each of the United States, and from the list of such persons each party shall alternately strike out one, the petitioners beginning, until the number shall be reduced to thirteen; and from that number not less than seven, nor more than nine names as Congress shall direct, shall in the presence of Congress be drawn out by lot, and the persons whose names shall be so drawn or any five of them, shall be commissioners or judges, to hear and finally determine the controversy, so always as a major part of the judges who shall hear the cause shall agree in the determination: and if either party shall neglect to attend at the day appointed, without showing reasons, which Congress shall judge sufficient, or being present shall refuse to strike, the Congress shall proceed to nominate three persons out of each State, and the secretary of Congress shall strike in behalf of such party absent or refusing; and the judgement and sentence of the court to be appointed, in the manner before prescribed, shall be final and conclusive; and if any of the parties shall refuse to submit to the authority of such court, or to appear or defend their claim or cause, the court shall nevertheless proceed to pronounce sentence, or judgement, which shall in like manner be final and decisive, the judgement or sentence and other proceedings being in either case transmitted to Congress, and lodged among the acts of Congress for the security of the parties concerned: provided that every commissioner, before he sits in judgement, shall take an oath to be administered by one of the judges of the supreme or superior court of the State, where the cause shall be tried, 'well and truly to hear and determine the matter in question, according to the best of his judgement, without favor, affection or hope of reward': provided also, that no State shall be deprived of territory for the benefit of the United States.

All controversies concerning the private right of soil claimed under different grants of two or more States, whose jurisdictions as they may respect such lands, and the States which passed such grants are adjusted, the said grants or either of them being at the same time claimed to have originated antecedent to such settlement of jurisdiction, shall on the petition of either party to the Congress of the United States, be finally determined as near as may be in the same manner as is before presecribed [*sic*] for deciding disputes respecting territorial jurisdiction between different States.

The United States in Congress assembled shall also have the sole and exclusive right and power of regulating the alloy and value of coin struck by their own authority, or by that of the respective States—fixing the standards of weights and measures throughout the United States—regulating the trade and managing all affairs with the Indians, not members of any of the States, provided that the legislative right of any State within its own limits be not infringed or violated—establishing or regulating post offices from one State to another, throughout all the United States, and exacting such postage on the papers passing through the same as may be requisite to defray the expenses of the said office—appointing all officers of the land forces, in the service of the United States, excepting regimental officers—appointing all the officers of the naval forces, and commissioning all officers whatever in the service of the United States—making rules for the government and regulation of the said land and naval forces, and directing their operations.

The United States in Congress assembled shall have authority to appoint a committee, to sit in the recess of Congress, to be denominated 'A Committee of the States', and to consist of one delegate from each State; and to appoint such other committees and civil officers as may be necessary for managing the general affairs of the United States under their direction

—to appoint one of their members to preside, provided that no person be allowed to serve in the office of president more than one year in any term of three years; to ascertain the necessary sums of money to be raised for the service of the United States, and to appropriate and apply the same for defraying the public expenses—to borrow money, or emit bills on the credit of the United States, transmitting every half-year to the respective States an account of the sums of money so borrowed or emitted—to build and equip a navy—to agree upon the number of land forces, and to make requisitions from each State for its quota, in proportion to the number of white inhabitants in such State; which requisition shall be binding, and thereupon the legislature of each State shall appoint the regimental officers, raise the men and cloath [*sic*], arm and equip them in a solid-like manner, at the expense of the United States; and the officers and men so cloathed [*sic*], armed and equipped shall march to the place appointed, and within the time agreed on by the United States in Congress assembled. But if the United States in Congress assembled shall, on consideration of circumstances judge proper that any State should not raise men, or should raise a smaller number of men than the quota thereof, such extra number shall be raised, officered, cloathed, armed and equipped in the same manner as the quota of each State, unless the legislature of such State shall judge that such extra number cannot be safely spread out in the same, in which case they shall raise, officer, cloath, arm and equip as many of such extra number as they judge can be safely spared. And the officers and men so cloathed, armed, and equipped, shall march to the place appointed, and within the time agreed on by the United States in Congress assembled.

The United States in Congress assembled shall never engage in a war, nor grant letters of marque or reprisal in time of peace, nor enter into any treaties or alliances, nor coin money, nor regulate the value thereof, nor ascertain the sums and expenses necessary for the defense and welfare of the United States, or any of them, nor emit bills, nor borrow money on the credit of the United States, nor appropriate money, nor agree upon the number of vessels of war, to be built or purchased, or the number of land or sea forces to be raised, nor appoint a commander in chief of the army or navy, unless nine States assent to the same: nor shall a question on any other point, except for adjourning from day to day be determined, unless by the votes of the majority of the United States in Congress assembled.

The Congress of the United States shall have power to adjourn to any time within the year, and to any place within the United States, so that no period of adjournment be for a longer duration than the space of six months, and shall publish the journal of their proceedings monthly, except such parts thereof relating to treaties, alliances or military operations, as in their judgement require secrecy; and the yeas and nays of the delegates of each State on any question shall be entered on the journal, when it is desired by any delegates of a State, or any of them, at his or their request shall be furnished with a transcript of the said journal, except such parts as are above excepted, to lay before the legislatures of the several States.

X. The Committee of the States, or any nine of them, shall be authorized to execute, in the recess of Congress, such of the powers of Congress as the United States in Congress assembled, by the consent of the nine States, shall from time to time think expedient to vest them with; provided that no power be delegated to the said Committee, for the exercise of which, by the Articles of Confederation, the voice of nine States in the Congress of the United States assembled be requisite.

XI. Canada acceding to this confederation, and adjoining in the measures of the United States, shall be admitted into, and entitled to all the advantages of this Union; but no other colony shall be admitted into the same, unless such admission be agreed to by nine States.

XII. All bills of credit emitted, monies borrowed, and debts contracted by, or under the authority of Congress, before the assembling of the United States, in pursuance of the present confederation, shall be deemed and considered as a charge against the United States, for payment and satisfaction whereof the said United States, and the public faith are hereby solemnly pleged [*sic*].

XIII. Every State shall abide by the determination of the United States in Congress assembled, on all questions which by this confederation are submitted to them. And the Articles of this Confederation shall be inviolably observed by every State, and the Union shall be perpetual; nor shall any alteration at any time hereafter be made in any of them; unless such alteration be agreed to in a Congress of the United States, and be afterwards confirmed by the legislatures of every State.

And Whereas it hath pleased the Great Governor of the World to incline the hearts of the legislatures we respectively represent in Congress, to approve of, and to authorize us to ratify the said Articles of Confederation and perpetual Union. Know Ye that we the undersigned delegates, by virtue of the power and authority to us given for that purpose, do by these presents, in the name and in behalf of our respective constituents, fully and entirely ratify and confirm each and every of the said Articles of Confederation and perpetual Union, and all and singular the matters and things therein contained: And we do further solemnly plight and engage the faith of our respective constituents, that they shall abide by the determinations of the United States in Congress assembled, on all questions, which by the said Confederation are submitted to them. And that the Articles thereof shall be inviolably observed by the States we respectively represent, and that the Union shall be perpetual.

In Witness whereof we have hereunto set our hands in Congress. Done at Philadelphia in the State of Pennsylvania the ninth day of July in the Year of our Lord One Thousand Seven Hundred and Seventy-Eight, and in the Third Year of the independence of America.

Agreed to by Congress 15 November 1777

In force after ratification by Maryland, 1 March 1781

ATTACHMENT C

The Constitution of the United States of America

We the people of the United States, in order to form a more perfect union, establish justice, insure domestic tranquility, provide for the common defense, promote the general welfare, and secure the blessings of liberty to ourselves and our posterity, do ordain and establish this Constitution for the United States of America.

Article I

Section 1. All legislative powers herein granted shall be vested in a Congress of the United States, which shall consist of a Senate and House of Representatives.

Section 2. The House of Representatives shall be composed of members chosen every second year by the people of the several states, and the electors in each state shall have the qualifications requisite for electors of the most numerous branch of the state legislature.

No person shall be a Representative who shall not have attained to the age of twenty five years, and been seven years a citizen of the United States, and who shall not, when elected, be an inhabitant of that state in which he shall be chosen.

Representatives and direct taxes shall be apportioned among the several states which may be included within this union, according to their respective numbers, which shall be determined by adding to the whole number of free persons, including those bound to service for a term of years, and excluding Indians not taxed, three fifths of all other Persons. The actual Enumeration shall be made within three years after the first meeting of the Congress of the United States, and within every subsequent term of ten years, in such manner as they shall by law direct. The number of Representatives shall not exceed one for every thirty thousand, but each state shall have at least one Representative; and until such enumeration shall be made, the state of New Hampshire shall be entitled to chuse [*sic*] three, Massachusetts eight, Rhode Island and Providence Plantations one, Connecticut five, New York six, New Jersey four, Pennsylvania eight, Delaware one, Maryland six, Virginia ten, North Carolina five, South Carolina five, and Georgia three.

When vacancies happen in the Representation from any state, the executive authority thereof shall issue writs of election to fill such vacancies.

The House of Representatives shall choose their speaker and other officers; and shall have the sole power of impeachment.

Section 3. The Senate of the United States shall be composed of two Senators from each state, chosen by the legislature thereof, for six years; and each Senator shall have one vote.

Immediately after they shall be assembled in consequence of the first election, they shall be divided as equally as may be into three classes. The seats of the Senators of the first class shall be vacated at the expiration of the second year, of the second class at the expiration of the fourth year, and the third class at the expiration of the sixth year, so that one third may be chosen every second year; and if vacancies happen by resignation, or otherwise, during the recess of the legislature of any state, the executive thereof may make temporary appointments until the next meeting of the legislature, which shall then fill such vacancies.

No person shall be a Senator who shall not have attained to the age of thirty years, and been nine years a citizen of the United States and who shall not, when elected, be an inhabitant of that state for which he shall be chosen.

The Vice President of the United States shall be President of the Senate, but shall have no vote, unless they be equally divided.

The Senate shall choose their other officers, and also a President pro tempore, in the absence of the Vice President, or when he shall exercise the office of President of the United States.

The Senate shall have the sole power to try all impeachments. When sitting for that purpose, they shall be on oath or affirmation. When the President of the United States is tried, the Chief Justice shall preside: And no person shall be convicted without the concurrence of two thirds of the members present.

Judgment in cases of impeachment shall not extend further than to removal from office, and disqualification to hold and enjoy any office of honor, trust or profit under the United States: but the party convicted shall nevertheless be liable and subject to indictment, trial, judgment and punishment, according to law.

Section 4. The times, places and manner of holding elections for Senators and Representatives, shall be prescribed in each state by the legislature thereof; but the Congress may at any time by law make or alter such regulations, except as to the places of choosing Senators.

The Congress shall assemble at least once in every year, and such meeting shall be on the first Monday in December, unless they shall by law appoint a different day.

Section 5. Each House shall be the judge of the elections, returns and qualifications of its own members, and a majority of each shall constitute a quorum to do business; but a smaller number may adjourn from day to day, and may be authorized to compel the attendance of absent members, in such manner, and under such penalties as each House may provide.

Each House may determine the rules of its proceedings, punish its members for disorderly behavior, and, with the concurrence of two thirds, expel a member.

Each House shall keep a journal of its proceedings, and from time to time publish the same, excepting such parts as may in their judgment require secrecy; and the yeas and nays of the members of either House on any question shall, at the desire of one fifth of those present, be entered on the journal. Neither House, during the session of Congress, shall, without the consent of the other, adjourn for more than three days, nor to any other place than that in which the two Houses shall be sitting.

Section 6. The Senators and Representatives shall receive a compensation for their services, to be ascertained by law, and paid out of the treasury of the United States. They shall in all cases, except treason, felony and breach of the peace, be privileged from arrest during their attendance at the session of their respective Houses, and in going to and returning from the same; and for any speech or debate in either House, they shall not be questioned in any other place.

No Senator or Representative shall, during the time for which he was elected, be appointed to any civil office under the authority of the United States, which shall have been created, or the emoluments whereof shall have been increased during such time: and no person holding any office under the United States, shall be a member of either House during his continuance in office.

Section 7. All bills for raising revenue shall originate in the House of Representatives; but the Senate may propose or concur with amendments as on other Bills.

Every bill which shall have passed the House of Representatives and the Senate, shall, before it become a law, be presented to the President of the United States; if he approve he shall sign it, but if not he shall return it, with his objections to that House in which it shall have originated, who shall enter the objections at large on their journal, and proceed to reconsider it. If after such reconsideration two thirds of that House shall agree to pass the bill, it shall be sent, together with the objections, to the other House, by which it shall likewise be reconsidered, and if approved by two thirds of that House, it shall become a law. But in all such cases the votes of both Houses shall be determined by yeas and nays, and the names of the persons voting for and against the bill shall be entered on the journal of each House respectively. If any bill shall not be returned by the President within ten days (Sundays excepted) after it shall have been presented to him, the same shall be a law, in like manner as if he had signed it, unless the Congress by their adjournment prevent its return, in which case it shall not be a law.

Every order, resolution, or vote to which the concurrence of the Senate and House of Representatives may be necessary (except on a question of adjournment) shall be presented to the President of the United States; and before the same shall take effect, shall be approved by him, or being disapproved by him, shall be repassed by two thirds of the Senate and House of Representatives, according to the rules and limitations prescribed in the case of a bill.

Section 8. The Congress shall have power to lay and collect taxes, duties, imposts and excises, to pay the debts and provide for the common defense and general welfare of the United States; but all duties, imposts and excises shall be uniform throughout the United States;

To borrow money on the credit of the United States;

To regulate commerce with foreign nations, and among the several states, and with the Indian tribes;

To establish a uniform rule of naturalization, and uniform laws on the subject of bankruptcies throughout the United States;

To coin money, regulate the value thereof, and of foreign coin, and fix the standard of weights and measures;

To provide for the punishment of counterfeiting the securities and current coin of the United States;

To establish post offices and post roads;

To promote the progress of science and useful arts, by securing for limited times to authors and inventors the exclusive right to their respective writings and discoveries;

To constitute tribunals inferior to the Supreme Court;

To define and punish piracies and felonies committed on the high seas, and offenses against the law of nations;

To declare war, grant letters of marque and reprisal, and make rules concerning captures on land and water;

To raise and support armies, but no appropriation of money to that use shall be for a longer term than two years;

To provide and maintain a navy;

To make rules for the government and regulation of the land and naval forces;

To provide for calling forth the militia to execute the laws of the union, suppress insurrections and repel invasions;

To provide for organizing, arming, and disciplining, the militia, and for governing such part of them as may be employed in the service of the United States, reserving to the states respectively, the appointment of the officers, and the authority of training the militia according to the discipline prescribed by Congress;

To exercise exclusive legislation in all cases whatsoever, over such District (not exceeding ten miles square) as may, by cession of particular states, and the acceptance of Congress, become the seat of the government of the

United States, and to exercise like authority over all places purchased by the consent of the legislature of the state in which the same shall be, for the erection of forts, magazines, arsenals, dockyards, and other needful buildings;—And

To make all laws which shall be necessary and proper for carrying into execution the foregoing powers, and all other powers vested by this Constitution in the government of the United States, or in any department or officer thereof.

Section 9. The migration or importation of such persons as any of the states now existing shall think proper to admit, shall not be prohibited by the Congress prior to the year one thousand eight hundred and eight, but a tax or duty may be imposed on such importation, not exceeding ten dollars for each person.

The privilege of the writ of habeas corpus shall not be suspended, unless when in cases of rebellion or invasion the public safety may require it.

No bill of attainder or ex post facto Law shall be passed.

No capitation, or other direct, tax shall be laid, unless in proportion to the census or enumeration herein before directed to be taken.

No tax or duty shall be laid on articles exported from any state.

No preference shall be given by any regulation of commerce or revenue to the ports of one state over those of another: nor shall vessels bound to, or from, one state, be obliged to enter, clear or pay duties in another.

No money shall be drawn from the treasury, but in consequence of appropriations made by law; and a regular statement and account of receipts and expenditures of all public money shall be published from time to time.

No title of nobility shall be granted by the United States: and no person holding any office of profit or trust under them, shall, without the consent of the Congress, accept of any present, emolument, office, or title, of any kind whatever, from any king, prince, or foreign state.

Section 10. No state shall enter into any treaty, alliance, or confederation; grant letters of marque and reprisal; coin money; emit bills of credit; make anything but gold and silver coin a tender in payment of debts; pass any bill of attainder, ex post facto law, or law impairing the obligation of contracts, or grant any title of nobility.

No state shall, without the consent of the Congress, lay any imposts or duties on imports or exports, except what may be absolutely necessary for executing it's inspection laws: and the net produce of all duties and imposts, laid by any state on imports or exports, shall be for the use of the treasury of the United States; and all such laws shall be subject to the revision and control of the Congress.

No state shall, without the consent of Congress, lay any duty of tonnage, keep troops, or ships of war in time of peace, enter into any agreement or compact with another state, or with a foreign power, or engage in war, unless actually invaded, or in such imminent danger as will not admit of delay.

Article II

Section 1. The executive power shall be vested in a President of the United States of America. He shall hold his office during the term of four years, and, together with the Vice President, chosen for the same term, be elected, as follows:

Each state shall appoint, in such manner as the Legislature thereof may direct, a number of electors, equal to the whole number of Senators and Representatives to which the State may be entitled in the Congress: but no Senator or Representative, or person holding an office of trust or profit under the United States, shall be appointed an elector.

The electors shall meet in their respective states, and vote by ballot for two persons, of whom one at least shall not be an inhabitant of the same state with themselves. And they shall make a list of all the persons voted for, and of the number of votes for each; which list they shall sign and certify, and transmit sealed to the seat of the government of the United States, directed to the President of the Senate. The President of the Senate shall, in the presence of the Senate and House of Representatives, open all the certificates, and the votes shall then be counted. The person having the greatest number of votes shall be the President, if such number be a majority of the whole number of electors appointed; and if there be more than one who have such majority, and have an equal number of votes, then the House of Representatives shall immediately choose by ballot one of them for President; and if no person have a majority, then from the five highest on the list the said House shall in like manner choose the President. But in choosing the President, the votes shall be taken by States, the representation from each state having one vote; A quorum for this purpose shall consist of a member or members from two thirds of the states, and a majority of all the states shall be necessary to a choice. In every case, after the choice of the President, the person having the greatest number of votes of the electors shall be the Vice President. But if there should remain two or more who have equal votes, the Senate shall choose from them by ballot the Vice President.

The Congress may determine the time of choosing the electors, and the day on which they shall give their votes; which day shall be the same throughout the United States.

No person except a natural born citizen, or a citizen of the United States, at the time of the adoption of this Constitution, shall be eligible to the office of President; neither shall any person be eligible to that office who shall not have attained to the age of thirty five years, and been fourteen Years a resident within the United States.

In case of the removal of the President from office, or of his death, resignation, or inability to discharge the powers and duties of the said office, the same shall devolve on the Vice President, and the Congress may by law provide for the case of removal, death, resignation or inability, both of the President and Vice President, declaring what officer shall then act as President, and such officer shall act accordingly, until the disability be removed, or a President shall be elected.

The President shall, at stated times, receive for his services, a compensation, which shall neither be increased nor diminished during the period for which he shall have been elected, and he shall not receive within that period any other emolument from the United States, or any of them.

Before he enter on the execution of his office, he shall take the following oath or affirmation:—"I do solemnly swear (or affirm) that I will faithfully execute the office of President of the United States, and will to the best of my ability, preserve, protect and defend the Constitution of the United States."

Section 2. The President shall be commander in chief of the Army and Navy of the United States, and of the militia of the several states, when called into the actual service of the United States; he may require the opinion, in writing, of the principal officer in each of the executive departments, upon any subject relating to the duties of their respective offices, and he shall have power to grant reprieves and pardons for offenses against the United States, except in cases of impeachment.

He shall have power, by and with the advice and consent of the Senate, to make treaties, provided two thirds of the Senators present concur; and he shall nominate, and by and with the advice and consent of the Senate, shall appoint ambassadors, other public ministers and consuls, judges of the Supreme Court, and all other officers of the United States, whose appointments are not herein otherwise provided for, and which shall be established by law: but the Congress may by law vest the appointment of such inferior officers, as they think proper, in the President alone, in the courts of law, or in the heads of departments.

The President shall have power to fill up all vacancies that may happen during the recess of the Senate, by granting commissions which shall expire at the end of their next session.

Section 3. He shall from time to time give to the Congress information of the state of the union, and recommend to their consideration such measures as he shall judge necessary and expedient; he may, on extraordinary occasions, convene both Houses, or either of them, and in case of disagreement between them, with respect to the time of adjournment, he may adjourn them to such time as he shall think proper; he shall receive ambassadors and other public ministers; he shall take care that the laws be faithfully executed, and shall commission all the officers of the United States.

Section 4. The President, Vice President and all civil officers of the United States, shall be removed from office on impeachment for, and conviction of, treason, bribery, or other high crimes and misdemeanors.

Article III

Section 1. The judicial power of the United States, shall be vested in one Supreme Court, and in such inferior courts as the Congress may from time to time ordain and establish. The judges, both of the supreme and inferior courts, shall hold their offices during good behaviour, and shall, at stated times, receive for their services, a compensation, which shall not be diminished during their continuance in office.

Section 2. The judicial power shall extend to all cases, in law and equity, arising under this Constitution, the laws of the United States, and treaties made, or which shall be made, under their authority;—to all cases affecting ambassadors, other public ministers and consuls;—to all cases of admiralty and maritime jurisdiction;—to controversies to which the United States shall be a party;—to controversies between two or more states;—between a state and citizens of another state;—between citizens of different states;—between citizens of the same state claiming lands under grants of different states, and between a state, or the citizens thereof, and foreign states, citizens or subjects.

In all cases affecting ambassadors, other public ministers and consuls, and those in which a state shall be party, the Supreme Court shall have original jurisdiction. In all the other cases before mentioned, the Supreme Court shall have appellate jurisdiction, both as to law and fact, with such exceptions, and under such regulations as the Congress shall make.

The trial of all crimes, except in cases of impeachment, shall be by jury; and such trial shall be held in the state where the said crimes shall have been committed; but when not committed within any state, the trial shall be at such place or places as the Congress may by law have directed.

Section 3. Treason against the United States, shall consist only in levying war against them, or in adhering to their enemies, giving them aid and comfort. No person shall be convicted of treason unless on the testimony of two witnesses to the same overt act, or on confession in open court.

The Congress shall have power to declare the punishment of treason, but no attainder of treason shall work corruption of blood, or forfeiture except during the life of the person attainted.

Article IV

Section 1. Full faith and credit shall be given in each state to the public acts, records, and judicial proceedings of every other state. And the Congress may by general laws prescribe the manner in which such acts, records, and proceedings shall be proved, and the effect thereof.

Section 2. The citizens of each state shall be entitled to all privileges and immunities of citizens in the several states.

A person charged in any state with treason, felony, or other crime, who shall flee from justice, and be found in another state, shall on demand of the executive authority of the state from which he fled, be delivered up, to be removed to the state having jurisdiction of the crime.

No person held to service or labor in one state, under the laws thereof, escaping into another, shall, in consequence of any law or regulation therein, be discharged from such service or labor, but shall be delivered up on claim of the party to whom such service or labor may be due.

Section 3. New states may be admitted by the Congress into this union; but no new states shall be formed or erected within the jurisdiction of any other state; nor any state be formed by the junction of two or more states, or parts of states, without the consent of the legislatures of the states concerned as well as of the Congress.

The Congress shall have power to dispose of and make all needful rules and regulations respecting the territory or other property belonging to the United States; and nothing in this Constitution shall be so construed as to prejudice any claims of the United States, or of any particular state.

Section 4. The United States shall guarantee to every state in this union a republican form of government, and shall protect each of them against invasion; and on application of the legislature, or of the executive (when the legislature cannot be convened) against domestic violence.

Article V

The Congress, whenever two thirds of both houses shall deem it necessary, shall propose amendments to this Constitution, or, on the application of the legislatures of two thirds of the several states, shall call a convention for proposing amendments, which, in either case, shall be valid to all intents and purposes, as part of this Constitution, when ratified by the legislatures of three fourths of the several states, or by conventions in three fourths thereof, as the one or the other mode of ratification may be proposed by the Congress; provided that no amendment which may be made prior to the year one thousand eight hundred and eight shall in any manner affect the first and fourth clauses in the ninth section of the first article; and that no state, without its consent, shall be deprived of its equal suffrage in the Senate.

Article VI

All debts contracted and engagements entered into, before the adoption of this Constitution, shall be as valid against the United States under this Constitution, as under the Confederation.

This Constitution, and the laws of the United States which shall be made in pursuance thereof; and all treaties made, or which shall be made, under the authority of the United States, shall be the supreme law of the land; and the judges in every state shall be bound thereby, anything in the Constitution or laws of any State to the contrary notwithstanding.

The Senators and Representatives before mentioned, and the members of the several state legislatures, and all executive and judicial officers, both of the United States and of the several states, shall be bound by oath or affirmation, to support this Constitution; but no religious test shall ever be required as a qualification to any office or public trust under the United States.

Article VII

The ratification of the conventions of nine states, shall be sufficient for the establishment of this Constitution between the states so ratifying the same.

Done in convention by the unanimous consent of the states present the seventeenth day of September in the year of our Lord one thousand seven hundred and eighty seven and of the independence of the United States of America the twelfth. In witness whereof We have hereunto subscribed our Names.

ATTACHMENT C-1

The Bill of Rights

The Conventions of a number of the States having, at the time of adopting the Constitution, expressed a desire, in order to prevent misconstruction or abuse of its powers, that further declaratory and restrictive clauses should be added, and as extending the ground of public confidence in the Government will best insure the beneficent ends of its institution;

Resolved, by the Senate and House of Representatives of the United States of America, in Congress assembled, two-thirds of both Houses concurring, that the following articles be proposed to the Legislatures of the several States, as amendments to the Constitution of the United States; all or any of which articles, when ratified by three-fourths of the said Legislatures, to be valid to all intents and purposes as part of the said Constitution, namely:

Amendment I

Congress shall make no law respecting an establishment of religion, or prohibiting the free exercise thereof; or abridging the freedom of speech, or of the press; or the right of the people peaceably to assemble, and to petition the government for a redress of grievances.

Amendment II

A well regulated militia, being necessary to the security of a free state, the right of the people to keep and bear arms, shall not be infringed.

Amendment III

No soldier shall, in time of peace be quartered in any house, without the consent of the owner, nor in time of war, but in a manner to be prescribed by law.

Amendment IV

The right of the people to be secure in their persons, houses, papers, and effects, against unreasonable searches and seizures, shall not be violated, and no warrants shall issue, but upon probable cause, supported by oath or affirmation, and particularly describing the place to be searched, and the persons or things to be seized.

Amendment V

No person shall be held to answer for a capital, or otherwise infamous crime, unless on a presentment or indictment of a grand jury, except in cases arising in the land or naval forces, or in the militia, when in actual service in time of war or public danger; nor shall any person be subject for the same offense to be twice put in jeopardy of life or limb; nor shall be compelled in any criminal case to be a witness against himself, nor be deprived of life, liberty, or property, without due process of law; nor shall private property be taken for public use, without just compensation.

Amendment VI

In all criminal prosecutions, the accused shall enjoy the right to a speedy and public trial, by an impartial jury of the state and district wherein the crime shall have been committed, which district shall have been previously ascertained by law, and to be informed of the nature and cause of the accusation; to be confronted with the witnesses against him; to have compulsory process for obtaining witnesses in his favor, and to have the assistance of counsel for his defense.

Amendment VII

In suits at common law, where the value in controversy shall exceed twenty dollars, the right of trial by jury shall be preserved, and no fact tried by a jury, shall be otherwise reexamined in any court of the United States, than according to the rules of the common law.

Amendment VIII

Excessive bail shall not be required, nor excessive fines imposed, nor cruel and unusual punishments inflicted.

Amendment IX

The enumeration in the Constitution, of certain rights, shall not be construed to deny or disparage others retained by the people.

Amendment X

The powers not delegated to the United States by the Constitution, nor prohibited by it to the states, are reserved to the states respectively, or to the people.

ATTACHMENT C-2

Constitutional Amendments 11–27

Amendment XI (1798)

The judicial power of the United States shall not be construed to extend to any suit in law
or
equity, commenced or prosecuted against one of the United States by citizens of another state, or by citizens or subjects of any foreign state.

Amendment XII (1804)

The electors shall meet in their respective states and vote by ballot for President and Vice-President, one of whom, at least, shall not be an inhabitant of the same state with themselves; they shall name in their ballots the person voted for as President, and in distinct ballots the person voted for as Vice-President, and they shall make distinct lists of all persons voted for as President, and of all persons voted for as Vice-President, and of the number of votes for each, which lists they shall sign and certify, and transmit sealed to the seat of the government of the United States, directed to the President of the Senate;—The President of the Senate shall, in the presence of the Senate and House of Representatives, open all the certificates and the votes shall then be counted;—the person having the greatest number of votes for President, shall be the President, if such number be a majority of the whole number of electors appointed; and if no person have such majority, then from the persons having the highest numbers not exceeding three on the list of those voted for as President, the House of Representatives shall choose immediately, by ballot, the President. But in choosing the President, the votes shall be taken by states, the representation from each state having one vote; a quorum for this purpose shall consist of a member or members from two-thirds of the states, and a majority of all the states shall be necessary to a choice. And if the House of Representatives shall not choose a President whenever the right of choice shall devolve upon them, before the fourth day of March next following, then the Vice-President shall act as President, as in the case of the death or other constitutional disability of the President. The person having the greatest number of votes as Vice-President, shall be the Vice-President, if such number be a majority of the whole number of electors appointed, and if no person have a majority, then from the two highest numbers on the list, the Senate shall choose the Vice-President; a quorum for the purpose shall consist of two-thirds of the whole number of Senators, and a majority of the whole number shall be necessary to a choice. But no person constitutionally ineligible to the office of President shall be eligible to that of Vice-President of the United States.

Amendment XIII (1865)

Section 1. Neither slavery nor involuntary servitude, except as a punishment for crime whereof the party shall have been duly convicted, shall exist within the United States, or any place subject to their jurisdiction.
Section 2. Congress shall have power to enforce this article by appropriate legislation.

Amendment XIV (1868)

Section 1. All persons born or naturalized in the United States, and subject to the jurisdiction thereof, are citizens of the United States and of the state wherein they reside. No state shall make or enforce any law which shall abridge the privileges or immunities of citizens of the United States; nor shall any state deprive any person of life, liberty, or property, without due process of law; nor deny to any person within its jurisdiction the equal protection of the laws.
Section 2. Representatives shall be apportioned among the several states according to their respective numbers, counting the whole number of persons in each state, excluding Indians not taxed. But when the right to vote at any election for the choice of electors for President and Vice President of the United States, Representatives in Congress, the executive and judicial officers of a state, or the members of the legislature thereof, is denied to any of the male inhabitants of such state, being twenty-one years of age, and citizens of the United States, or in any way abridged, except for participation in rebellion, or other crime, the basis of representation therein shall be reduced in the proportion which the number of such male citizens shall bear to the whole number of male citizens twenty-one years of age in such state.
Section 3. No person shall be a Senator or Representative in Congress, or elector of President and Vice President, or hold any office, civil or military, under the United States, or under any state, who, having previously taken an oath, as a member of Congress, or as an officer of the United States, or as a member of any state legislature, or as an executive or judicial officer of any state, to support the Constitution of the United States, shall have engaged in insurrection or rebellion against the same, or given aid or comfort to the enemies thereof. But Congress may by a vote of two-thirds of each House, remove such disability.
Section 4. The validity of the public debt of the United States, authorized by law, including debts incurred for payment of pensions and bounties for services in suppressing insurrection or rebellion, shall not be questioned. But neither the United States nor any state shall assume or pay any debt or

obligation incurred in aid of insurrection or rebellion against the United States, or any claim for the loss or emancipation of any slave; but all such debts, obligations and claims shall be held illegal and void.
Section 5. The Congress shall have power to enforce, by appropriate legislation, the provisions of this article.

Amendment XV (1870)

Section 1. The right of citizens of the United States to vote shall not be denied or abridged by the United States or by any state on account of race, color, or previous condition of servitude.
Section 2. The Congress shall have power to enforce this article by appropriate legislation.

Amendment XVI (1913)

The Congress shall have power to lay and collect taxes on incomes, from whatever source derived, without apportionment among the several states, and without regard to any census of enumeration.

Amendment XVII (1913)

The Senate of the United States shall be composed of two Senators from each state, elected by the people thereof, for six years; and each Senator shall have one vote. The electors in each state shall have the qualifications requisite for electors of the most numerous branch of the state legislatures.

When vacancies happen in the representation of any state in the Senate, the executive authority of such state shall issue writs of election to fill such vacancies: Provided, that the legislature of any state may empower the executive thereof to make temporary appointments until the people fill the vacancies by election as the legislature may direct.

This amendment shall not be so construed as to affect the election or term of any Senator chosen before it becomes valid as part of the Constitution.

Amendment XVIII (1919)

Section 1. After one year from the ratification of this article the manufacture, sale, or transportation of intoxicating liquors within, the importation thereof into, or the exportation thereof from the United States and all territory subject to the jurisdiction thereof for beverage purposes is hereby prohibited.
Section 2. The Congress and the several states shall have concurrent power to enforce this article by appropriate legislation.

Section 3. This article shall be inoperative unless it shall have been ratified as an amendment to the Constitution by the legislatures of the several states, as provided in the Constitution, within seven years from the date of the submission hereof to the states by the Congress.

Amendment XIX (1920)

The right of citizens of the United States to vote shall not be denied or abridged by the United States or by any state on account of sex.

Congress shall have power to enforce this article by appropriate legislation.

Amendment XX (1933)

Section 1. The terms of the President and Vice President shall end at noon on the 20th day of January, and the terms of Senators and Representatives at noon on the 3d day of January, of the years in which such terms would have ended if this article had not been ratified; and the terms of their successors shall then begin.

Section 2. The Congress shall assemble at least once in every year, and such meeting shall begin at noon on the 3d day of January, unless they shall by law appoint a different day.

Section 3. If, at the time fixed for the beginning of the term of the President, the President elect shall have died, the Vice President elect shall become President. If a President shall not have been chosen before the time fixed for the beginning of his term, or if the President elect shall have failed to qualify, then the Vice President elect shall act as President until a President shall have qualified; and the Congress may by law provide for the case wherein neither a President elect nor a Vice President elect shall have qualified, declaring who shall then act as President, or the manner in which one who is to act shall be selected, and such person shall act accordingly until a President or Vice President shall have qualified.

Section 4. The Congress may by law provide for the case of the death of any of the persons from whom the House of Representatives may choose a President whenever the right of choice shall have devolved upon them, and for the case of the death of any of the persons from whom the Senate may choose a Vice President whenever the right of choice shall have devolved upon them.

Section 5. Sections 1 and 2 shall take effect on the 15th day of October following the ratification of this article.

Section 6. This article shall be inoperative unless it shall have been ratified as an amendment to the Constitution by the legislatures of three-fourths of the several states within seven years from the date of its submission.

Amendment XXI (1933)

Section 1. The eighteenth article of amendment to the Constitution of the United States is hereby repealed.
Section 2. The transportation or importation into any state, territory, or possession of the United States for delivery or use therein of intoxicating liquors, in violation of the laws thereof, is hereby prohibited.
Section 3. This article shall be inoperative unless it shall have been ratified as an amendment to the Constitution by conventions in the several states, as provided in the Constitution, within seven years from the date of the submission hereof to the states by the Congress.

Amendment XXII (1951)

Section 1. No person shall be elected to the office of the President more than twice, and no person who has held the office of President, or acted as President, for more than two years of a term to which some other person was elected President shall be elected to the office of the President more than once. But this article shall not apply to any person holding the office of President when this article was proposed by the Congress, and shall not prevent any person who may be holding the office of President, or acting as President, during the term within which this article becomes operative from holding the office of President or acting as President during the remainder of such term.
Section 2. This article shall be inoperative unless it shall have been ratified as an amendment to the Constitution by the legislatures of three-fourths of the several states within seven years from the date of its submission to the states by the Congress.

Amendment XXIII (1961)

Section 1. The District constituting the seat of government of the United States shall appoint in such manner as the Congress may direct:

A number of electors of President and Vice President equal to the whole number of Senators and Representatives in Congress to which the District would be entitled if it were a state, but in no event more than the least populous state; they shall be in addition to those appointed by the states, but they shall be considered, for the purposes of the election of President and Vice President, to be electors appointed by a state; and they shall meet in the District and perform such duties as provided by the twelfth article of amendment.
Section 2. The Congress shall have power to enforce this article by appropriate legislation.

Amendment XXIV (1964)

Section 1. The right of citizens of the United States to vote in any primary or other election for President or Vice President, for electors for President or Vice President, or for Senator or Representative in Congress, shall not be denied or abridged by the United States or any state by reason of failure to pay any poll tax or other tax.

Section 2. The Congress shall have power to enforce this article by appropriate legislation.

Amendment XXV (1967)

Section 1. In case of the removal of the President from office or of his death or resignation, the Vice President shall become President.

Section 2. Whenever there is a vacancy in the office of the Vice President, the President shall nominate a Vice President who shall take office upon confirmation by a majority vote of both Houses of Congress.

Section 3. Whenever the President transmits to the President pro tempore of the Senate and the Speaker of the House of Representatives his written declaration that he is unable to discharge the powers and duties of his office, and until he transmits to them a written declaration to the contrary, such powers and duties shall be discharged by the Vice President as Acting President.

Section 4. Whenever the Vice President and a majority of either the principal officers of the executive departments or of such other body as Congress may by law provide, transmit to the President pro tempore of the Senate and the Speaker of the House of Representatives their written declaration that the President is unable to discharge the powers and duties of his office, the Vice President shall immediately assume the powers and duties of the office as Acting President.

Thereafter, when the President transmits to the President pro tempore of the Senate and the Speaker of the House of Representatives his written declaration that no inability exists, he shall resume the powers and duties of his office unless the Vice President and a majority of either the principal officers of the executive department or of such other body as Congress may by law provide, transmit within four days to the President pro tempore of the Senate and the Speaker of the House of Representatives their written declaration that the President is unable to discharge the powers and duties of his office. Thereupon Congress shall decide the issue, assembling within forty-eight hours for that purpose if not in session. If the Congress, within twenty-one days after receipt of the latter written declaration, or, if Congress is not in session, within twenty-one days after Congress is required to assemble, determines by two-thirds vote of both Houses that the President is unable to discharge the powers and duties of his office, the Vice President shall continue to discharge the same as Acting

President; otherwise, the President shall resume the powers and duties of his office.

Amendment XXVI (1971)

Section 1. The right of citizens of the United States, who are 18 years of age or older, to vote, shall not be denied or abridged by the United States or any state on account of age.
Section 2. The Congress shall have the power to enforce this article by appropriate legislation.

Amendment XXVII (1992)

No law varying the compensation for the services of the Senators and Representatives shall take effect until an election of Representatives shall have intervened.

ATTACHMENT D

Individual Rights Found in the Text of the Constitution Excluding the Amendments

As collected by Professor Chemerinsky, Constitutional Law, at pp. 477–479.

Article I, § 9

The privilege of the Writ of Habeas Corpus shall not be suspended, unless when in Cases of Rebellion or Invasion, the public Safety may require it.
   No Bill of Attainder or ex post facto Law shall be passed.

Article I, § 10

No State shall ... pass any Bill of Attainder, ex post facto Law, or law impairing the Obligation of Contracts.

Article III, § 2

The trial of all Crimes, except in Cases of Impeachment, shall be by jury; and such Trial shall be held in the State where the said Crimes shall have been committed.

Article III, § 3

Treason against the United States, shall consist only in levying War against them or, in adhering to their Enemies, giving them Aid and Comfort. No person shall be convicted of Treason unless on the Testimony of two Witnesses to the same overt Act, or on Confession in open Court. The Congress shall have Power to declare the Punishment of Treason, but no Attainder of Treason shall work Corruption of Blood, or Forfeiture except during the Life of the Person attained.

Article IV, § 2

The Citizens of each State shall be entitled to all Privileges and Immunities of Citizens in the several States.

Article VI, cl. 3:

[N]o religious Test shall ever be required as a Qualification to any Office of public Trust under the United States.

ATTACHMENT E

The Emancipation Proclamation (1863)

By the President of the United States of America:
A PROCLAMATION
Whereas on the 22nd day of September, A.D. 1862, a proclamation was issued by the President of the United States, containing, among other things, the following, to wit:

"That on the 1st day of January, A.D. 1863, all persons held as slaves within any State or designated part of a State the people whereof shall then be in rebellion against the United States shall be then, thenceforward, and forever free; and the executive government of the United States, including the military and naval authority thereof, will recognize and maintain the freedom of such persons and will do no act or acts to repress such persons, or any of them, in any efforts they may make for their actual freedom.

"That the executive will on the 1st day of January aforesaid, by proclamation, designate the States and parts of States, if any, in which the people thereof, respectively, shall then be in rebellion against the United States; and the fact that any State or the people thereof shall on that day be in good faith represented in the Congress of the United States by members chosen thereto at elections wherein a majority of the qualified voters of such States shall have participated shall, in the absence of strong countervailing testimony, be deemed conclusive evidence that such State and the people thereof are not then in rebellion against the United States."

Now, therefore, I, Abraham Lincoln, President of the United States, by virtue of the power in me vested as Commander-In-Chief of the Army and Navy of the United States in time of actual armed rebellion against the authority and government of the United States, and as a fit and necessary war measure for supressing [sic] said rebellion, do, on this 1st day of January, A.D. 1863, and in accordance with my purpose so to do, publicly proclaimed for the full period of one hundred days from the first day above mentioned, order and designate as the States and parts of States wherein the people thereof, respectively, are this day in rebellion against the United States the following, to wit:

Arkansas, Texas, Louisiana (except the parishes of St. Bernard, Palquemines, Jefferson, St. John, St. Charles, St. James, Ascension, Assumption, Terrebone, Lafourche, St. Mary, St. Martin, and Orleans, including the city of New Orleans), Mississippi, Alabama, Florida, Georgia, South Carolina, North Carolina, and Virginia (except the forty-eight counties designated as West Virginia, and also the counties of Berkeley, Accomac, Morthhampton,

Elizabeth City, York, Princess Anne, and Norfolk, including the cities of Norfolk and Portsmouth), and which excepted parts are for the present left precisely as if this proclamation were not issued.

And by virtue of the power and for the purpose aforesaid, I do order and declare that all persons held as slaves within said designated States and parts of States are, and henceforward shall be, free; and that the Executive Government of the United States, including the military and naval authorities thereof, will recognize and maintain the freedom of said persons.

And I hereby enjoin upon the people so declared to be free to abstain from all violence, unless in necessary self-defence; and I recommend to them that, in all case when allowed, they labor faithfully for reasonable wages.

And I further declare and make known that such persons of suitable condition will be received into the armed service of the United States to garrison forts, positions, stations, and other places, and to man vessels of all sorts in said service.

And upon this act, sincerely believed to be an act of justice, warranted by the Constitution upon military necessity, I invoke the considerate judgment of mankind and the gracious favor of Almighty God.

BIBLIOGRAPHY

Bibliography of most important books consulted in the preparation of this edition, whether or not cited in the text. Articles listed are those cited in the text.

Ackerman, Bruce A. *We the People: Foundations* (1991).
Black, Jr., Charles L. *Impeachment: A Handbook* (1974).
Bork, Robert H. *The Tempting of America: The Political Seduction of the Law* (1990).
Chemerinsky, Erwin. *Parity Reconsidered: Defining a Role for the Federal Judiciary*, 36 University of California Los Angeles Law Review 233 (1988).
Chemerinsky, Erwin. *Constitutional Law: Principles and Policies* (3d ed. 2006).
Choper, Jesse H. *Judicial Review and the National Political Process* (1980).
Crandall, Samuel Benjamin. *Treaties: Their Making and Enforcement* (2005).
Currie, David P. *The Constitution of the Federal Republic of Germany* (1994).
Dahl, Robert. *On Democracy* (1999).
Daniels, Roger. *Concentration Camps North America: Japanese in the United States and Canada during World War II* (reprint ed. 1993).
Eberle, Edward J. *Public Discourse in Contemporary Germany*, 47 Case Western Reserve 797 (1977).
Ely, John Hart. *Democracy and Distrust* (1980).
Epstein, Richard A. *Forbidden Grounds: The Case Against Employment Discrimination Laws* (1992).
Farber, Daniel A., and Suzanna Sherry. *A History of the American Constitution* (1990).
Farrand, Max. *The Records of the Federal Convention of 1787*, vol. 1 (1913).
Fischer, Katrina L. *Harnessing the Treaty Power in Support of Environmental Regulation of Activities that Don't "Substantially Affect Interstate Commerce": Recognizing the Realities of the New Federalism*, 22 Virginia Environmental Law Journal 167 (2004).
Fiss, Owen, *Groups and the Equal Protection Clause*, 5 Philosophy & Public Affairs 107 (1976).
Fletcher, George P. *Basic Concepts of Legal Thought* (1996).
Friedman, Lawrence M. *A History of American Law* (2d ed. 1985).
Gardner, James A. *The Positivist Revolution that Wasn't: Constitutional Universalism in the States*, 4 Roger Williams Law Review 109 (1998).
Gaulding, Jill. *Note: Race, Sex, and Genetic Discrimination in Insurance: What's Fair?*, 80 Cornell Law Review 1646 (1995).
Gunther, Gerald. *Foreword: In Search of Evolving Doctrine on a Changing Court: A Model for a Newer Equal Protection*, 86 Harvard Law Review 1 (1972).
Gunther, Gerald, and Kathleen M. Sullivan. *Constitutional Law* (16th ed. 2007).
Hadek, David V. *Why the Policy Behind the Irrebuttable Presumption of Paternity Will Never Die*, 26 Southwestern University Law Review 359 (1997).
Hall, Kermit, William Wiecek, and Paul Finkelman. *American Legal History: Cases and Materials* (2d ed. 1996).

Hamilton, Alexander, John Jay, and James Madison. *The Federalist: A Commentary on The Constitution of the United States, being A Collection of Essays written in Support of the Constitution agreed upon September 17, 1787*, by The Federal Convention (H.C. Lodge, ed. 1888).

Hayek, Friedrich A. *The Constitution of Liberty* (1960).

Hughes, Charles Evans. Speech before the Elmira [N.Y.] Chamber of Commerce, May 3, 1907, in Addresses and Papers of Charles Evans Hughes 133 (1908).

Issacharoff, Samuel, and Erica Worth Harris. *Is Age Discrimination Really Age Discrimination?: The ADEA's Unnatural Solution*, 72 New York University Law Review 780 (1997).

Jackson, Vicki C. *Federalism and the Uses and Limits of Law: Printz and Principle?*, 111 Harvard Law Review 2180 (1998).

Jaffa, Harry V. *Original Intent and the Framers of the Constitution: A Disputed Question* (1994).

Kahn, Paul W. *Commentary: Interpretation and Authority in State Constitutionalism*, 106 Harvard Law Review 1147 (1993).

Koh, Harold. The National Security Constitution (1990).

Kramer, Donald T. *American Jurisprudence* (2d ed. 2007).

Kramer, Larry. *The Lawmaking Power of the Federal Courts*, 12 Pace L. Rev. 263 (1992).

Larson, Lex K. *Employment Discrimination*, vol. 3 (2d ed. 1994).

Locke, John. *Of Civil Government* (London 1936).

Lundmark, Thomas. *East Germans' Conversion to Democracy*, 20 Fordham International Law Journal 384 (1996).

Lundmark, Thomas. *Forms and Legitimacy of States*, 6 Juridisk Tidskrift vid Stockholms Universitet 647 (1994–95).

Lundmark, Thomas, Juristische Technik und Methodik des Common Law (Münster 1998).

Lundmark, Thomas, and John B. McNeece. *State and Local Government Participation in Solving Environmental Problems at the U.S.-Mexican Border*, 3 Journal of Environmental Law & Practice 37 (1995).

Lundmark, Thomas. *Landscape, Recreation, and Takings in German and American Law* (Stuttgart 1997).

Lundmark, Thomas. *Regulation of Private Logging in California*, 5 Ecology Law Quarterly 139 (1975).

Lundmark, Thomas, *Die Freiheit der Werbung und der Grundsatz der Verhältnismäßigkeit in der amerikanischen Rechtsprechung*, 1994 Verwaltungs-Archiv 522.

Lupu, Ira C. *Untangling the Strands of the Fourteenth Amendment*, 77 Michigan Law Review 981 (1979).

Maloney, Kerrie E. *Gender-Motivated Violence and the Commerce Clause: The Civil Rights Provision of the Violence Against Women Act After Lopez*, 96 Columbia Law Review 1876 (1996).

Massey, Calvin. *Getting There: A Brief History of the Politics of Supreme Court Appointments*, 19 Hastings Constitutional Law Quarterly 1 (1991).

McKinley, Stacey L. *The Violence Against Women Act After United States v. Lopez: Will Domestic Violence Jurisdiction be Returned to the States?*, 44 Cleveland State Law Review 345 (1996).

McTaggart, Kelli C. *The Violence Against Women Act: Recognizing a Federal Civil Right to be Free from Violence*, 86 Georgetown Law Journal 1123 (1998).

Merryman, John Henry. *The French Deviation*, 44 American Journal of Comparative Law 109 (1996).
Mikva, Abner J. *Doubting Our Claims to Democracy*, 39 Arizona Law Review 793 (1997).
Montesquieu, Charles Louis de Secondat. *De l'esprit des loix, ou du rapport que les loix doivent avoir avec la constitution de chaque gouvernement, les moeurs, le climat, la religion, le commerce,* 1–3 (1749).
Mosk, Richard M. *The Jurisprudence of Ratings Symposium Part I: Motion Picture Ratings in the United States,* 15 Cardozo Arts & Entertainment Law Journal 135 (1997).
Nowak, John E., and Ronald D. Rotunda. *Constitutional Law* (5th ed. 1995).
Perlin, Michael L. *Individual Rights and Reasonable Accommodations under the Americans with Disabilities Act: "Make Promises by the Hour": Sex, Drugs, the ADA, and Psychiatric Hospitalization,* 46 DePaul Law Review 947 (1997).
Ross, William G. *The Supreme Court Appointment Process: A Search for a Synthesis,* 57 Albany Law Review 993 (1994).
Rotunda, Ronald D., *Independent Counsel and the Charges of Leaking: A Brief Case Study,* 68 Fordham Law Review 869 (1999).
Rubin, Edward L., and Malcolm Feeley. *Federalism: Some Notes on a National Neurosis,* 41 University of California Los Angeles Law Review 903 (1994).
Rubin, Edward L. *The Fundamentality and Irrelevance of Federalism,* 13 Georgia State University Law Review 1009 (1997).
Schlesinger, Arthur M., Jr. *The Disuniting of America: Reflections on a Multicultural Society* (1992).
Shaman, Jeffrey. *Cracks in the Structure: The Coming Breakdown of the Levels of Scrutiny,* 45 Ohio State Law Journal 161 (1984).
Stuckey, Tara M. *Jurisdictional Hooks in the Wake of Raich: On Properly Interpreting Federal Regulations of Interstate Commerce,* 81 Notre Dame Law Review 2101 (2006).
Simon, Larry G. *The Authority of the Framers of the Constitution: Can Original Interpretation Be Justified?,* 73 California Law Review 1482 (1985).
Singer, Joseph William. *No Right to Exclude: Public Accommodations and Private Property,* 90 Northwestern University Law Review 1283 (1996).
Smith, Rogers M. *Liberalism and American Constitutional Law* (1990).
Solimine, Michael E., and James L. Walker. *Federalism, Liberty and State Constitutional Law,* 23 Ohio Northern University Law Review 1457 (1997).
Stone, Geoffrey R., Louis M. Seidman, Cass R. Sunstein, and Mark V. Tushnet. *Constitutional Law* (5th ed., 2005).
Toobin, Jeffrey. *A Vast Conspiracy: The Real Story of the Sex Scandal that Nearly Brought Down the President* (2000).
Treanor, William Michael, *Fame, The Founding, and the Power to Declare War,* 82 Cornell L. Rev. 694 (1997).
Tribe, Laurence H. *American Constitutional Law* (3d ed., 2000).
U.S. Bureau of Labor Statistics and the Census Bureau, Current Population Survey (CPS) Table A-1, Reported Voting and Registration by Race, Hispanic Origin, Sex, and Age Groups: November 1964 to 2004.
Williams, Robert F. *State Constitutional Law Processes,* 24 William & Mary Law Review 169 (1983).
Wright, Robert. *The Moral Animal: Evolutionary Psychology and Everyday Life* (1995).

Table of Cases

Excerpted cases are in boldface type.

44 Liquormart, Inc. v. Rhode Island 151

Aetna Life Insurance Co. v. Haworth........................... 77
Agostini v. Felton... 155
Alabama v. Garrett 100
Allegheny, County of, v. American Civil Liberties Union
    Greater Pittsburgh Chapter 153
Allegheny Pittsburgh Coal Co. v. County Commission............ 117
Ambach v. Norwick... 193
American Party of Texas v. White,wz 118
Apodaca v. Oregon... 112
Arnett v. Kennedy... 126

Baggett v. Bullitt 151
Bailey v. Alabama... 113
Baker v. Carr 78, 90
Bakke, Regents of the University of California v. 182
Baldwin v. Fish and Game Comm'n of Mont...................... 199
Bates v. State Bar of Arizona................................. 150
Batson v. Kentucky 185
Bayside Timber Co. v. Board of Supervisors 64
Beal v. Doe... 116
Beauharnais v. Illinois....................................... 135
Bell v. Burson.. 126
Bigelow v. Virginia... 150
BMW of North America, Inc. v. Gore 117
Board of Regents v. Roth 126
Board of Trustees of the University of Alabama v. Garrett....... 53, 109
Boddie v. Connecticut... 196
Boerne, City of, v. Flores.................................... 53

239

Bolger v. Youngs Drug Products Corp. 150
Bolling v. Sharpe. 128, 174, 185
Bonham's Case 80
Boos v. Barry 147
Bounds v. Smith. 163
Bowers v. Hardwick. 174
Brandenburg v. Ohio 2, **133**, 173
Broadrick v. Oklahoma. 151
Brown v. Board of Education [Brown I] 2, **188**, 191
Brown v. Board of Education [Brown II] 2, **191**, 192
Brown v. Oklahoma. 138
Buckley v. Valeo. 19, 129
Burton v. Wilmington Parking Authority 115
Butler v. Perry 195

Caban v. Mohammed 195
Califano v. Webster 195
California v. LaRue 142
Campbell v. Louisiana. 173
Cantwell v. Connecticut 142
Carey v. Population Services
    International 150
Carter v. Carter Coal Co. 21
Castaneda v. Partida 184
Central Hudson Gas & Electric Corp. v. Public Service
    Commission of New York 120, 150
Chaplinsky v. New Hampshire 136, 144
Cheffer v. Reno 36
Chicago, City of, v. Int'l College of Surgeons 173
Chicago & Grand Trunk Railway v. Wellman 78
Chicago Police Department v. Mosley. 146
Church of the Lukumi Babalu Aye, Inc. v. City of Hialeah 156
City of Boerne v. Flores. 53
City of Chicago v. Int'l College of Surgeons 173
City of Dallas v. Stanglin 129
City of Ladue v. Gilleo. 147
City of Renton v. Playtime Theatres, Inc. 146
City of Richmond v. J.A. Croson Co.. . . . . 2, 173, **179**
Civil Rights Cases 23
Clark v. Allen. 55
Cleburne v. Cleburne Living Center, Inc. 196
Clinton v. Jones. 2, **70**
Cohen v. California. 129, 132

Coleman v. Miller 90
Collin v. Smith.. 135
Connell v. Higginbotham.. 151
Cornelius v. NAACP Legal Defense & Education Fund 148
County of Allegheny v. American Civil Liberties Union
    Greater Pittsburgh Chapter 153
Cox v. New Hampshire....................................... 142, 147
Craig v. Boren 120, 195
Cruzan v. Director.. 163

Dallas, City of, v. Stanglin...................................... 129
Dames & Moore v. Regan.. 55
Dawson v. Delaware... 129, 151
DeBartolo Corp. v. Florida Gulf Coast Building and
    Construction Trades Council 130
Dennis v. United States.. 133
DeShaney v. Winnebago County Department of Social Services..... 113
Doe v. McMillan 15
Dr. Bonham's Case 80
Duke Power Co. v. Carolina Environmental Study Group, Inc...... 117
Dun & Bradstreet, Inc. v. Greenmoss Builders, Inc............... 136
Duncan v. Louisiana 97
Dunn v. Blumstein.. 118

Edenfield v. Fane.. 150
Edmonson v. Leesville Concrete Co................................ 115
Edwards v. California .... .97
Edwards v. South Carolina 147
Eisenstadt v. Baird.. 165
Employment Division v. Smith.................................... 156
Equal Opportunity Employment Commission v. Wyoming............. 100
Erznoznik v. City of Jacksonville................................ 147
Evans v. Abney... 115

Federal Energy Regulatory Commission v. Mississippi............. 100
Fiallo v. Bell... 194
Flast v. Cohen .... .78
Fletcher v. Peck.. .86
Foley v. Connelie.. 193
44 Liquormart, Inc. v. Rhode Island 151
Freeman v. Maryland 148, 149
Frontiero v. Richardson 195
Fullilove v. Klutznick... 180

Gade v. National Solid Waste Management Association. 98
Garcia v. San Antonio Metropolitan Transit Authority. 100
Geduldig v. Aiello 195
Gertz v. Robert Welch, Inc. 136
Gibbons v. Ogden 20
Gibbs v. Babbitt 34
Gitlow v. New York. 127, 133
Goldberg v. Kelly. 126
Goldwater v. Carter 91
Gomez v. Perez 194
Gomillion v. Lightfoot 184
Gonzales v. Carhart. **52**
Gonzales v. Raich 2, **20**, 32
Gooding v. Wilson. 137
Goss v. Lopez. 126
Graham v. Richardson 193
Gravel v. United States 15
Gregory v. Ashcroft 26, 77, 100
Griffiths, In re 193
Griswold v. Connecticut. 162, 163, 165

Hague v. Committee for Industrial Organization. 142, 147
Hamdi v. Rumsfeld 62
Hammer v. Dagenhart 21
Hampton v. Mow Sun Wong. 112, 174
Harper & Row v. Nation Enterprises 135
Harris v. McRae 196
Head Money Cases 55
Heart of Atlanta Motel v. United States 2, 18, **22**, 27, 28, 35
Heffron v. International Society for
    Krishna Consciousness. 146, 147, 148
Helvering v. Davis 18
Hernandez v. Texas. 188
Hirabayashi v. United States. 175
Hodel v. Virginia Surface Mining &
    Reclamation Assn., Inc. 22, 27, 30, 35, 100
Hoffman Homes, Inc. v. EPA 34
Holmgren v. United States 102
Hughes v. Oklahoma. 20
Hustler Magazine, Inc. v. Falwell 132
Hutardo v. California 128
Hutchinson v. Proxmire 15
Hynes v. Mayor of Oradell 146

Immigration and Naturalization Service v. Chadha 64
In re Winship. 163

Jackman v. Bodine. 90
Jacobellis v. Ohio. 139
J.E.B. v. Alabama 185
Jenkins v. Georgia. 2, **139**, 141
Jones & Laughlin Steel 26, 27
Jones v. Clinton 74

Kahn v. Shevin. 195
Katzenbach v. McClung 22, 27
Kelley v. Johnson. 173
Keyes v. School Dist. No. 1 . . . . 186, 192
Kidd v. Pearson 20
Kilroy v. Winter 36
Kimel v. Florida Board of Regents 53, 100, 109
Kleindienst v. Mandel 14
Knox v. Lee 14
Kolender v. Lawson. 146
Korematsu v. United States 2, **175**, 179
Kovacs v. Cooper. 146

Ladue, City of, v. Gilleo. 147
Lallix v. Lallix 194
Lawrence v. Texas 163, 174
Lebron v. National Railroad Passenger Corporation 112
Lee v. Weisman 152, 153
Lehr v. Robertson 120, 126
Leon v. Kurtzman 152
Levy v. Louisiana 194
Lewis v. City of New Orleans. 138
Liner v. Jafcom, Inc. 78
Linmark Associates, Inc. v. Township of Willingboro 151
Lloyd v. Tanner 109
Lochner v. New York. 162, 173
Logan v. Zimmerman Brush Co. 126
Lorillard Tobacco Co. v. Reilly 151
Lovell v. City of Griffin 142, 148
Loving v. Virginia 163, 165, 173
Lubin v. Parrish. 163
Lugar v. Edmondson Oil Co. 115

Lujan v. Defenders of Wildlife 79
Lynch v. Donnelly 152

Marbury v. Madison 2, **72**, 81, 86, 116
Marcus v. Search Warrant 149
Marina Point, Ltd. v. Wolfson 109
Marsh v. Alabama 115
Marsh v. Chambers 153
Marston v. Lewis 118
Martin v. Hunter's Lessee 2, **87**
Martin v. Mott 91
Massachusetts Board of Retirement v. Murgia 196
Mathews v. Diaz 193
McCray v. United States 17
McCulloch v. Maryland 2, **37**, 38
McGowan v. Maryland 153
McIntyre v. Ohio Elections Commission 130
McLaurin v. Oklahoma 190
Medtronic, Inc. v. Lohr 98
Memoirs v. Massachusetts 139
Memorial Hospital v. Maricopa County 118
Memphis Light, Gas & Water Division v. Craft 126
Metromedia, Inc. v. City of San Diego 146
Meyer v. Nebraska 160, 163, 165
Michael H. v. Gerald D. 194
Michael M. v. Sonoma
    County Superior Court 195
Miller v. California 139, 140, 141
Miller v. Johnson 118
Minneapolis & St. Louis R.R. Co. v. Bombolis 112, 128
Mississippi University for Women v. Hogan 195
Missouri ex rel. Gaines v. Canada 188
Missouri v. Holland 35, 53
Moore v. City of East Cleveland 163
Moore v. Ogilvie 78
Morrison v. Olson 2, **35**, 53, 68
Morton v. Mancari 188
Mueller v. Allen 155, 156
Myers v. United States 8, 67

National Labor Relations Board v. Jones
    Laughlin Steel Corporation 22
Near v. Minnesota 148, 149

New State Ice Co. v. Liebman..93
New York Times Co. v. Sullivan 136, 138
New York Times v. United States 149
New York v. Ferber 139
New York v. United States..............................99, 100, 105
Nixon v. Fitzgerald 70
Nixon v. United States 14, 67, 90
Nyquist v. Mauclet..193

Ogden v. Saunders 112
O'Hare Truck Service, Inc. v. City of Northlake..................151
Ohralik v. Ohio 150
Oregon v. Mitchell 116

Palko v. Connecticut..128
Panama Refining Co. v. Ryan..64
Parents Involved in Community Schools v. Seattle
    School District No. 1..193
Parham v. Hughes..195
Paris Adult Theatre I v. Slaton 140
Penthouse International Ltd. v. McAuliffe 142
Perez v. Campbell..98
Perez v. United States..22, 27
Perry Education Association
    v. Perry Local Educators' Association 147
Philadelphia Newspaper, Inc. v. Hepps..........................136
Pierce v. Society of Sisters......................158, 159, 163, 165
Plessy v. Ferguson 188, 189, 190
Plyler v. Doe 2, **120**, 122, 163
Poe v. Ullman 78
Pollock v. Farmers' Loan & Trust Co. 17, 116
Presser v. Illinois...128
Prince v. Massachusetts..165
Printz v. United States 2, **101**
Prize Cases..56

Railroad Retirement Board v. Alton Railway Co................25
R.A.V. v. City of St. Paul...................................2, **143**
Reed v. Reed 195
Regents, Board of, v. Roth 126
Regents of the University of California v. Bakke..............182
Renton, City of, v. Playtime Theatres, Inc. 146
Rescue Army v. Municipal Court 78

Richmond, City of, v. J.A. Croson Co. 2, 173, **179**
Robins v. Pruneyard Shopping Center 109
Roe v. Wade. 2, **163**, 164
Rosenblatt v. Baer 136
Rosenfeld v. New Jersey 137
Rostker v. Goldberg. 195
Roth v. United States. 138
Roudebush v. Hartke 90
Rubin v. Coors Brewing Co.. 119
Rubin v. United States. 70
Russell v. United States. 22
Rutan v. Republican Party of Illinois 151

Sabri v. United States 51
Saenz v. Roe. 2, 163, **197**
San Antonio Independent School
    District v. Rodriguez 109, 118, 125, 163
Santosky v. Kramer 163
Schad v. Borough of Mt. Ephraim 146
Schaumburg, Village of, v. Citizens for a Better Environment. 129
Schechter Poultry Corp. v. United States 21, 64
Schlessinger v. Ballard 195
Schneider v. State of New Jersey. 142, 147
Serrano v. Priest. 109
Shapiro v. Thompson 118, 198, 200
Sheldon v. Sill 75
Shelley v. Kraemer. 115, 171
Sibron v. New York 78
Skinner v. Oklahoma 163, 165
Slaughterhouse Cases 127
Smith v. Allwright 115
Sonzinsky v. United States 34
Spence v. Washington. 130
Stanley v. Georgia 139, 163, 165
Steward Machine Co. v. Davis. 18
Stone v. Graham 152
Strauder v. West Virginia. 186
Sturges v. Crowninshield 97
Sugarman v. Dougall. 193
Swann v. Charlotte-Mecklenburg Board of Education 192
Sweatt v. Painter 190
Swift & Co. v. United States 30

Talley v. California..130
Terminiello v. Chicago..132
Terry v. Adams..115
Testa v. Klatt..101
Texas v. Johnson...131
Toll v. Moreno...193
Train v. New York..63

United States v. Bajakajian....................................119
United States v. Belmont..55
United States v. Bishop...36
United States v. Bongiorno......................................36
United States v. Brewster.......................................15
United States v. Carolene
    Products Co................................117, 162, 172
United States v. Cummings.......................................36
United States v. Curtiss-Wright Export Corp.....................16
United States v. Darby.....................................99, 100
United States v. Denalli..36
United States v. Dorris...36
United States v. E.C. Knight Co............................20, 21
United States v. Eichman.......................**2, 131**, 173
United States v. Faasse...36
United States v. Gallimore......................................36
United States v. Gerlach Live Stock Co..........................17
United States v. Grace...147
United States v. Guest...198
United States v. Guy W. Capps, Inc..............................55
United States v. Johnson....................................15, 36
United States v. Jones...102
United States v. Lewko..36
United States v. Lopez...........2, 20, 25, 31, 32, 33, 34, 35, 36, 51, 116
United States v. Monts..36
United States v. Morrison..............................32, 51, 52
United States v. Mussari..36
United States v. Napier...36
United States v. Nixon..70
United States v. O'Brien.......................................150
United States v. Pappadopoulos..................................36
United States v. Pink...55
United States v. SCRAP..78
United States v. Seeger..156
United States v. Virginia.......................**2, 123**, 195

United States v. Wilks 36
United Transportation Union v. Long Island R.R. Co 100
University of Alabama, Board of Trustees of, v. Garrett 53

Veazie Bank v. Fenno 16
Veazie v. Moor 20
Village of Schaumburg v. Citizens for a Better Environment 129
Virginia State Board of Pharmacy v. Virginia Citizens
    Consumer Council, Inc. 150
Virginia v. Black 145
Vitek v. Jones 126
Vlandis v. Kline 199

Wallace v. Jaffree 152
Ward v. Rock Against Racism 120
Ware v. Hylton 35
Washington v. Davis 2, 175, **185**
Washington v. Glucksberg 173
Watts v. United States 138
Weber v. Aetna Casualty & Surety Co. 194
Welton v. Missouri 97
West Coast Hotel v. Parrish 162
West Virginia State Board of Education v. Barnette 130
Whitney v. California 128
Wickard v. Filburn 20, 22, 27, 100
Williams v. Rhodes 65
Williams v. Vermont 117
Williamson v. Lee Optical Co. 117, 173
Wisconsin v. Yoder 2, **157**, 173
Witters v. Washington Department of Services for the Blind 155, 156
Woods v. Cloyd W. Miller Co. 14
Wooley v. Maynard 130
Wright v. Rockefeller 186
Wrightwood Dairy 33
Wygant v. Jackson Board of Education 118, 182, 183

Yankus v. United States 64
Yates v. United States 133
Yick Wo v. Hopkins 173, 184, 186
Youngstown Sheet & Tube Co. v. Sawyer 2, **58**, 72

Zelman v. Simmons-Harris 2, **153**
Zobel v. Williams 172
Zobrest v. Catalina Foothills School District 155, 156
Zorach v. Clauson 152